D0463482

A Generation
of Women

A Generation of Women

Education in the Lives of Progressive Reformers

Ellen Condliffe Lagemann

HARVARD UNIVERSITY PRESS
Cambridge, Massachusetts
and London, England
1979

Copyright © 1979 by the President and Fellows of Harvard College
All rights reserved
Printed in the United States of America

Library of Congress Cataloging in Publication Data

Lagemann, Ellen Condliffe, 1945-
 A generation of women.

 Includes bibliographical references and index.
  1. Feminists—United States—Biography. 2. Social
reformers—United States—Biography. 3. Education of
women—United States—Biography. I. Title.
HQ1412.L33   301.24'2'0922 [B]   79-13528
ISBN 0-674-34471-5

For Kord

Acknowledgments

I first became interested in the women of the progressive period when I wrote an essay on Vida Scudder almost fifteen years ago. That essay included a section called "A Generation of Women," in which I compared Scudder to Jane Addams and Lillian Wald, and in a sense that marked the beginning of this book. Since then, however, many people have helped me expand and refine my interests and a few deserve special thanks.

Lawrence A. Cremin introduced me to educational history. By listening, questioning, encouraging, and letting me share in his work, he has made it possible for me to develop my own ideas. At times, he has believed in this book even more than I have, and he has helped in innumerable ways to bring it into being. Hope Jensen Leichter, Robert A. Nisbet, Douglas Sloan, and Richard F. W. Whittemore discussed the study with me and raised interesting questions, many of which were far too searching to be answered in a single book. My grandfather, John B. Condliffe, was forthright, gentle, and determined in his efforts to improve my writing. Joyce Antler, Virginia Brereton, Harriet Cuffaro, and Steven Schlossman read the manuscript at an early stage, and their criticisms and suggestions were as thoughtful as their interest was encouraging.

The archivists and curators of the following libraries facilitated my research, and, whenever necessary, they have granted me permission to quote from the manuscript collections they hold: Special Collections, Teachers College Library, Columbia University (Grace H. Dodge Papers); Archives of the National Board of the Young Women's Christian Association of the U.S.A. (Grace H. Dodge Collection and Records Files Collection); Schlesinger Library, Radcliffe College (Maud Nathan and Leonora O'Reilly Papers); Manuscript and Archives Division, New York Public Library, Astor, Lenox and Tilden Foundation (Lillian D. Wald Papers); Rare Book and Manuscript Library, Columbia University (Lillian D. Wald Papers); Archives of the Visiting Nurse Service of New York (Lillian D. Wald Papers); Tamiment Library, New York University (Rose Schneiderman Papers); Swarthmore College Peace Collection (Jane Addams Papers); Franklin D. Roosevelt Library, Hyde Park (Eleanor Roosevelt Papers); American Jewish Archives, Hebrew Union College (Annie Nathan Meyer Papers); New York State Department of Labor Research Library (Women's Trade Union League of New York Papers). Lucy Goldthwaite has been kind enough to give me permission to quote from *All for One* (New York: Paul S. Eriksson, 1967), and Doris Daniels, Nancy Schrom Dye, and Allan Edward Reznick have allowed me to quote from their unpublished dissertations which are cited in the notes.

Finally, to my husband, Kord, whose patience, perspective, and good humor have been abundant, and to my son, Nicky, whose laughter has been infectious, I would simply say, many thanks for many things.

E.C.L.

Contents

Introduction   1
1. Grace Hoadley Dodge, 1856-1914   9
2. Maud Nathan, 1862-1946   33
3. Lillian D. Wald, 1867-1940   59
4. Leonora O'Reilly, 1870-1927   89
5. Rose Schneiderman, 1882-1972   115
6. The Education of a Generation   138
   A Note on Method and Sources   167

Notes   181
Index   201

Illustrations

Grace Dodge about 1907   8
Courtesy of Cleveland E. Dodge.

Maud Nathan about 1933   32
From Maud Nathan, *Once Upon a Time and Today* (New York: G. P. Putnam's Sons, 1933).

Lillian Wald about 1917   58
From R. L. Duffus, *Lillian Wald: Neighbor and Crusader* (New York: The Macmillan Company, 1938).

Leonora O'Reilly about 1910   88
From Barbara Mayer Wertheimer, *We Were There: The Story of Working Women in America* (New York: Pantheon, 1977). Used with the permission of the author and Pauline Newman.

Rose Schneiderman about 1912   114
From Barbara Mayer Wertheimer, *We Were There: The Story of Working Women in America* (New York: Pantheon, 1977). Used with the permission of the author and Pauline Newman.

A Generation
of Women

Introduction

GRACE DODGE, Maud Nathan, Lillian Wald, Leonora O'Reilly, and Rose Schneiderman were prominent progressive social reformers. Grace Dodge was a major figure in the early years of the working girls' clubs, of Teachers College, Columbia University, and of the National Board of the Young Women's Christian Association. Maud Nathan was for many years president of the New York Consumers' League and a leader in the campaign for women's suffrage. Lillian Wald was the founder of the Henry Street Settlement and of the Visiting Nurse Service. Leonora O'Reilly was an influential member of the Women's Trade Union League. And Rose Schneiderman was not only president of the National Women's Trade Union League, she was also a member of the Labor Advisory Board of the National Industrial Recovery Administration and secretary of the New York State Department of Labor. What can the life histories of these five women tell us about the history of women's education? What can their education tell us about a generation of women?

Like so many women born during the latter half of the nineteenth century, Dodge, Nathan, Wald, O'Reilly, and Schneiderman responded with optimism, vigor, and humanity to the inequities and suffering they found in their society, and saw opportunity and challenge in their chance to rebuild the world. They were not a precise chronological cohort. Grace Dodge was born in 1856; Rose

Schneiderman in 1882. But they stood in a similar relationship to their times, and were in that sense a generation. With Jane Addams, they believed that social action was a "subjective necessity," and this belief framed all aspects of their adult lives. The distinguishing feature of the progressive generation was a compelling interest in finding solutions to the social problems of their day, and the life histories of Grace Dodge, Maud Nathan, Lillian Wald, Leonora O'Reilly, and Rose Schneiderman allow one to inquire into the relationship between education and the attitudes and achievements associated with that group.[1]

Of course, the progressive generation was not the first generation of women to feel a sense of social calling. During the Civil War, untold numbers of women had joined in the effort to provision the Union and Confederate armies. And even before the Civil War, large numbers of women had expressed a sense of social duty in church-related benevolent work. What is more, in an earlier day many women had seen their domestic activities as a direct effort to serve the welfare of the nation. For them, the achievement of harmony within the family was coincident with the achievement of order and stability in society, and that was a necessary precondition to the realization of America's unique mission in history. Despite these continuities, however, there is merit in Maud Nathan's assertion that the progressive generation was a "pioneer" generation in the history of American women.[2]

It was, in the first place, the generation that won the right for women to vote. The campaign for women's suffrage began in the United States in the 1840s. But it was the progressive generation that brought that effort to a successful conclusion. And as a woman journalist writing in 1910 explained, suffrage was what eight million women wanted, because women of this generation aspired to much that their mothers had not had. Equal pay for equal work and formal collegiate education were but two of the goals that became common during the lifetime of the progressive generation.[3]

As had been true earlier, women of the progressive generation found in benevolence an avenue for work outside their homes. Yet for many women of this generation, such work became more important—it now was more likely to become a career—and for an even larger number, it transformed the cultural pursuits that had traditionally defined "the lady." An interest in art, literature, or music often became an interest in the social and educational value of culture. To women of this generation, the writings of art critics like John Ruskin were a call to social action, and Shakespeare clubs were way stations to participation in school reform, good government campaigns, and the many other activities that were a part of the progressive response to growing cities, increasing industrialization, and constantly larger and more diverse patterns of immigration.

The progressive generation also made great strides in opening other nondomestic pursuits to women. By 1900, there were at least a few women in all but 8 of the 303 occupational categories of the U.S. Census, whereas sixty years earlier a foreign traveler had observed that only 7 occupations were open to women. Occupational choice was still severely limited for women of the progressive generation, but the conditions of life in turn-of-the-century America offered women novel opportunities, and their response to these changed their views, their lives, and our history.[4]

Education was important in the lives of progressive women. It was part of what defined what they could and could not do. And the education of Grace Dodge, Maud Nathan, Lillian Wald, Leonora O'Reilly, and Rose Schneiderman is significant even beyond its relevance to their individual achievements. Because these five women were leaders in a movement that was distinctive to their era, and also because in their backgrounds they represent a broad spectrum of late nineteenth- and early twentieth-century American society, their education can help us understand the generation of women to which they belonged.[5]

Dodge, Nathan, Wald, O'Reilly, and Schneiderman came from different economic, social, religious, and ethnic groups. At birth they had little in common except gender. Nevertheless, when one compares the education of the five, it becomes apparent that among them there were a number of very significant similarities (which I shall discuss in detail in Chapter 6). In each instance, these similarities originated from the intersection of culture and social structure that defined the expectations and opportunities relevant to each woman. Education was not determined by the objective coordinates of identity that described each woman's place in the world, but it was shaped by what was and was not available to a woman of such position. Consequently, if the similarities one finds in the education of these women arose from cultural traditions, intellectual constructs, and economic and social structures that were widespread in American society at the time, it is reasonable to argue that their education reflects much that was common to the education of progressive women in general.[6]

The degree to which any individual or small group can be "typical," "representative," or even "characteristic" of a much larger group is always problematical. Yet in spite of this, there are compelling historiographical reasons to use biography as a means of approach to the history of education. The logic for studies that can deal not only with schooling, but with all of the various institutions that together, in changing balance over time, have been involved with the transmission of culture is by now well known. The need for research that focuses upon personal documents (diaries, autobiographies, memoirs, letters), and does so from the perspective of the "learner," has also been widely noted. And the value of looking at any aspect of the history of women, including the history of women's education, in ways that make it possible to overstep traditional canons of historical significance is increasingly clear. Recent work in women's history strongly suggests that the history of women will remain unrecorded if public politics, wage-related economic activity, and recognized intellectual achievements are considered at the expense of, or in isolation from, the private and personal events, activities, and experiences that have been so important to women. Biography is a sensible approach to the educational history of progressive women, then, for at least two reasons. First, it allows one to examine education as a broad process, to map the variety of settings in which education can take place, to analyze the personal and social factors that define the educative meaning of a wide range of experiences, and to trace the effects of these experiences over time. And second, it permits one to judge significance, in this case educative significance, in terms of personal and subjectively meaningful growth.[7]

For these reasons, I have written a series of educational biographies and in conclusion drawn from them a generational portrait. My primary purpose is to describe the education of five individual women and through that to illustrate the kinds of educative experiences that women like Dodge, Nathan, Wald, O'Reilly, and Schneiderman had in common. In addition, I hope to show how one can structure a life history so that it can serve as a means of educational analysis. The method I have used, which is further described in the Note on Method and Sources that follows the text, can add an important increment not only to the educational history of women, but to the history of education as a whole.

Educational biography is different from literary biography in that it emphasizes only one aspect of a life: education. Like psychobiography, it focuses on an individual's growth and development throughout the course of the life cycle. Unlike psychobiography, however, educational biography is primarily concerned with conscious processes, and its explanatory categories are drawn from educational theory rather than psychoanalytic theory. Inevitably, much that is considered in an educational biography would also be considered within a psychobiography or a literary biography. To draw a clear line between the conscious and the unconscious or between life and education is not always possible. More important, it is not always desirable. Such distinctions, while perhaps useful in defining a discipline, can be empirically inaccurate. Indeed, it is because an educational biography deals with the experience of education, the process of education as an integral part of an individual's life, that it can add a new dimension to the history of education. The questions around which one frames an educational biography must therefore be made explicit. They are important if one is to understand this book.

In writing a biography that focuses on education, an educational biography, one must pose the kind of questions any biographer would ask. Thus, to the evidence remaining from the lives of Grace Dodge, Maud Nathan, Lillian Wald, Leonora O'Reilly, and Rose Schneiderman, I have put the following broad queries. Who was this woman? Where did she come from? What did she do? How did she see herself? How was she seen by others? But since my first concern has been the education of these women, in reconstructing their lives I have always also asked as part of the above: what were the educationally significant influences throughout each woman's life, how were these educational and significant, and what, if any, was the relationship between education and accomplishment, subjectively meaningful accomplishment as well as publicly recognized accomplishment?

Obviously, to deal with these questions, to write an educational biography, it is necessary to have a clear understanding of the process that is education. In studying the lives of Grace Dodge, Maud Nathan, Lillian Wald, Leonora O'Reilly, and Rose Schneiderman, therefore, I have thought of education as a continuous, cumulative, essentially lifelong process of growth. To put it in theoretical terms, my analysis of each life has been built around the notion that education is a process of interaction by which individual potential (instincts, propensities, talents) is activated, shaped, or channeled and a change (an observable or consciously felt difference) thereby produced in the self.

Any number of different definitions could be used by an educational biographer, but this definition is especially helpful for several reasons. First, it is very broad. As a result, it can serve to anchor one's inquiry in a theoretical understanding of education without restricting the scope of that inquiry to those relationships and encounters that have generally been equated with education. In writing an educational biography, one cannot assume that formal schooling, to name the most obvious example, was unimportant. But since one's purpose is to derive the educationally significant from actual experience, one also cannot assume that any particular experience had to be educative. Thus, a broad definition of education enables one to bring into view anything and everything that was a source of education.

Education in its broadest sense is, of course, teaching and learning. Conceivably, therefore, one could simply say that an educational biography is a life history that emphasizes that. Yet it is valuable to be more specific than this, as a brief explanation of what my definition specifies will show.

By defining education as a process of interaction that activates, shapes, and channels the potential with which a person is born, one directs attention to the effects of experience on the individual under consideration. As a result, teaching that does not result in learning becomes irrelevant, while experience that was incidentally educative—in other words, experience that was rendered educative by the intent of the learner rather than the purposes of the teacher or the inherent structure of the situation—and experience that became educative by subsequent recognition of meaning, become central. Similarly, by positing that changes in the self are the essential feature of educative experience, one indicates that a particular kind of learning will be of special concern.

As I have used the term, the self has to do with the strains of continuity or stability that give an individual's identity a degree of "sameness" over time and across situations. The self has many facets; for instance, it includes one's sense of physical and emotional being as well as one's felt connections to other people and to things. To paraphrase William James, the self is all that one means by "I" and "me" and all that one implies when describing something as "mine." To focus on learning that in some way or other changes the self is, therefore, to focus on intentional learning, learning that is motivated primarily by the interests connected to one's ideal sense of self. By specifying the center of my analysis, then, I have signaled that I consider purposeful striving to be more important to education than conditioned animal drives, and that has helped clarify my study. [8]

One could dwell at length on the meaning involved in all of the terms used above. But further detail is unnecessary since the most essential features of an educational biography, as well as the scope of the ones presented here, should be clear already. An educational biography is a life history that has a special purpose. And that purpose is informed by educational theory. Unless one knows what it is that education does, one cannot achieve the focus, the emphasis, that allows a life history to tell about education. An educational biography is a means to an end. It attempts to fuse art and science, the writing of life history and the study of education, but its ultimate goal is to enrich our knowledge of history and our understanding of that part of human growth that is education.

1
Grace Hoadley Dodge
1856-1914

GRACE HOADLEY DODGE was born in New York City on May 21, 1856. She was the first daughter and oldest child of Sarah Hoadley and William Earl Dodge, Jr. At birth she inherited a distinguished family tradition, one that was rooted in a larger tradition of evangelical Protestantism. Her paternal grandfather was known as the "Christian Merchant." With his father-in-law he had started Phelps, Dodge and Co., a metals trading firm that became one of the largest in the country. Following his own father, who had been a founder of the New York Peace Society and a member of the Young Men's Missionary Society, he had also attended faithfully to his duties as a servant of God. He was active, for example, in the Young Men's Christian Association and the American Board of Commissioners for Foreign Missions; he was a leading figure in the temperance movement, and when Grace was a child, he served for a term in the U. S. House of Representatives. He also fathered nine children, the oldest of whom was Grace Dodge's father.[1]

Within the Protestant evangelical tradition, a woman's responsibilities were distinctly different from a man's. In early nineteenth-century New England this tradition had helped to popularize the notion of "spheres," the idea that gender made different activities peculiarly appropriate to each of the sexes. According to the Dodge heritage, therefore, the domestic was considered a

9

woman's special province, and if it was thought admirable for a woman to work for the church and to be active in related auxiliaries, it was clear nevertheless that she was to be first and foremost a wife, mother, teacher, nurse—a minister within the home.

All of this was, of course, taught to Grace Dodge by her parents, and all of it was learned. But Grace Dodge was to take the belief that one had a responsibility to use one's "talents" for the service of God somewhat differently than Dodge women had done before. Grace Dodge devoted her life to building institutions, particularly institutions that would help women use their "talents" to serve God in many different ways.[2]

Grace Dodge's work is clearly set forth in the diary that she called her "Record book." It begins in 1874 when she "left school in January," and proceeds to outline the landmarks of her subsequent career. It states, for example, that in February of 1884, she "organized [the] first Working Girls' Society"; on November 1, 1886, she was "appointed Commissioner of the Board of Education"; in April of 1887, she "resigned as acting President of [the] Industrial Education Association"; and in 1906, she became "Pres'd. Nat. Bd. Y.W.C. Ass'n. U.S. of A."[3]

Dodge's "Record book" is a factual chronicle. It was designed to tell what she had done, although it inadvertently tells a good deal more. On the prefatory page Dodge wrote: "The following pages cover the special new movements or developments of old, or the change of relationship occurring in the year recorded— The continuation of work, or normal growth is not put down—The record has been kept to help memory remember when special movements, events, or my relationship to them took place." Thus, the volume indicates that Dodge was proud of what she had done and wanted "memory" to "remember," even though its terse, objective, skeletal form also shows that Dodge was inclined to obscure herself as a person. Her work is there, in the "Record," but in a sense she is not. Her career is presented as an objective happening and is never described for its personal significance. In a listing that runs for thirty-one crowded pages, the pronoun "I" never appears.

The tension between pride and humility that marks Grace Dodge's "Record book" illustrates a conflict that was central to her life. With uncharacteristic candor, Dodge once said: "I usually repress myself . . . I want to be the humble follower and yet at times it is hard to keep in when I feel I could help a wee bit." The effects of Grace Dodge's education can be seen in this statement. Her educational biography is the story of the way her "talents" were nurtured and repressed, extended beyond but confined within the "sphere" to which she was assigned by virtue of her sex and her family's tradition.[4]

The process began in childhood and was significantly influenced by self-conscious parental teaching. As William Dodge once explained in relation to philanthropy, though his statement implied a more general intent, the six Dodge children were "educated . . . to feel it a privilege and joy to give liberally and largely, in proportion to their means, for the advancement of the cause of our blessed Redeemer and for all humane and benevolent objects." William and Sarah Dodge instructed their children constantly, comprehensively, in a variety of ways, and always with intended gentleness and affection.[5]

While away from home during the Civil War, for example, William Dodge wrote his children frequent letters. The letters described his activities, but they also expressed his aspirations for the children: "I want very much to have you learn to sing and to play on the piano . . . But more than anything else I want you . . . to learn to love our precious Savior." In addition, the letters told of his pleasure in their progress: "I was made very happy the other day by opening an envelope and finding your nice letter all spelled out in big letters and looking so beautifully." And they always conveyed his deep and abiding affection: "How sorry I felt not to go to Sunday School with you this beautiful morning . . . Don't forget to write to me very soon again because I love you and your little letters very much." Similarly, when he was at home, William Dodge spent Sunday evenings telling his children "Nobody Nothin' " stories, which always had more than an incidental pedagogical purpose. The stories were drawn from the children's behavior of the previous week, and in them misfortune followed disobedience as surely as good fortune followed the reverse. Beyond this, William and Sarah Dodge also taught by example, inviting their children to join them at tea, for instance, so the children could observe their behavior and listen to their conversation. And finally, the Dodges hired surrogates to carry out the specifics of their intent: Bella, an Irish nurse, to maintain law and order; Miss Flint, to tutor Grace in writing and spelling and to impose punctuality; Mr. Muller, to teach music.[6]

In response to this ubiquitous synthesis of clear demands and strong affection, Grace Dodge became a child who was devoted to her parents and to learning all that they set forth. The Bible verses, Psalms, indeed the whole constellation of beliefs, values, and standards of behavior drawn from religious precept came easily. Despite zealous effort, however, some more specific tasks presented difficulty. Grace tried to learn to play the piano, but failed to do so, at least well; she did learn to write "beautifully" and to spell correctly but the process was arduous. The source of her difficulty cannot be reconstructed, because it was not understood at the time, but its effects are far less elusive. Grace Dodge became a painfully shy person who expected and feared humiliation. Her relative incompetence in mastering some of what her parents asked probably contributed to this, as it may have also to her desire to win approval in other, less conspicuous, more comfortable ways. Grace was not only a well-behaved, dutiful child, she was a child who was doggedly determined to be good. And her seriousness of purpose was increased even further by her place in the sibling hierarchy.

Grace Dodge was the oldest of six. Her three brothers and two sisters saw her as a "giant," and felt that there was "a loneliness in her life" that separated her from them. In part, their perceptions reflected Grace's physical size. As the oldest, she was naturally larger than they, and she was also larger than other children of her age. Moreover, sibling awareness and comment upon Grace's size, which may have been accompanied by clumsiness on her part and teasing on theirs, was magnified by the responsibilities Grace was asked to assume. By the time she was fifteen, Grace had moved from the child who helped Bella, the nurse, get her charges across the street, to her mother's substitute at the tea table and to the position of running the entire household during the several months that her parents spent in Europe. Thus, as Grace's responsibilities grew—as the pleasure Grace found in parental satisfaction brought forth increased competence and in turn a further escalation of duties—so too did her siblings' larger-than-life perceptions. Grace was not one of them. The consequences of this situation can be seen in a story Dodge's biographer, Abbie Graham, recounts.[7]

One day when she was sick in bed, the Dodge children managed to bring Grace's pony up the back stairs to her room to visit. Grace supposedly expressed "vast satisfaction" at the sight of "Nettie," although her brothers and sisters left with the feeling that she lived within "a gulf of solitude." What she did to convey this impression is not known, yet one can imagine what was involved. To Grace, full enjoyment of a prank, whether felt or expressed, would have been likely to imply complicity; complicity would have threatened responsibility; and the fulfillment of responsibility was the way in which Grace had learned to please her parents, and through their pleasure, to satisfy her own wish to be loved. Thus, in acting as she did, Grace came to resemble the "giant" she was in the minds of her siblings; and as they in turn acted toward her according to their perceptions, her self-consciousness became more acute and isolating; the distance between them increased; and so too, consequently, did Grace's need for her parents' approval, as well as her reliance upon the pattern of behavior that was most likely to win it. The point is not that Grace did not get along with her brothers and sisters. The point is that she acted differently from the way they did—more responsibly, less spontaneously; and the difference grew over time.[8]

That there was not only affection and loyalty but also distance —"a gulf of solitude"—between Grace Dodge and her siblings is verifiably true, although the pattern of interaction I have described is, of course, based on inference. One learns who one is through reflected images. Especially during childhood, one's sense of self is largely derived from the reactions one elicits in those to whom one is most closely attached. Thus, when Grace Dodge's siblings referred to her as a "giant" they were telling her how she appeared to them: they were teaching her who she was. Similarly, when her parents acted on their view of her by giving her adult responsibilities they were also teaching her about herself: they were telling her where they saw her in relation to themselves and to her brothers and sisters, her familial peers. And since the interplay over time between these views and the ways in which she acted were a large part of what defined Grace Dodge, what one can infer from nicknames, childhood escapades, and the like is as much a part of her educational biography as the learning one can trace to intentional parental teaching.

Two people in addition to her siblings and parents also deserve mention in reconstructing the early years of Grace Dodge's education. Her paternal grandparents lived nearby, and they set an example that all of their children and grandchildren admired. Melissa Phelps Dodge, Grace's grandmother, was a devoted wife and mother as well as her husband's faithful partner in benevolence. She was a strong person, and became an important role model for her granddaughter.

Grace's mother, Sarah Dodge, was a semiinvalid. From the very start, therefore, because Grace was a healthy, energetic child, she was more like her grandmother than her mother. The effects of this are not entirely clear, but it does seem probable that the likenesses Grace could see between the ways in which her grandmother functioned and the ways in which she herself liked to behave heightened the value she could see in herself. After all, Sarah Dodge's example could not have affirmed Grace in the competence she was developing and her grandmother's could. More than likely, therefore, the presence of a healthy, active, and revered female figure helped Grace see promise implicit in her gender. The grandmother Grace looked up to, was fond of, and knew well proved that one could be a woman, an admired woman, at the same time that one was an effective person. Melissa Dodge, then, was another source of reflected images, ones that were projective, and perhaps therefore especially important in nurturing Grace's sense of possibility.[9]

All that I have described above took place within a context, one that actually gave Grace a place within her immediate family that was not totally dissimilar from the one her grandmother held within hers. Her mother's condition, coupled with the fact that the Dodges, in addition to raising six children, kept up two houses and entertained a constant stream of visitors, placed unusually heavy burdens on their eldest daughter. In the nineteenth century, understudy, serving as an aid, companion, and confidante to one's mother, was a common and highly regarded form of education for young girls. Nonetheless, in asking Grace not only to help with, but to assume fully many of the tasks her mother was unable to perform, the Dodges forcefully supported the direction of their daughter's growth.

William Dodge was a partner of Phelps, Dodge and Co. and active in a number of civic and philanthropic organizations— the Young Men's Christian Association, the Evangelical Alliance, the American Sunday School Union, the National Arbitration Committee, and many more. As her mother's substitute at tea or dinner, therefore, Grace was able to listen to her father and his associates discuss politics and business and to watch them plan all kinds of civic projects and missionizing campaigns. When Dwight L. Moody stayed with the Dodges during the 1876 New York City religious revivals, for example, Grace's position within the household allowed her to talk with him more often and on a more equal basis than might have been true if her mother had been able to be a more active hostess. Thus, the tasks that fell to Grace exposed her to her father's world, at the same time that they allowed her to amass a wide range of administrative and domestic skills in ways that built on her wish (and ability) to be responsible, without activating her acute self-consciousness. And this experience, combined with the other important influences of childhood, nurtured in Grace Dodge a sense of comfort, competence, and mastery in the performance of real, necessary, useful tasks that turned her disinclination for self-display and public notice into an equally strong propensity for quiet, useful work: for activity in which she could lose herself sufficiently to act freely, according to the demands of the task at hand, rather than self-consciously, according to the anxieties associated with her image of herself as a misfit, a giant.[10]

Grace Dodge's earliest experience had one additional outcome of paramount significance. Through the growth of a strong, unshakable religious faith, coupled with the freedom she found in the fulfillment of responsibility and the admiration she felt for her father and grandparents, Dodge family tradition took on vital relevance to Grace Dodge's life. Service to others prompted by knowledge of one's duties as Christ's servant on earth became the vehicle through which she found meaning in life. The vision she had inherited from her family became Grace Dodge's chosen purpose. Through it she sought to find a life that was suitable to the dictates of her own special "talents." Had she been a man, this would have been easier to do. As some of her brothers would do, she could have worked at Phelps, Dodge and continued the philanthropic causes of her great-grandfather, grandfather, and father. Being a woman, however, she had to find a way to express her aspirations and abilities in a manner that was appropriate to her ''sphere.''

Later on in life, Grace Dodge became especially interested in the problems of young women. And with hindsight one can see that her interest partly grew out of the difficulties she herself had encountered in growing up. Before she was sixteen, however, Dodge probably thought little about what she would do. Indeed, it is more than likely that the question became important for the first time during the year and a half she spent at Miss Porter's School in Farmington, Connecticut, where she was sent in 1872. Dodge was far too private a person to have discussed such things even in letters to her family. But everything about her sojourn at the school argues that the time was one of deep reflection.

Before she went to Miss Porter's, Grace's schooling had been taken care of at home. She had always had private tutors, and because she was so shy and preferred work to play, she had had relatively little contact with other children. When she went to Miss Porter's, she was extremely homesick and spent a good deal of time riding alone on the horse she had brought from home. Having to live in close and constant contact with other people seems to have heightened Grace's sense that she was different and added to the loneliness of which her siblings were so aware.[11]

Miss Porter, the school's founder and headmistress, was the daughter of a prominent Farmington Congregational minister and the sister of Noah Porter, the philosopher who had become president of Yale in 1870. Her school carried the imprint of her personality. Miss Porter was a scholar of unusual knowledge and training and her school offered a wide array of academic subjects: Latin, French, German, chemistry, natural philosophy, rhetoric, mathematics, history, geography, music. So far as one can tell, however, the school's academic offerings held little interest for Grace. Whatever her intellectual capacities might have been, her training heretofore had not taught her to use her mind freely, with no utilitarian end in mind. Truth had been given, not discovered; learning had been a duty, not a pleasure. Furthermore, since learning was generally considered ornamental for a woman of Dodge's background, and since she had little wish to be so adorned, it is hard to imagine that her academic motivation was strong. Most likely, therefore, Dodge mastered as much of Miss Porter's curriculum as she was obliged to, but acquired little in this respect that was of lasting value.[12]

Miss Porter's personality, however, was extremely educative for Grace Dodge. Unlike Sarah Dodge, Miss Porter was an extraordinarily energetic person. At one time she herself had taught the school's entire curriculum, and during Dodge's time at the school, she continued to teach some classes—she was Grace's composition teacher—and also joined the girls in study hall, ate with them in the dining room, took them on picnics, and intimately involved herself in all aspects of their lives. In addition, Miss Porter, who was highly esteemed among the people the Dodges knew best, exemplified all of the virtues Grace had been taught to respect. Her deep sense of piety and religious faith were mirrored in the school's daily Bible readings and Sunday sermons as well as in her firm insistence that her students act as good Protestant gentlewomen in all aspects of their lives. Thus, in many ways, Miss Porter was like Grace's grandmother, although she was a devoted and well-loved teacher, rather than a mother and a wife. Miss Porter's example was presented within a school environment that was conducive to emulation; it was presented at a time when Grace was acutely lonely; it was compatible with Grace's already established aspirations, while quite different from any example she had been systematically exposed to before. Consequently, even though Grace Dodge never said that Miss Porter was one of the important role models in her life, one may surely assume that this was the case. It cannot be coincidental that there are striking resemblances between Miss Porter as she was when Dodge was at Farmington and Dodge as she became after her time at the school. It has been claimed, for example, that Miss Porter's activity "seemed . . . to be wholly without friction. She was rarely hurried or worried . . . she used her whole strength for the business in hand . . . She was habitually prompt in decision, and immediate in execution . . . [and therefore was capable of] continuous and intense effort." So too, for the same reasons, was Dodge. A friend of Miss Porter's also once wrote that "the lesson she most thoroughly inculcated by her influence was moderation; a few studies at a time, each task well learned, and all combined into a whole, complete as far as it went; pleasure sufficient for intellectual and moral recuperation; work as a vocation, and not incidental to life; piety within the bounds of personal responsibility." And it was in this style that Dodge also lived, and it was this that she herself would teach.[13]

Another older woman was also very important in helping Grace Dodge find the path she would follow. Dodge's "Record book" begins in the year she left school (1874), and if Miss Porter's was partly responsible for its beginning, Louisa Lee Schuyler deserves a good deal of credit for its later design. Schuyler did not become important in Dodge's education, however, until approximately 1880.

After attending Farmington and spending several months in Europe, Grace Dodge returned to New York City and quickly filled her days with an unusually large number of essentially charitable activities. She became a teacher in the Sunday school and the sewing school of the Madison Square (Presbyterian) Chapel and in the industrial schools of the Children's Aid Society. She became a volunteer reader in the Yonkers Hospital, led Sunday afternoon services in the Women's Homeopathic Hospital, and was appointed a manager of the New York Infirmary. As had been true before she went to Miss Porter's, she also took over the management of the household and assisted her father with some of his projects, notably the religious revival led by Dwight L. Moody in 1876, of which he was a prominent sponsor. According to Dodge's biographer, however, Grace was unable to make clear to her father the kind of life she wanted until she explained to him that she did not want a traditional debut. "You have taught me to be a follower of Jesus, to love God and man," she is supposed to have said. "I must love through work." It was soon thereafter that William Dodge arranged for Grace to meet the woman who would become her mentor.[14]

Louisa Lee Schuyler was nineteen years older than Grace Dodge. Personal style, philosophy, social position, and good works had made her a leader among the men and women of William Dodge's generation. During the Civil War, she had been chairman of the Committee of Correspondence of the Women's Central Association of Relief and had organized all of the gathering of supplies in the New York area for the Sanitary Commission. In the 1870s, she had established the State Charities Aid Association, through which she hoped to establish a "visiting committee" for every public welfare institution in the state. In both ventures, William Dodge had been one of her most faithful assistants.

Clearly, then, Grace's father knew that Schuyler had "disingenuous managerial skill . . . coupled with . . . immense energy and efficiency" and that she was a woman of devout religious faith and gracious hospitality. In the meeting he arranged one can see an acknowledgement on his part of Grace as she was in 1880: a woman of conviction and ability who would use what he had taught in ways he had not envisioned.[15]

In that year and the following one, in addition to organizing the Kitchen Garden Association (from which Teachers College ultimately developed) and a Tuesday evening class of working girls (from which the Working Girls' Association originated), Grace Dodge "became a Manager of the Bellevue Training School for Nurses, and Chairman of its House Committee." The Bellevue Training School was one of Schuyler's special interests. It had been established in 1873, via the Bellevue Hospital Visiting Committee of the State Charities Aid Association. Its aim was to train "professional" nurses to replace the attendants that Schuyler described as the " 'helpers'—all of them ignorant, many of them degraded" (and most of then newly arrived immigrants), upon whom she placed the blame for Bellevue's "deficient" state.[16]

Serving first as a manager of the nursing school, and then as chairman of the State Charities Aid Association's Committee for the Elevation of the Poor in Their Homes, allowed Grace Dodge to watch her father's old friend at work. For all that they were similar in terms of competence, Louisa Lee Schuyler was a very different person from Grace Dodge, and much that she offered by way of example did not suit Dodge's temperament. Schuyler's style, for example, was leisurely and upper class. Long retreats to Europe, Mt. Desert, Lenox, and Newport were a regular part of her routine. Dodge, by contrast, found pleasure in denying herself anything more than two weeks of vacation a year. Schuyler's view of herself as a general in command of an elite corps was equally unsuitable to a woman who increasingly preferred to be seen as one among many working girl "friends." Differences notwithstanding, Schuyler's example taught Grace Dodge that a woman need not restrict herself to serving others directly. She could be a "true woman," as Schuyler was thought to be, and admired for her good works, even if she acted in the more masculine role of architect or planner, even if she were a philanthropist who helped others deliver services she herself did not provide. Dodge had seen her father and her grandfather act in this way. Until she met Schuyler, however, all of the female models in her life, including her grandmother and Miss Porter, had fulfilled more traditional, more service-oriented, feminine roles.

The lesson was important. At the outset of her career, Dodge had not been able to act in this way. She had been a teacher in many different settings, as well as a hospital reader and lay church leader. Yet earlier still, she had acquired all of the skills necessary to the managerial role that she was now increasingly assuming. Apparently, therefore, Schuyler's example helped her recognize that she could act as she was most able to do, without violating the canons in which she had been taught to believe. And the advice that one may presume Schuyler gave Dodge directly, as she superintended her functioning within her personal empire, the State Charities Aid Association, added to the general lesson implicit in her example, the personal realization that she, Grace Dodge, could indeed plan and organize and execute outside of her home as well as within.

In 1886, Dodge informed the Board of Managers of the State Charities Aid Association that "owing to other very important duties," she would have to resign. By that time all of her "duties" had expanded. Like the State Charities Aid Association Committee for the Elevation of the Poor in Their Homes, the scope of which had been enlarged under her leadership, the Kitchen Garden Association and the Tuesday evening class had taken on functions well beyond those originally set forth in 1880 and 1881. As they grew, the demands upon Dodge's time necessitated an economy of purpose. After 1886 Dodge would involve herself in many different organizations and causes. She was claimed as a founder by the Travelers' Aid Association, the American Social Hygiene Association, and the Riverdale Neighborhood and Library Association; she played a part in the early years of the Consumers' League and the Women's Municipal League; she was a trustee of the Constantinople Woman's College and contributed in one way or another to hundreds of additional organizations. But she invested herself most fully in the Working Girls' Association, Teachers College, and the Young Women's Christian Association.[17]

All of these organizations, *as she saw them*, had similar goals. They were all, even Teachers College, which admitted men, dedicated to the education of women and through the "influence" of their graduates to the advancement of the nation. The State Charities Aid Association was quite different. It focused on promoting efficiency in custodial care and charity, not education. Its medium of influence was the upper class, not women of all classes. And its philosophy was more oriented toward stabilizing society through individual rehabilitation than reforming it by promoting social change. Grace Dodge was no revolutionary; nor was she overt or militant in her feminism. But the choice she made when she resigned from the State Charities Aid Association illustrates how much she had learned during the first years of her career. By 1874 Dodge had apparently already decided that she would work. But it was only during the years after she left Miss Porter's School that she developed a clear notion of what this meant. Her purpose was always the same: service to others as service to God. Nevertheless, between 1874 and 1886 she learned how best she might serve, and through that, how she might dedicate others to the same end.[18]

During this period, Dodge learned a great deal from Louisa Lee Schuyler, although the activities she pursued independently of her mentor were equally educative. Dodge's education, perhaps especially in this period when the question of vocation was so important, consisted of a variety of different experiences, all of which bore relationship not only to those of the past and the future but also to each other. Indeed, with the perspective that time affords, one can see that it was the fit between the insights Dodge acquired as Schuyler's apprentice and those that came from developing the Tuesday evening class and the Kitchen Garden Association that allowed for the clarity of purpose evident in her resignation from the State Charities Aid Association.

By 1886, the Tuesday evening class that had first gathered in 1881 had become the 38th Street Working Girls' Society and had spawned eleven similar clubs and, in the previous year, the New York Association of Working Girls' Societies. Transforming a single unsuccessful class into an organization that attracted a relatively large number of young women provided Grade Dodge with several lessons of enduring value.[19]

The experience taught, first, that one could not teach through imposition. This is clear from the simple fact that the class became a club. More important, the atmosphere that followed from this, the esprit de corps a club fostered, enabled Dodge to develop a medium by which she could style her pedagogy differently than she probably had done at the start. Little is known about her initial class, but one would imagine that the hostile reaction Dodge encountered was at least to some extent the result of stiff, formal preaching on her part. The ''Practical Talks'' that became the central feature of all working girls' clubs were therefore designed to teach in a less exhortatory fashion. What is especially interesting about the ''Practical Talks,'' in terms of Grace Dodge's education, however, is that they provided a setting in which she felt comfortable enough to articulate what it was that she wanted to do.[20]

In 1887, Dodge published a book entitled *A Bundle of Letters to Busy Girls on Practical Matters*. The letters were drawn from the ''Practical Talks.'' They were written for women who could not reach a club. Three themes run throughout: that everything on earth comes from God and should in some way serve to glorify Him; that women by virtue of their sex have special ''influence''; and that the world is full of temptation and problems, the solution of which is the special responsibility of women. In the book, Dodge argued that if they were pure, modest, virtuous, and knowledgeable, women who married could exercise their ''influence'' directly and naturally through their homes, while women who did not marry could do the same ''in caring for nieces, nephews, either real or adopted.'' Furthermore, in discussing the unmarried, Dodge also noted that ''a bright, helpful life can be theirs, and as a true, pure woman they can bring cheer and gladness into *many* a home instead of only one'' (emphasis added).[21]

As tended to be true with Dodge, the statement was indirect, to say the least. Nevertheless, that Dodge came as close as she did to explaining her personal aspirations is worth considering. From childhood on, Dodge had been least self-conscious and most effective when serving the needs of others, and her self-perceptions also seem to have been most acute when directed to this end. It is not surprising, therefore, that in trying to understand the needs of young women factory workers, Dodge came to understand herself. Through ''Practical Talks,'' Grace Dodge not only learned what she wanted to do, she also discovered the rationale for her work: the premise upon which she could base her belief that her ''talents'' made suitable the kind of life she had chosen.

''Practical Talks'' were built on the assumption that a club leader was ''not working *for*, but *with*'' the ''girls.'' The assumption reflected the gender-based identity Dodge found with working women as she translated the conditions they described into generic problems: problems that might be solved by the improvement of character; problems that were uniquely and universally female; problems that were susceptible to "influence." To say, as Dodge did, that she was a working girl who simply had " 'wages earned for her in advance' . . . by grandfather or father" was to gloss over a great deal. Vida Scudder was right: Grace Dodge had "no appreciation, in the modern sense, of the reaction of economic circumstances on personality." Nevertheless, the persona Dodge developed and sincerely believed in was useful in her career, and important to her education.[22]

Dodge's identification with working women enabled her to lead without self-consciousness. It also allowed her to advocate greater freedom and more opportunity for women without doing so in what she would have considered an unbecoming, unfeminine way. "To my special friends, 'the girls,' " Dodge could say, "I can understand how you are misunderstood, how you want to do so many things that you cannot." And having voiced the problem she herself faced, "with" the "girls" she could work for change as she could not have done more directly or on her own.[23]

The identification Dodge felt with working girls also opened her to the thought of other reformers of her generation. On occasion, for example, she compared working girls' clubs to social settlements; the only difference between the two, she believed, was that club work was accessible to women who could not leave their families to take up residence elsewhere. To an extent her analogy was appropriate. Settlement residents also felt a community of interest with the people they served. Though she could not renounce "the family claim" and saw the care of her parents as an essential and self-imposed part of her responsibilities as a woman, Dodge's sense of "working with the girls" helped her align herself with one of the most influential movements of the day. And in so doing, she was able to find support and confirmation for what she discovered "with" the "girls" as she might not have, had she stayed within the philanthropic rationale, the presumption of noblesse oblige, that characterized the benevolence of her father's and Schuyler's generation. Grace Dodge was deeply in debt to the factory women who had joined her club. And she herself acknowledged this frequently, as when she said: "I would tell you of some of my girl friends, those who have educated me. I was never privileged to go to college and to be educated as today young women feel they must be, but I started the petty responsibilities of life when I was very young and learned and gained by my friends. We studied life, the problems of life, together, they helping me much more than I could help them.''[24]

Fruitful as Dodge's working-girl self-image was, at least for her own education, it had severe limitations as a career base. This Grace Dodge would discover later on at Teachers College. At the outset, however, the educative value of Dodge's involvement with the organizations that became Teachers College appears to have derived primarily from the fact that the experience offered her the chance to try out what she was learning elsewhere. In a sense, it provided her with a laboratory for testing, among other things, the managerial orientation toward benevolence that she was simultaneously learning from her mentor.

Teachers College began when Grace Dodge organized the Kitchen Garden Association in 1880. The association's purpose was ''the promotion of the Domestic Industrial Arts . . . according to the principles of the Kitchen Garden System,'' an essentially Froebelian technique for teaching household skills to children who would become domestic servants. The system had been developed by Emily Huntington through her work in the Wilson Industrial School on the Lower East Side and most likely came to Dodge's attention (in fact she became one of Huntington's volunteer teachers) when she taught in the industrial schools of the Children's Aid Society. The association was abundantly successful. The method may have been an idea whose time had come—vocational schooling of all kinds was drawing increasing attention in the 1880s—but the association's publications and classes for teachers facilitated the method's adoption in cities and states well beyond the New York area, and allowed Grace Dodge to enlarge the project.[25]

In 1884, the Kitchen Garden Association gave way to the Industrial Education Association and the organization's goal was expanded to include industrial training of every kind, although its ultimate purpose of creating ''self-supporting'' people was maintained. Until 1886, the Industrial Education Association, which Dodge organized in much the same way as the State Charities Aid Association, was relatively unsuccessful in its effort to convince the New York City Board of Education to sponsor domestic and industrial training. The situation changed markedly, however, after an exhibition of industrial work done by children drew thousands of visitors to Cosmopolitan Hall during the first week of April 1886 and received a great deal of attention from the press.

In November of 1886, Dodge was appointed to the Board of Education. The exhibition had embarrassed the administration of Mayor William R. Grace because none of the work had been done in the New York City schools. By appointing Dodge, who was "Acting President" of the Industrial Education Association, under General Alexander S. Webb, president of the College of the City of New York, the board hoped to silence public furor. And by giving Grace Dodge a new job, the board gave her an opportunity to extend the identification she had discovered through the working girls' clubs. During her three terms on the board, Dodge visited all of the city's public schools. In addition, she made it her business to become acquainted with as many teachers as possible, and frequently encouraged them to come to her home to discuss their concerns. Thus, via informal contact—discourse among "friends" —Grace Dodge was once again able to elicit the information most relevant to her interests. "With" the "girls" she was able to pursue her goals; from the "girls" she learned that teachers needed more and better training.[26]

Soon after Dodge's appointment to the Board of Education, which coincided with her resignation from the State Charities Aid Association, she reorganized the Industrial Education Association. Schuyler had trained Dodge well, and she was now learning to give scope to her executive ability. The Industrial Education Association's Board of Managers was discarded in favor of a smaller group of trustees. And, as Dodge remembered it, "the taking of the Acting President out of detail work [because of her responsibilities to the Board of Education] . . . and the growth of the work, resulting from higher educational ideals," made apparent the necessity for "a strong, salaried President." Consequently, when George Vanderbilt evidenced an interest in the organization, Dodge persuaded him to give her money for "brains" instead of a library. Nicholas Murray Butler, the young protégé of President Frederick A. P. Barnard of Columbia, was chosen for the job. He was known to be a strong advocate of professional teacher training, both at Columbia and in general, as well as a supporter of public school classes in manual training. The Industrial Education Association quickly became first The New York College for the Training of Teachers and then Teachers College. What Grace Dodge had observed in watching her father at work, filtered through what she had seen in Louisa Lee Schuyler, was obvious in the way in which she built Teachers College. Grace Dodge knew the basis for evangelical campaigns of any kind: that a simple idea successfully promoted can become enlarged in the process. She would later use the same technique to create the National Board of the YWCA.[27]

To test a principle is to learn its limits, and it would seem that at Teachers College, Grace Dodge became increasingly aware of hers. At the time Butler became president of the Industrial Education Association, things could have gone a different way. Grace Dodge was not a "professional" educator, and on occasion she expressed self-consciousness about her lack of formal schooling. Many years later, for example, when Mt. Holyoke offered her an honorary degree, she told friends that she would decline because she was "not educated." Had she seen herself differently, however, she might have become president of the Industrial Education Association herself. She had been a teacher; she was a member of the Board of Education; and she had been involved with the association since its inception. Clearly, therefore, Butler's appointment and Dodge's support for it indicate that at the college she felt able to be a philanthropist, a trustee, but not a professional, not a person who could claim special expertise. Dodge may or may not have considered the possibility that she was as qualified as Butler, if differently so, to become president of the Industrial Education Association. Most likely, however, if the idea crossed her mind she downed it with a good deal of vehemence. Louisa Lee Schuyler and her "girl friends" had legitimated her wish to have a career and had helped her see that women, through highly acceptable forms of self-development and "influence," could be powerful beyond their own homes. But nothing in Dodge's education had prepared her for the kind of leadership she apparently believed the college now needed.[28]

After Butler became president of the Industrial Education Association, Dodge increasingly assumed an exclusively trustee role. Her view of what she could and could not do was tutored significantly, first by Butler and then by James Earl Russell, who followed Butler and then Walter L. Hervey as head of the college.

Whatever Butler told Dodge in private, one thing is clear.

Butler was an aggressive man of strong ideas, who saw in the Industrial Education Association an opportunity to achieve his own,
and President Barnard's, aims at Columbia. He had little sympathy with the organization's initial philanthropic goals and, at
least in his retrospective writing, totally obscured the import of
Grace Dodge's role. In the chapter of his memoirs called "Founding Teachers College," he described Dodge as one of a number of
"eager women" who had organized the Kitchen Garden Association; in a piece called the "Beginnings of Teachers College," he
did not even mention her, and referred to the Industrial Education
Association as a "body organized to strengthen and develop some
admirable work in manual training of various sorts . . . begun by a
group of farsighted and public-spirited women." It seems likely,
therefore, that Butler did little to involve Dodge in the further
programmatic design of the institution. In fact, she herself implied
this when she wrote in 1899 that although she was "the only one
holding official relationship with the College who had been with it
from the beginning . . . another than myself can better sketch the
educational history from 1889 to the present time." Thus, Butler's
perceptions of the role Dodge might play at Teachers College reinforced her own willingness to retreat to a "sphere."[29]

Unlike Butler, Russell was generous in his recognition of the
role Dodge had played in starting Teachers College and well aware
of how much the college had come to mean to her. It was Russell,
in fact, who described Teachers College as Grace Dodge's "oldest
child." Sensitive though he was, however, Russell also found it
necessary to remind Dodge that she was a trustee and therefore
should "keep in." Once, for example, Dodge tried to alert Russell
to the "dangerous influences" he was harboring in the kindergarten department, where, she believed, there was too little discipline
and not enough stress on neatness and order. But having been re-
buked by the dean, in a letter that explained the situation in terms
of pedagogical philosophy—professional expertise—Dodge re-
sumed the "self-restraint" that even Russell recognized as "remarkable" considering the duration and degree of her involvement. The incident "marked the end of [all] external influence
upon the professional policies of the faculty." Dodge had been
moving in this direction at least since the year Butler had been
hired to give the college "brains," but from the late 1890s forward
she restricted herself almost entirely to fund raising. Perhaps be-

cause she could not "influence" the college otherwise, Dodge threw herself completely into the job of capitalizing the venture, and as a result, acquired invaluable knowledge in that area.[30]

As a trustee of Teachers College, Grace Dodge became an extraordinarly good fund raiser. In her "Record book" she once noted, for example, "1894—Between March and July raised $100,000 for College Building," and the figure does not even include what she raised during and after those months or in other years. Much that this effort involved had little to do with Dodge's immediate experience. Many of the necessary personal attributes, persistence, for example, she had been taught to value and cultivate many years before. Nevertheless, the recognition that one must spend "generously" to obtain a future return in growth was one that Dodge herself credited to her work for the college. It was this kind of insight that allowed Grace Dodge to extend and transform the managerial lessons of her childhood to suit the philanthropic role.[31]

Grace Dodge's experience at Teachers College also taught that a person could not act as effectively as possible without formal training. Dodge had felt competent to take the college only so far, and then she had felt compelled to turn it over to "professionals" —to men with "brains." Her "influence" had been limited by the "self-restraint" that, especially when encouraged, she had felt obliged to exercise. As a result, Grace Dodge became even more interested in the education of women than she had been before.

She remained an active trustee of Teachers College until her death in 1914, although her continuing involvement added little to her education. Indeed, by 1905, when she offered her services as mediator to the two branches of the YWCA, Dodge's education was essentially at an end. The years she put into the YWCA, of course, solidified the "talents" she had previously acquired. Yet her work for the YWCA, however important historically, however satisfying personally, is most important to her educational biography as a measure of cumulative growth.

The National Board of the YWCA that was formed as a result of Dodge's intervention brought together what had been the American Committee and the International Board. The differences between the organizations may seem slight today but they were not perceived as such by either group at the time. To create an alliance, therefore, Dodge had to act forcefully, which she did.

She called the leaders of both groups together and convinced them that it would serve them both to unite. A "Joint Committee" with Dodge at its head was set up to work out the details of the merger. It met daily for ten months. Dodge presided at every meeting. According to one of the participants, "when debate grew sharper and edged with unfriendly wit, Miss Dodge from her *Presiding Platform* would say, 'This is very difficult Ladies. Let us ask God to help us, will you join me in prayer?' And the most determined among us could do no less than bow in prayer as Miss Dodge and others voiced our need for *wisdom* and *kindliness* and *spiritual vision.*" Throughout the negotiations and her subsequent term as president of the National Board (1906-1914), Dodge acted with skill, determination, and clarity of purpose. All that she had learned in her previous work was put to use in this, her last new venture.[32]

In a letter she wrote at the beginning of the joint committee's meetings, Dodge stated that "work for and among girls has for thirty years been of great interest. From early womanhood I have felt the lives of my fellow sisters, and I have been allowed in a wonderful way to enter into their problems." She then went on to describe her admiration for women "from all ranks of life," and to point out that "from all these friends I have gained a great deal." Finally, before going into the details with which the joint committee would be concerned, she added: "during the past years . . . I have felt more and more strongly that the SPIRITUAL life of young women needs to be more emphasized, and that when it comes to direct Christian work, we should associate together those who stand on the same platform and also upon the basis of the Young Men's Christian Association. Since early childhood I have been deeply interested in the work of the Young Men's Christian Association movement. My father, brothers, and many friends gave so much of their lives to this work . . . I have known it from the inside as well as the out . . . I have wished many times that the work for young women could have been more united and more on the lines of that for young men." It would seem, therefore, that at the YWCA Grace Dodge saw herself as the female equivalent of her father. During her childhood, her father had united the YMCAs at the Portland Convention, and she was attempting to do the same for the YWCAs. At least within a world of women, Grace Dodge was now able to act publicly and powerfully. She was an architect as Louisa Lee Schuyler had hoped she might be, and to be large in capacity—a giant—was no longer a source of shame.[33]

Beyond this, however, the letter also shows that Grace Dodge never renounced the values of her childhood. "SPIRITUAL life" had been central within her own education and she continued to believe that it was a necessary, perhaps the most necessary, component of a woman's education. Institutions like Teachers College might school a woman's "brains" and certify her "professional" expertise, but as the college had developed, it did not emphasize the kind of discipline in which Dodge believed. Dodge never publicly criticized the college for this, but one can infer at least oblique disappointment from her letter, and since service was to Grace Dodge a religious duty, and service, at home and outside, was also in her opinion what defined "true womanhood," it was entirely logical to believe that "SPIRITUAL life" should be an "emphasized" aspect of the education of women. Furthermore, although the process cannot be reconstructed, reading the Bible and, through prayer and meditation, reflecting constantly were central to Grace Dodge's own education. She could not have done what she did without this, and she quite obviously believed that "SPIRITUAL life" could serve other women as it had served her. The YWCA, then, represents more than Grace Dodge's effort to do what her father had done. It represents her effort to establish an institution over which she could preside in every way and thereby insure that it would educate women to the extent of their abilities, which meant according to their "true," female, nature. At the YWCA, Grace Dodge expressed all that she had learned throughout the course of her education. The legacy of Miss Porter, even more that of her parents, grandparents, and their tradition, remained with Grace Dodge to the end.[34]

In Grace Dodge's work at the YWCA, one can also see the educative effects of her career. As president of the National Board, Dodge established a school to give "secretaries" (field workers) advanced training, and encouraged research on employment opportunities for women and working conditions in predominantly female industries. Her experience had taught that even women could not "influence" as far as they ought without scientific knowledge and formal mental discipline. In 1910 Grace Dodge wrote, "knowledge gives confidence and power," and to enhance women's ability to serve, she intended the YWCA to offer knowledge to women from all walks of life. As president of the National Board, Dodge also urged secretaries to recruit and guide other women as she had tried to do at the working girls' clubs. She even suggested that they use the "Practical Talks" format she had originated so many years before. "Practical Talks," she told them, were a means by which knowledge could be conveyed to women (like herself) who "would not feel equal to taking up for discussion literary or scientific subjects." Through them, she argued, one could "give to young women a shield to resist temptation. Bring out the thought of the dignity and value of labor, get each young worker to feel that she has a part to play in the world's history, and that the world will be either better or worse for the fact of her living in it. Keep up her courage, give her thoughts outside of herself and her work, and by all this lay the foundation for a true womanhood; in a word, teach each member to become 'mistress of herself.' "[35]

At the YWCA, Grace Dodge made it clear that over the years she had learned that a woman's "sphere" need not be domestic. Her education had nurtured interests and abilities that had taken her outside her home, and it had helped her pursue these as a means of service to others. Her achievements were large, perhaps larger than we know. Much that she did, she did quietly and unobtrusively; much that she did went unrecorded. However that may be, Dodge's purpose at the YWCA also shows that her education had not taken her beyond the notion that as a woman she did have special obligations, which were, in a sense, a "sphere." What was she offered that would have allowed her to question this? Not much, it seems. And experiences like the one at Teachers College, regardless of the more positive lessons also conveyed, compounded by her shyness and fear of humiliation, probably undercut whatever she did encounter that might otherwise have taken her even further than she went. Through service, then, Grace Dodge was able to make the most of many of the "talents entrusted" to her, although there were no doubt others that were eclipsed as she tried to be "the humble follower" and willed herself to "keep in."

2

Maud Nathan
1862-1946

AUD NATHAN, like Grace Dodge, was a woman of energy and efficiency. The two women knew each other, and Dodge, in characteristic fashion, generously admired Nathan's work with the Consumers' League, an organization to which she also belonged. Unlike Grace Dodge, however, Maud Nathan was a woman of driving ambition. The reticence, humility, self-restraint, and self-effacement that were so much a part of Grace Dodge were antithetical to Nathan. Grace Dodge, for example, never wrote an autobiography. The closest she came was her "Record book." Maud Nathan, however, did write one, and even this, which tells the story of her childhood, her years as president of the New York Consumers' League, her many speeches in favor of women's suffrage, her leadership among Jewish women, her long and happy marriage, and her busy schedule of travel, parties, concerts, and the like, appears to have been written to document one point: that Maud Nathan had been a woman of outstanding achievement.[1]

In presenting her life as she did, Nathan had a rather obvious didactic purpose. Her autobiography was entitled *Once upon a Time and Today* in order to evoke a fairy-tale allusion that might charm and inspire as a means of instruction. The book was intended to show what a woman could do, especially what a Jewish woman could do. It was published in 1933. The era in which the book was written helped to define the message Nathan wished to impart. In the 1930s, it was unfortunately but acutely necessary to speak out against anti-Semitism, as it was also important to remind the public that "the new woman" had originated from a serious-minded "pioneer" generation. The autobiography indicates, therefore, that its author was the kind of person who could respond directly, personally, and forcefully to the challenges of her day. *Once upon a Time and Today* is a telling document. It reflects qualities that need to be considered in reconstructing Maud Nathan's education, and its form and content set the agenda for her educational biography, which must examine the origins of her outlook, the ways in which this was sustained and modified over time, and the consequences it had both for her life and for her education.

Maud Nathan was born in New York City on October 20, 1862. Her father, Robert Weeks Nathan, was a stockbroker whose usually unsuccessful speculations caused financial problems throughout Maud's childhood and finally, when she was twelve and he had lost his seat on the Exchange, forced his family to move to Green Bay, Wisconsin, where he had been given a job as general passenger agent for a small midwestern railroad. Added to this, Robert Nathan was a man of pleasure, who enjoyed whist, singing duets with well-known sopranos, spending time at the Union Club, and becoming involved in love affairs, often with his wife's friends. He spent little time with his children, although he demanded their laughter and applause whenever they were present during one of his many practical jokes. In short, Robert Nathan was a handsome, genial man but a dismal failure as a husband, father, and head of a family.[2]

Annie Florance Nathan, Maud's mother, was quite different. Although she enjoyed and cultivated a number of male friends and admirers and actively pursued her interest in music and theater, she was a conscientious parent. It was she who taught Maud to read and write; it was she who supervised Maud's daily life; and it was she to whom Maud and her sister and two brothers had to account for their behavior. Annie Florance Nathan always said prayers with her children in the evening. It was from her mother that Maud learned all of the customs of the Nathans' religious heritage: the observance of the sabbath according to the literal interpretation of the biblical commandments, the celebration of the holidays, and the maintenance of strict dietary laws. Annie Florance Nathan, then, was the central adult figure in Maud's early education, and her teaching had a strong influence on her daughter.[3]

High standards were implicit in all that Annie Florance Nathan taught. High standards helped to instill in Maud a wish to excel. When she took Maud to synagogue, for example, Annie Florance Nathan was teaching her that she had something important to live up to. The Nathan family was a prominent one in the New York City Sephardic Jewish community. Maud Nathan's ancestors had arrived on the *St. Charles* in 1654. Her lineage included men like Gershom Mendes Seixas, her maternal great-grandfather, who had been the leader of Shearith Israel (the oldest synagogue in New York City), a trustee of what was then King's College, and a friend of George Washington. Through religious instruction, therefore, Annie Florance Nathan inspired Maud to reach for the goals her ancestors had set. It is hardly coincidental that *Once upon a Time and Today* begins with a description of Maud's family heritage. Giants "quicken youthful imagination," she claimed, and then quickly added: "Surely the descendants of these Jewish Pilgrims are entitled to consider themselves one hundred per cent Americans equally with the descendants of the *Mayflower* Pilgrims. The rights of citizenship sought by the *St. Charles* group were not attained without a struggle, but they came eventually in full measure. Their ideal to become an integral part of the community has been realized."[4]

Ideals and principles were a part of Annie Florance Nathan's curriculum, but religion was not the only vehicle for the aspirations she transmitted. Because her example presented a goal, one that could not be reached without considerable exertion, it also served this function. Before her "exile" to Green Bay, Annie Florance Nathan had been the much admired "center of a brilliant literary and musical coterie." She wrote poems and plays; she was accomplished as a pianist; and she was very beautiful. Maud adored her mother and was proud of her. That she worked very hard to emulate her example is hardly surprising. And since Annie Florance Nathan's example taught that a successful woman was a sought-after woman, in whom learning, "culture," charm, and beauty were a means to an end, Maud became a child who was zealous in her efforts to acquire the skills and posture of a lady.[5]

Annie Florance Nathan believed in Maud. She apparently thought of her as taking on all of the "charms" she herself possessed. And this, combined with Maud's capacity to master what her mother wished, was also important in teaching Maud who she was and what she could do. As a child (and an adult) Maud Nathan was facile with language and physically well coordinated. There is no evidence that she had trouble learning anything. However high Annie Florance Nathan's expectations, therefore, Maud grew up with the feeling that she could reach for the "heights."[6]

To be eager to learn and keen to strive requires strength. In her relationship with her mother, Maud Nathan developed confidence in herself and pride in her family, both of which nurtured a sense of aspiration. Yet in the drive Maud brought first to the business of growing up and then to the other tasks she undertook, one can see a degree of intensity that also needs to be examined. Maud Nathan was an extremely competitive person. She became that way as a child. And in the development of this particular facet of Nathan's personality, the influence of some of the other aspects of her early experience is readily apparent. It is here that Maud's relationships with her father, her siblings, and her peers come into the picture.

Though Maud tended to be silent about her relationship with her father, one should not assume that Robert Nathan was insignificant educationally. It is indicative, for instance, that one of Maud's most cherished childhood dreams was to become "a world renowned cantatrice." For if her mother's example contributed to this, so too, one may presume, did her own longing to attract her father's eye. What is more, Maud's lifelong enjoyment of the coquette role probably came from the same mix of influences. However deficient Robert Nathan was as a father, therefore, one can see nonetheless that his tastes and behaviors had a part in defining those of his daughter. Beyond this, logic would argue that Robert Nathan's disinterest and detachment contributed to Maud's attempts to win the attention she needed from other sources. Consequently, one may conclude that Robert Nathan's failings as a parent injected a measure of vehemence and of determination into the tenacity with which Maud tried to fulfill what was asked of her. As a little girl, Maud wanted to perform well, and she may also have hoped that if she did perform well, exceptionally well, she would gain the notice she craved. Assuming, then, that Maud was in fact the precocious child that she claimed to have been—and there is no reason to disbelieve her assertion—one can see that both her mother and her father encouraged her to learn early to talk, to sing, and to behave as a lady. Differences notwithstanding, both relationships had a powerful effect on Maud.[7]

In retrospect it is also evident that sibling rivalry was a part of Maud Nathan's education and that this too added an increment to her energy and ambition. Annie Florance Nathan had four children, an irresponsible husband, and time-consuming ambitions of her own. The Nathan children had a lot to compete with to hold their mother's interest. Had their mother, let alone their father, been able to give them more time and attention, or had one of their numerous relatives acted as surrogate, Maud might have become a less rivalrous person. As it was, however, Maud, who was a middle child (she was preceded by a brother and followed by another brother and a sister), grew up constantly on guard lest she be outdone by her siblings and more than a little pleased when she was given the chance to feel superior. As a young child she felt impelled to accept her older brother's "dare" to crawl across a plank between two apartment buildings; until "much later" she felt slighted because her two brothers had new silver mugs while she had only a family heirloom belonging to her father; and she greatly enjoyed the time in Green Bay when she was given charge of the pantry keys and her younger brother and sister had to come to her for cookies.[8]

Maud never said much about the interaction between herself and her siblings, although her sister, Annie Nathan Meyer, discussed the relationship between the two of them in her own autobiography. In describing the time immediately following their mother's death in 1878, Annie claimed, for example, that Maud had received abundant sympathy and attention from relatives, while she had been ignored and neglected. "What a difference a little attention would have made in our lives," she wrote. "The seeds of jealousy were planted then and there—a jealousy of my sister which was largely responsible for spoiling our relationship for many years. It was a jealousy all the more bitter because I knew I was Mama's favorite, as I have said, so much nearer her in looks and in temperament." The statement may exaggerate the significance of this one event, and one may question Annie's view of her superior place in their mother's affections. After all, Maud was older than Annie by five years. Thus, if either of them was "nearer" to their mother, at least in prerogatives, if not in "looks and temperament," it was probably Maud. That aside, the statement clearly documents the "jealousy" that existed between all four of the Nathan children, and especially between the two sisters. Annie, like Maud, would become a woman of unusual accomplishment. She was the founder of Barnard College, an author, a playwright, and a vociferous antisuffragist. To argue that either woman's achievements sprang only from her desire to outshine the other would be simplistic, although it would be equally naive to overlook the spurring effect rivalry had on both of them. Competition at home undoubtedly increased Maud's efforts to do whatever was necessary to gain and hold the attention of others.[9]

Anxious for acceptance and notice, eager for success, and already on guard lest she be slighted, Maud was acutely vulnerable to the status consciousness that was increasingly widespread in that part of the late nineteenth-century New York City world in which she spent her first twelve years. Her companions during her daily outings in Central Park and on Fifth Avenue, at Mrs. Ogden Hoffman's School and then at the Gardiner Institute, and at her dancing lessons at Dodsworth's and Hlasko's dancing schools were Protestant and "fashionable." Hence, the "irksome . . . religious observances . . . which made me seem different in the eyes of my playmates" brought resentment. Furthermore, when the Nathans moved from 36th Street one block off Fifth Avenue to 46th Street west of Eighth Avenue, and Maud's school friends "lifted their eyebrows superciliously and tilted their noses," the knowledge that she was "regarded as being outside the social pale" caused acute pain.[10]

Instead of leading to retreat, however, the snub heightened Maud Nathan's ambition. As an adult she purposefully chose to participate in Protestant (or nonsectarian) organizations beyond the confines of what she called "a narrow communal circle" (by which she meant Jewish philanthropy) partly to make a point. Clearly, then, Maud brought to her initial forays in the outside world the attitudes that she had developed in response to both the intended and the inadvertent pedagogy of her family. She once wrote: "some venturesome, indiscreet imp has always urged me on, even to the brink of folly, when suggestion has been put in the form of a 'dare' . . . The childish taunt, 'You daren't do what I've done,' has always made me feel: 'What others have done, I too can do.' '' The belief that she could meet challenges as well as the presumption that restriction meant challenge was extended to the world at large early in her life.[11]

The anti-Semitism and snobbishness Maud encountered in her peers was unquestionably real and cruel. Yet it is important to recognize that Maud may have helped to elicit the response she met both in the park and at school. She had developed a rather consistent style early in life. The eagerness, competitiveness, and determination—the ambition—that was so typical of her was evident even in the nursery. It obviously influenced her interaction with her siblings; it may have also influenced her interaction with her peers.

An individual's style, her physical appearance, her choice of words, her posture toward other people, often has this effect. Because Maud's style was a challenging one, therefore, the way she presented herself to her playmates may have urged them to see her as they did. In short, the strength of Maud's wish for acceptance may have influenced her childhood companions as much as the sting of their insults influenced her. In her style, Maud Nathan carried already established patterns of seeing, believing, and behaving with her as her education began to move outside of her home. Her style had a continuing influence on the way in which she interacted with the people and the experiences from which her education was derived.[12]

More than many individuals, Maud was aware of this. She recognized, for example, that her response to a "dare" had been "an impelling force" in her life. And she stated directly that her accomplishments were the result of persistence. Interestingly too, she claimed that her life had been greatly influenced by "having been brought up in a small country town," where there were fewer "conventions" and more "freedom" than in New York City. The openness and democracy of life in Green Bay, Wisconsin, Maud wrote, "gave me a broad outlook."[13]

The years she spent in Green Bay were indeed an important part of Maud Nathan's education, especially perhaps in terms of schooling. When the Nathans moved there in 1874, Maud and her older brother were sent to the local high school. Offered a curriculum of Latin and geography and the U. S. Constitution, as opposed to the French and rhetoric and "cultural smattering" that had been her previous fare, and urged on by the presence of boys as well as girls, Nathan found her time in the classroom pleasant and challenging. Typically, when the Latin teacher warned that "hic, haec, hoc" would be a difficult declension to learn, Maud mastered it so well that she was able to recite it "glibly." Within two years she had completed the requirements for graduation. Her examination scores were perfect. She was chosen class salutatorian. As she later explained, the experience became a kind of touchstone to which she could and did return whenever her confidence faltered in later years. Her success, and the acclaim and notice that came with it, added to the conviction that with effort she could accomplish whatever she set out to do.[14]

The years in Green Bay were significant to Nathan's education in still another way. Her earliest experience had established a specific view of femininity, which was sustained by her activities during these years. In high school, Maud discovered that women in Wyoming had been given the right to vote. But if this information in any way modified her notion of what it meant to be a woman, the rest of her experience did not.

When she finished school at fourteen and a half, Maud was allowed to "put up" her hair and to join in adult parties, concerts, and lectures. She also took piano lessons, read literature, history, and French with her mother to "round out her cultural outlook," sang with the Green Bay choral society, took part in amateur theatricals, and helped with the management of the household. In other words, she was provided with further training for the traditional conception of the role of leisure-class lady but with no way to gain status other than through her position in society. And since there was also nothing to dampen Maud's wish for recognition—if anything her high school experience taught her how satisfying recognition could be—she returned to New York City as eager to be a "young lady in society" as when she left four years earlier. Considering the intellectual ability Maud evidenced in high school, one cannot help wondering what might have happened if she had gone on to college. Because it was still extremely rare for women to go to college, however, and Annie Florance Nathan believed that girls of college age needed constant maternal attention and supervision, Maud's formal schooling was not continued.[15]

When one places her experience in Green Bay within the context of what came before and after, one discovers, therefore, that what Maud learned at this time made her better able to reach for what she wanted, although there was little in "the freer life of a small western village" to change her direction. How, then, is one to understand her assertion that her experience at this time nurtured a "broad outlook," an outlook that led her to devote her life to creating a more open society, a society in which all people would have the chance to be judged on the basis of their talent and character, rather than according to their place in the social hierarchy? Her claim must be read, on one level, as a plea for such a society, as an argument for the kind of community Nathan was advocating in her autobiography; and on another level, it must be read as an accurate interpretation of her experience, in that subsequent developments made it possible for Nathan to gain from the memory of this period the "broad outlook" she attributed to it. At the time, however, her experience was most important because it increased her confidence, which should not be underrated in considering her continuing ability to grow. And the same may be said of the years immediately following the ones in the Midwest.[16]

The Nathan family left Green Bay in 1878. Shortly thereafter, Annie Florance Nathan became seriously ill and died. Just before hearing the news of her mother's death, Maud, who was staying at the Florance home in New York City, met Frederick Nathan, a first cousin, twenty years her senior, whom she described as "a handsome man . . . a member of the Union, Knickerbocker, Manhattan, New York and Racquet Clubs, and of the Seventh Regiment Veteran Association . . . [and a bachelor who was] very popular with the ladies." The two became engaged on Thanksgiving Day, 1879, and were married at Shearith Israel on April 7, 1880.[17]

In the dedication of her autobiography, Maud referred to her husband as "the Fairy Prince of this tale." Throughout the thirty-eight years of their marriage, Frederick Nathan provided her with the emotional support and financial security she had had so little of as a child. In her marriage, Maud Nathan found the opportunity to vindicate herself in traditional female roles and, as she took on increasing interest in other activities, the sustenance and help that was also so vital to her career. Lillian Wald once described Frederick Nathan as Maud's "staunch comrade in public service." Another friend wrote that the Nathans' marriage provided "a fine illustration of what marriage ideally ought to be . . .

a partnership between comrades who, while keeping their own rights as individuals, work together for the same high ends." Maud Nathan's husband was an important figure in her continuing education.[18]

Frederick Nathan did in fact work with his wife. He joined her, for instance, in her efforts for women's suffrage. He traveled with her when she went on speaking tours; he was an early and active member of the Men's League for Equal Suffrage; and he patiently and unflappably responded in the affirmative when asked whether marriage to a suffragist was supportable. So far as one can discern, Frederick Nathan was not at all threatened by his wife's attention to outside issues; instead, he seems to have reveled in Maud's triumphs. Why this was so, what made the Nathans' marriage such a successful "partnership," is difficult to know, but Frederick Nathan's self-confidence and his lack of comparably passionate interests probably had an effect, as did Maud's ability to move easily and with equal enjoyment from a suffrage rally or a Consumers' League meeting to a totally frivolous caper, costume parties being among her favorite activities. In any event, the reasons for the marriage's success are less important for an understanding of Maud Nathan's education than are the effects of Frederick Nathan's devotion and respect, which helped Maud develop a mature style that combined her wish to be a "lady in society" and her desire to express herself as she saw fit. In her husband, Maud Nathan found an ever-attentive audience whose estimate was consistently and genuinely favorable, and highly valued. Frederick Nathan and the experience Maud had as a result of their marriage took her in new directions much more than did life in Green Bay, Wisconsin.[19]

Imagine, for example, what the parties and shopping that preceded the Nathans' wedding showed Maud. Immediately following the announcement of their engagement, she became the center of attention, "fêted on all sides." She was taken to the opera, given dinners at Delmonico's, allowed the use of her fiancé's coupé, and showered with hundreds of wedding presents. "The display of silverware was bewildering," she remembered, and the entire experience dazzling. Even the tone of the section of *Once upon a Time and Today* that describes this period (she called the chapter "The Fairy Prince and the Land of Enchantment") conveys the excitement she apparently felt. Suddenly and at a young age (she was seventeen at the time of her marriage), Maud had become the recipient of all that her mother had wished for her and all that she had learned from her mother to wish for herself. Annie Florance Nathan had told Frederick Nathan, when Maud was still a baby, that he should wait for her; she would make him a good wife. She had also once written a poem in which she expressed the hope that Maud would receive "the homage and the culture" that was her "due." During the weeks before the Nathans' wedding, Maud entered the world for which she had been prepared. Those weeks could not have failed to show her how worthwhile all of her previous efforts had been.[20]

The same lesson was also implicit in the following sixteen months in Europe, during which Maud's sense that she was now a desirable woman, admired and sought-after wherever she went, was further magnified. She remembered, for example, that in London, Edward VII, then the Prince of Wales, had stared at her at the opera and asked that she join him for breakfast on the royal yacht at Cowes; that in Paris, during her one excursion without her maid, she had been persistently pursued by an "unknown admirer"; that at dances in Nice, she had been "whirled about by a French or Italian cavalier who was a complete stranger"; and that in Venice, she had felt like "royalty." The time was apparently one of consolidation. Maud was finding out that her aspirations were not impossible dreams. The integration that began with her betrothal was to remain the central agenda of her education for some time to come.[21]

When the Nathans returned from Europe, Maud became totally immersed in buying furniture, supervising the maids, going personally to the market, and making her own pickles and preserves. Unlike many of the women with whom she would later join in her work as a reformer, Maud Nathan seems not to have chafed at a conventional life. During the early years of her marriage, Maud was not agonizing over what she would do or how she would serve. Rather, she enjoyed planning for the frequent visitors who arrived just in time to be invited for a meal, or who came to her Wednesday afternoons "at home," or one of the "soirées musicales" that she and her husband gave together. She felt pride in the discovery that "by being systematic" she could finish her household duties in an hour or two, leaving more time for the embroidery, piano playing, singing, shopping, and calls that filled the rest of her day. And during the summer when she and her husband went to Saratoga or another of the then popular summer resorts, she happily sat on the piazza with the other women, gossiping and planning future entertainments—a charity concert for the New York Diet Kitchen, a garden party, a Saturday evening cotillion. As one might expect in light of her previous education, all Maud Nathan wanted at this time was "to be a sweet songstress, and an ideal housekeeper." Her education had not led to what Jane Addams would later call a "snare of preparation." Maud Nathan was not now and never would be burdened by introspection or by the inability to act.[22]

The years before Nathan became an active reformer were ones of important growth. To become fully aware, and sure, that she was a woman who could be all that her mother had been may even have been a necessary precondition to her pursuit of other additional ambitions. And the charity work that was a natural, even a necessary, aspect of Nathan's newly acquired status of matron offered a kind of training she had not had before as well as exposure to problems she had not previously known about.

When the Nathans returned from Europe, Maud's aunt asked her to join the Board of Directors of the Mt. Sinai Hospital nursing school. Soon thereafter, she also became chairman of the subcommittee on kindergartens of the Hebrew Free School Association. As was true for so many women of her class, the need to provide services for the steadily increasing stream of East European immigrants was for Maud a significant educational opportunity. She took her new responsibilities earnestly and worked very hard. At the least her new jobs solidified her sense of maturity, and subsequently the experience also may have helped her recognize the satisfaction greater service might provide. More important still, it was at this time that Maud became associated with the New York Exchange for Women's Work, and the educative significance of this association is unmistakable.[23]

When Nathan was asked to become a manager of the exchange she was given a place on a board that was made up of established Protestant New Yorkers. The organization's purpose, to provide a retail outlet for the needlework of "impoverished gentlewomen," had little, if anything, to do with the problems of newly arrived Jewish immigrants. As she herself pointed out, her work for the board provided a first lesson in politics; Nathan corresponded with the New York congressional delegation to urge the defeat of the Dingley Tariff Bill, which would have decreased the market for the goods sold by the exchange. In addition, her position on the board exposed her, through Mrs. William G. Choate's example, to a model of board chairmanship that combined business and social ties in a fashion that she found appealing. But in light of her earlier experience, the affiliation strikes one as having been most significant because it proved that Maud need not restrict herself to work for her coreligionists. Maud had always had the strength of will to strive for what she wished. Yet in joining the board of the New York Exchange for Women's Work she no doubt felt a kind of vindication that helps to account for her increasing ability to find the kind of acceptance she sought. It is not that Maud wanted to shun Jewish philanthropy. She was the first president of the sisterhood of Shearith Israel and active in the National Council of Jewish Women. But she did want to prove her worth as a member of a pluralistic community and not simply as a faithful adherent to Judaism. At the New York Exchange, Maud had a chance for association with women of non-Jewish background in work that had to do with "civic" as opposed to "communal" problems. And in part it was this that led to her growing interest in social reform.[24]

Many things influenced Maud Nathan's increasing participation in "civic" activities—above all else the friendship she developed with Josephine Shaw Lowell. The Nathans first met Lowell when they spent an evening listening to her read a paper on prison reform at the home of a mutual friend. Though the subject had been of little interest to Maud previously, she claimed to have been "deeply affected" by the conditions Lowell described. Lowell, who was a revered and romantic figure in New York society, was the type of person who could capture and hold Maud Nathan's attention and admiration.[25]

As the sister of Robert Gould Shaw, a Civil War hero who had died in command of the first Negro regiment to be sent to the front, and the widow of Charles Russell Lowell, who had given his life for "the [Union] cause" one year after their marriage, Josephine Shaw Lowell was a symbol of feminine altruism and sacrifice. Through her work, she had also achieved an elevated position within the hierarchy of New York City reformers. Her career had begun with the Sanitary Commission and Louisa Lee Schuyler's State Charities Aid Association. Her efforts for those organizations

had brought her an appointment to the New York State Board of
Charities; the survey she undertook for the board in turn had led
her to organize the New York Charity Organization Society to co-
ordinate and promote greater efficiency among existing charity
groups. Lowell's competence and public prominence held great
appeal for Nathan.[26]

Since at this time Lowell still held to the standard assumptions concerning the essentially moral nature of social "rehabilitation," her point of view also made sense to Nathan. Despite the
very significant differences involved, one can see in Lowell's presumption that she, and others like her, had to control paupers,
tramps, and immigrants for their own good as well as that of society, the same kind of thinking "that made it necessary," as Maud
Nathan put it, "for the Jews of New York to form committees . . .
[in the 1880s and 1890s] in order to devise means of distributing
. . . [the] sudden avalanche of hitherto ghetto-imprisoned . . . for-
eigners over the country and of endeavoring to Americanize them
as rapidly as possible."[27]

Between Josephine Shaw Lowell and Maud Nathan, then,
there was a good deal of rapport in terms of temperament and outlook; there was also a significant differential in knowledge and
skill; and on each side, there was cause to invest in the other. Maud
Nathan's curiosity, quickness, and ambition were no doubt as appealing to Lowell as Lowell's position was to Nathan. And all of
this helped to make it possible for Lowell to become Maud Nathan's chosen mentor. For approximately ten years, Nathan worked
closely with Lowell. Lowell helped Nathan expand her understanding of what a lady in society must do.

Josephine Shaw Lowell put long and hard hours into her work
and expected serious engagement on the part of her colleagues.
"Charity organization is not a work to which any man should put
his hand, unless he is prepared to give it some measure of devotion," she said in describing the "duties of friendly visitors." "It
is hard work which we have undertaken; work requiring time, and
thought, and patience and judgment." The attitude was a far cry
from the one that had characterized Maud's charitable activities
before she met Lowell. She had taken her various board member-
ships seriously, but by her own admission she had been leading the
kind of life typical of a leisure-class lady. "I was interested in my
husband, my little girl, my home," she wrote later. "Only in rela-

tion to them and to the wider family circle did I recognize any duties and responsibilities.'' The range of Maud's interests was to change, however, through Lowell's example and that of the other women with whom she became associated in the establishment of the Consumers' League; through the expectations Lowell held out for her as her colleague; through her own increasing awareness of the desperate conditions under which many less fortunate women lived and worked, the skills and knowledge she was able to bring to the effort to change these, and the satisfaction she achieved as a result. The process was one of slow, cumulative learning. Maturation contributed its part. Maud was in her twenties when she first met Lowell; she was thirty-four when she became president of the New York Consumers' League. But without Josephine Shaw Lowell, Maud Nathan's aspirations might have taken her in another direction.[28]

As one can see in looking at the years during which Nathan and Lowell were closely allied, it would be difficult to overrate the part Lowell played in Nathan's education. On Lowell's invitation, for example, Nathan was present at a mass meeting in May of 1890 that was called to hear a report on working conditions in large department stores. The report had grown out of investigations undertaken by the Working Women's Society, a group of factory workers and salesgirls (one of whose leaders was Leonora O'Reilly) who had met regularly since 1886 to share information and to do what they could to improve all aspects of their employment. The report shocked and horrified the people who heard it. Nine months later the Consumers' League was formally established. Its object was ''by public opinion, by law, and by the action of consumers . . . to ameliorate the conditions of the women and children employed in the retail houses of New York City.'' Maud Nathan was one of its original directors. Through Lowell, therefore, she was able to join in the founding of an organization, one that was directed toward the solution of ''civic'' problems.[29]

The report that Nathan heard at the original Chickering Hall meeting opened a ''new vista of life'' for her. From it she learned that, albeit unwittingly, she had contributed to the conditions it described and therefore had a responsibility to change them. Lowell may have had a hand in styling the report; at the time she was acting as an adviser to the Working Women's Society. However that may be, she obviously knew what women like Maud

Nathan needed to hear in order to develop the kind of commitment necessary to sustain an organization. Nathan's first acquaintance with the realities of life on the Lower East Side, through her work with the Hebrew Free School Association, whose kindergarten subcommittee she headed during the period when extreme need had forced it to become involved with the distribution of shoes, clothing, food, and other necessities, had not provoked the kind and depth of responsibility she now felt. But her reaction to this report was no less electrifying than the reaction of the audience in general. The meeting Lowell organized was attended by some women who were already aware of their social responsibilities and some who were like Nathan in that they were just beginning to see them. Being similar, however, in their recognition of a call to action, seasoned reformer and neophyte alike served to promote the "new vista of life" that Nathan realized. Josephine Shaw Lowell had created a situation in which Maud Nathan, and others, could learn for themselves.[30]

Finally, and most important, Lowell took Nathan on as an assistant and understudy. During the first years of its existence when Lowell was its president, the Consumers' League concentrated on the establishment of a "White List" of retail firms that met its standards of working hours, sanitary conditions, and the like. Additionally, the league supported the Working Women's Society's effort to have a bill regulating the employment of women and children passed by the New York state legislature. Helping Lowell in both activities increased Maud's knowledge of the working woman's world and of the lack of concern for working conditions frequently manifested by businessmen. With Lowell, who quite literally, as Nathan put it, "took me by the hand and led me forward in the work," Nathan wrote thousands of letters, visited stores all over the city, and talked with hundreds of saleswomen. By 1895, she had become expert enough so that she was "the only one" who could give the Rhinehart Commission the information it needed to justify support of the bill the Working Women's Society favored. If her "devotion" and importance had not been clear before, they were now. When Lowell urged Maud to appear at the hearing in Albany, despite the recent death of her only child—a daughter, who had been born in 1886—she did. Soon thereafter, Lowell resigned as president of the league. The office was passed on to Nathan. In 1899, when the National Consumers' League was organized, she became a vice president of that as well. Josephine Shaw Lowell and her friends were the right people and they came at the right time to change Maud Nathan's life.[31]

Having learned that work, serious work, could be personally satisfying as well as enhancing to a woman's position in society, Maud Nathan was able to find in her job at the Consumers' League opportunities that were profoundly educative. By 1933, when she wrote her autobiography, she had obviously come to believe that learning, "culture," charm, and beauty were not simply a means by which a woman might win compliments; they were part of the arsenal upon which she might draw to recall the nation to its ideals. The difference in belief was a fundamental one. It grew out of what she learned during the twenty years that she was president of the Consumers' League.

Having assumed that post from her mentor, Nathan quickly suited the job to her own personality. Unlike Josephine Shaw Lowell, who was most skillful as an investigator and lobbyist, Maud Nathan preferred the role of publicist. She used her position to transform the Consumers' League into a national movement. As president of the group, Maud traveled throughout the United States and Europe; she spoke wherever she was offered a platform. By 1926, there were ninety local leagues, twenty state leagues, thirty-five school and college branches, thirty-five auxiliary leagues, and an International Conference of American and Foreign Consumers' Leagues, most of which she had helped to initiate.[32]

From her travels, Maud Nathan drew an important insight: "that all the people need is for someone to go about the country 'prodding them up.' " Most people, she had discovered, knew little about the conditions in which the goods they bought were manufactured and sold. But when they were told about these and helped to see their part in creating and maintaining them, their willingness to change was sincere. At least to Maud, the rapid organizational success of the Consumers' League proved this. Thus, Maud's experience with the Consumers' League confirmed her in her self-designed role. Her job, as she saw it, was to arouse the conscience of the nation.[33]

Because this discovery gave direction to Maud Nathan's career, it was one of the most essential lessons of her adult life, and a number of other experiences fed into it. Through her husband, for example, a devout Jew who seems to have joined in "civic" as well

as "communal" groups more easily and with less initial self-consciousness than she did, Maud learned to understand Judaism differently than she had as a child. At that point in her life, she had
sometimes found the religious customs of her family "irksome";
as an adult, their faith became an important resource. In fact, it
was in what she termed the "heart of Judaism"—"righteousness
and justice, mercy and loving-kindness"—that she saw "the salvation of a nation." Through her husband, who remained faithful in
his devotion to and admiration for her as a woman, Maud also realized that the femininity she had worked so hard to develop as a girl
had become an integral part of her identity. In various ways, then,
Frederick Nathan helped his wife understand that her initial goals
had been achieved. Learning to see herself as her husband did
helped Maud Nathan speak out with ease and grace. Her speeches
were always witty and incisive and embellished with well-chosen
quotations. As she grew in poise and social presence, she was able
to put to good use the foreign languages, literature, and history
she had learned years before. Her increasing capacity to call forth
all of her abilities was in large measure the result of the confidence
and self-acceptance she developed through her marriage.[34]

The sense of achievement that was nurtured in Maud by her
husband had a profound effect on her style as this, too, was subtly
transformed over the years. Its most essential elements remained
unchanged. As president of the Consumers' League, Maud was no
less determined and ambitious than she had been as a child, but
now these qualities reflected more than an assertion of will and of
right. In Maud Nathan's mature style one can see a presumption of
wisdom and insight that had not been there before. As Maud explained the Consumers' League to audiences throughout the country, she repeatedly asserted that her purpose and the organization's
purpose were primarily educational. What she called "preventive
philanthropy"—"the general elevation of the working classes by
means of proper compensation for work done, as distinguished
from the method of underpaying them and later caring for them in
poorhouses and public hospitals"—was worthwhile; but since
shopping involved "ethical" questions, the more important aspect
of her goal was to teach people that spending money, no less than
making it, demanded that one shun short-term personal gain—
"bargains"—and consider instead the long-term welfare of the
entire community, "buying only that which is moral and healthful

to the producer and consumer; only that which is made and sold under good conditions."[35]

One might argue that as president of the Consumers' League, Nathan thought of herself as something of a prophet. She had learned that "the key to the solution of all social and economic problems is to make our personal wants at one with the supreme good of the entire universe," and through her speeches, it was her job to bring the word to others. However that may be, it is certainly clear that Nathan's style expressed the confident assumption that she had something fundamentally true, moral, right, and of course important to share with others. And since her style as a mature woman continued to shape her experience as much as her experience shaped her, her style helped to bring forth in the people to whom she spoke echoes of the lesson she herself projected. In other words, Nathan learned, or was increasingly confirmed in her sense, that it was her job to arouse the conscience of the nation, partly because she presented herself as carrying out that task. And she did so as a result most immediately of what she had acquired in her relationships with Lowell and her husband. Maud Nathan's earlier definition of her mission in life—"to be a sweet songstress, and an ideal housekeeper"—was quite different. The desire to be listened to and to be seen as exemplary are evident in both, although the distance between them also reflects all aspects of Nathan's education, which, during these years, included at least one additional influence.[36]

Individuals can educate, but so too can groups, and the group of women with whom Maud Nathan became associated in the Consumers' League played an important educational function in her life. Many of these women were suffragists; all were in some way concerned and involved with the plight of working women and children, corruption in municipal government, public school politics, and civil service reform; and a number of them were extremely articulate feminists. Mary Putnam Jacobi, for example, was a doctor and the author of a clever and influential pamphlet entitled " 'Common Sense' Applied to Woman Suffrage." Soon after Maud became president of the Consumers' League, Mary Putnam Jacobi asked her also to become president of the New York State Suffrage Association. She declined that post, although the offer illustrates the way in which her Consumers' League friendships served to lead her beyond that organization. Educa-

tionally, however, it is even more important that Mary Putnam
Jacobi and a number of others, indeed Maud's female colleagues as
a whole, became a reference group for her. To travel throughout
the country, preaching the "ethics" of the bargain counter, was to
act on the belief that women had a right and responsibility to
speak out, which was a notion that was increasingly common
among the women who had become Maud Nathan's friends.
Maud acted as she did, therefore, partly because the women she respected admired her for doing so. Their views supported, to an
extent even directed, the change Maud underwent in slowly relin-
quishing a rather traditional, essentially decorative notion of femininity for one that was more socially responsible and service
oriented.[37]

Maud Nathan's associates, her husband, and her mentor were
the significant others of her adult life. Their views and knowledge
as well as their behavior were vital sources of education, even if
their influence was constantly filtered through Maud's own experience.

Maud Nathan's interest in suffrage, for example, was stimulated by the women with whom she worked in the Consumers'
League, but it was increased still further by her own contact with
politicians. The Consumers' League's effort to get the Mercantile
Inspection Act passed by the New York state legislature, though
successful, taught her, she claimed, that without the vote, women's political influence would be minimal. And that experience
was prefatory to many similar ones. In 1915, Nathan told a re-
porter: "Each time that I have gone to Albany to plead for more
progressive legislation in behalf of working women, I have returned home a more ardent suffragist." The people whose admiration Maud wanted, the people with whom she identified, pushed
her to work for the franchise, but so too did the men who failed to
give her the hearing she felt entitled to. No doubt their inatten-
tion activated the kind of defiant reaction that Maud had first
developed in response to the challenges of her childhood. And this
certainly made it easier for her to understand and adopt the prosuffrage arguments she heard all around her.[38]

Nathan's participation in the suffrage campaign was consistent with the direction in which her education had been taking her
at least since the late 1880s. As a suffragist, however, Maud did
little that involved knowledge or skill she did not already possess.

It was she who gained the support of Mrs. Clarence Mackay, the first of the "so-called 'society women' " to become involved in the cause and subsequently the founder of the Equal Franchise Society, whose board included well-known men (John Dewey, Stephen Wise, and so on) as well as women. But the effort this required of her, explaining the cause to Mackay and then to the women Mackay gathered at a lunch at the Colony Club, was no different from the kind of effort she had put into the parlor meetings the Consumers' League organized. Similarly, her frequent speeches, however witty, amusing, and persuasive, called for nothing more than the ones she also made for the league. Finally, although she won a one hundred dollar prize for submitting the best letter in support of suffrage to a *New York Herald* contest, Maud had had many previous letters and articles published by this time and her argument said little that was original among suffragists or novel within the logic she had used to explain any number of other subjects. She wrote: "I believe in suffrage because it is just and because it is expedient." She might have substituted shorter working hours or civil service reform for suffrage. She had already lobbied for these on essentially the same grounds.[39]

The point is not to denigrate Nathan's work. Her name was included by the New York League of Women Voters in the state honor roll inscribed on a bronze tablet in the capital in Albany, and deserved to be. She was chairman of the Women's Suffrage Committee of the National Progressive party and a vice president of the Equal Suffrage League of New York City. She put unusual time and energy as well as competence and experience into the fight. In itself, however, the suffrage campaign seems to have taught her little more than participation in the Women's Auxiliary of the Civil Service Reform Association, the Advisory Board of the Industrial Committee of the General Federation of Women's Clubs, the Women's Health Protective League, the Southern Library Fund, the Central Park Protection Committee, and so on.[40]

Two considerations are relevant in understanding this. First, suffrage work, like all of the above, had become Maud Nathan's daily life. The crucial, most determinative junctures had been negotiated before she became an active suffragist. Hence, the insights suffrage work brought, whatever they may have been, were so incremental in effect that they are extremely difficult to recover. Second, Maud Nathan enjoyed a fight. She had always, by her own admission, taken it upon herself to attempt whatever others had achieved. Often, therefore, she focused more attentively on winning a fight—on tactics—than on the philosophical questions involved. And since her tactical skills were already well developed by the time she became a suffragist, there was little the campaign could offer in terms of new awareness. Again, this is not to say that she did not learn anything from suffrage work. Nor is it to say that Nathan cared only for triumph. But it is to say that the ambition and striving that energized her education also limited it.

From the beginning, Maud Nathan had set out to win recognition, a goal that certainly encouraged her efforts to become excellent in all that she did. This wish took Nathan a long way. It was this that allowed her to meet the challenges of life head on, and it was in her effort to do this that she became a precocious little girl, an outstanding student, a popular hostess, and a competent, socially responsible woman who was a leading figure in turn-of-the-century New York City. To respond to life as Nathan did had obvious advantages in terms of education, although the same tendencies may have deprived her of the opportunity to stand back and consider freely and on her own what it was that she really wanted and why what she chose to do really mattered. Little in Maud Nathan's education had encouraged her to reflect, to question, to ponder; much in Maud Nathan's education had encouraged her to act quickly and effectively. She was extraordinarily attuned to the expectations and judgments of other people, and as a result highly susceptible to the trends, fashions, and controversies of the world in which she lived. Maud liked to think of herself as an exceptionally independent person. Was she really so independent? In light of her education, one cannot be so sure.

Think even of the pace of her life, which, until Frederick Nathan died in December of 1918, continued in the pattern established in the 1890s. Her days were filled with meetings and speeches; her evenings and afternoons with parties, receptions, and family gatherings. During the summer, the Nathans continued to spend four or five months away from New York City, most often traveling in Europe and usually combining purely social visiting, sightseeing, and attendance at congresses, conventions, and meetings where Maud had been asked to speak. Their years together were busy, and over its entire span, Maud's life had few periods of quiescence. She pushed herself hard, once even to the point of breakdown (in the winter of 1912-13). She had married soon after her mother's death; she had become president of the Consumers' League in the year following her daughter's death; and in the spring of 1919, she was "very glad" to have been chosen as a delegate to the Woman Suffrage Convention in St. Louis, at which the National American Woman Suffrage Association was transformed into the League of Women Voters. Widowhood involved a difficult "readjustment" for Maud, but it did little to change her approach to life. She wrote of the time after her husband's death: "My life seemed empty. I was no longer President of the Consumers' League . . . The struggle for equal suffrage seemed to be nearing its goal. The happy incentive of home-making no longer existed. [And] the home that my husband and I had made together seemed so big, so lonely, that I fled to a small apartment." Activist that she was, however, Nathan managed to fill the void. She relied increasingly upon friends to provide support and companionship; she took a trip through the Far East; and she wrote her autobiography. *Once upon a Time and Today* is hard to read as the work of a person who was as autonomous and self-determined as Nathan claimed to have been.[41]

The book was intended to be a chronicle of triumph, and it is. It features the major events of Nathan's life; it tells of her persistence; and, at the end, in a "note of prophecy," it assures its readers that "the world *does* change," if one is willing to turn "stumbling blocks" to "stepping stones" on the road "to further achievement." In the book, Nathan was quite explicit in pointing to what she considered the major stumbling blocks of her day, anti-Semitism and a lack of community being high on her list. Her goal in writing the book, as I mentioned at the start, appears to have been didactic. She was offering her life as an example to help others find the right road. Her purpose, therefore, was of a piece with her life, and one suspects that the act of writing the book was equally representative of her education.[42]

The autobiography is a selective document and obviously carefully crafted. As always, therefore, Nathan probably worked hard on the book and marshaled all of her abilities to do the job well. At times the book is clever, and throughout the narrative is clear and direct. In general, however, *Once upon a Time and Today* is a chronicle, rather than a searching, enlightening self-study. The meaning and significance of the people Nathan mentions are not always clear, and she was far more inclined to describe and assert than she was to explain. Even in writing her autobiography, therefore, Nathan does not seem to have developed the ability to see beyond herself and her immediate goal. Her education allowed her to do many things, but if *Once upon a Time and Today* is the measure, it did not nurture the kind of thinking necessary to incisive self-scrutiny. Maud Nathan was an able and ambitious woman, one who preferred action to contemplation. Thus, her autobiography clearly describes the limits of her education. In it one can see what Maud Nathan was and was not able to achieve as a woman who strove with persistence for the recognition she wanted, and deserved.

3

Lilliaɲ D. Wald
1867-1940

AFTER JANE ADDAMS, Lillian Wald may be
the best-known woman of the progressive gen-
eration. She was the founder of the Henry Street Settlement and of
the Visiting Nurse Service. She became with Addams one of the
leading spokeswomen for progressive social reform of all kinds. In
terms of accomplishment Wald was clearly a giant. To the people
who knew her, Lilliam Wald was an approachable, fun-loving,
extraordinarily generous, perceptive, and humane person. She was
respected for the abilities that made her a leader, but she was loved
for those that made her an unusual human being. Few people are
accorded the kind of admiration and affection that one finds in so
many contemporary descriptions of Wald.

Lillian Wald's education was no less remarkable than her life.
Wald was able to strive for and accomplish almost all that she
wanted. She was able to move through disappointment and success
with equal equanimity. Most important of all, she was able to
choose what she did and did not want to be and to do with unusual
ease and intelligence. In a sense, therefore, Lillian Wald's educational biography is a simple chronicle. Her education took her a
long way, but it was not a complex process.

Lillian Wald was born on March 10, 1867, in Cincinnati,
Ohio. She was the third of the four children of Max D. and Minnie
Schwarz Wald. Her childhood was spent in Cincinnati and Dayton,

Ohio, and then Rochester, New York. In Dayton, Wald attended a local "seminary"; in Rochester, Miss Cruttenden's School. At sixteen Wald applied to Vassar College, but was rejected on the grounds that she was too young. Six years later she left Rochester to begin eighteen months of training at the New York Hospital School of Nursing. Her family was not pleased by her decision, but it was primarily their influence that made it possible.

Wald never attributed such influence to her family. She said only that they had spoiled and indulged her. Her refusal to probe further was characteristic. Lillian Wald did not like to analyze the sources of her motivation or to survey her life to draw from it a moral for others. "Self-analysis . . . [is] prone to hinder and to dwarf wholesome instincts," Wald wrote in *The House on Henry Street*, and more often than not abjured such reflection (or its public statement) throughout her life. The importance of Wald's family is clear, however, when one examines the nature of their life together as well as the enduring effects of this life upon Wald's subsequent education in nursing school, at the settlement she founded on Henry Street, and within the wider circles into which she was eventually drawn. It is with a description of the Wald family, therefore, that her educational biography must begin.[1]

The Wald household consisted of Max and Minnie Wald, Goodman Schwarz, Lillian's maternal grandfather, Samuel Schwarz, an uncle who visited often, and the four children. Max Wald was a dealer in optical goods. He had come to the United States from Germany in 1848, at the age of ten. He was a person of quiet and calm temperament who was often overshadowed by the more flamboyant members of his family. He was also a person of great gentleness, whose totally unselfish attitude toward his family and complete dependability led them to take him for granted. Minnie Wald, by contrast, was strong-willed, colorful, even a little eccentric. She had an almost childlike love of beauty, and her generosity and faith in the goodness of human nature knew no bounds. Her willingness to feed the hungry and to give money to the destitute caused problems for her family but was also regarded with affectionate, even proud indulgence. Minnie Wald, not Max, was the dominant figure in the Walds' familial life.[2]

Favey, as Grandfather Schwarz was called, had been a successful merchant, but his greatest loves were "the works of Schiller, folk tales, old furniture and silver, birds," and making his grandchildren happy. He was a constant source of candy and pocket money, ice cream and stories, and he also gave the Wald children a number of ponies and a life-size playhouse replica of the Prussian houses he had known as a child. The visiting uncle, Samuel Schwarz, had been trained as a doctor. Following an accidental, self-prescribed overdose of medicine taken at the beginning of his career, he became a semiinvalid. The sympathy elicited by his "misfortune," as well as his charm, enabled him to play the role of gentle tyrant, expropriating Max Wald's favorite chair whenever he visited, for example, and prevailing upon Lillian's older brother, Alfred, to postpone going to college so that he (Uncle Samuel) could leave his business affairs and go to Baden-Baden for a cure. Notwithstanding these impositions, Uncle Samuel was also generous and jolly. Whenever he came to visit he brought a bag full of books for the children and entertained them with Shakespearean verse, the speeches of Marcus Aurelius, and the Psalms of David.[3]

The four Wald children were no less colorful. The oldest was Alfred, who was supposed to have inherited his uncle's "brilliance as well as his charm." He was bright, "prudent," forgiving, and Lillian's constant and adored companion. Next there was Julia, "the daring and mischievous older sister," and then, following Lillian, there was Gus, the baby of the family, who later became Lillian's special charge.[4]

From these family portraits, which are taken from those Wald drew for R. L. Duffus, her official biographer, it is clear that Lillian Wald as an adult was much like the adults who were most important to her as a child. Max and Minnie Wald, Favey, and Uncle Samuel were generous people. Minnie Wald may have extended her largesse beyond the family circle more commonly and less discriminately than the others, but a willingness to give of themselves and of their possessions and a sensitivity to the needs of others were traits more or less common to all. Beyond this, all valued literature, poetry, music, and beautiful things, and valued them especially for the pleasure they could give to other people; all loved children and enjoyed their presence; and all, Max Wald perhaps being an exception, were strong willed and determined. In her character, in her role as "Leading Lady" of the Henry Street "family," and even in her belief in action prompted by unanalyzed, unselfconscious "instincts," Wald would become most like her mother. Nevertheless, as she herself indicated by memories that stressed a general tone—being spoiled and indulged—the attitudes and values of all the adults in Wald's family as well as their personalities and relationships to one another, were the central curriculum of Lillian Wald's earliest education, and one that was learned by a kind of osmosis: by observing and patterning herself after the two-generation adult group with whom she lived.

Learning of this kind was supported by the dynamics of family interaction. The Walds were a closely knit, happy group. Their life together was peaceable, comfortable, lively, and loving. The adults taught by sharing their interests with the children, as Favey did, for example, when he took them all to see Schiller's plays performed; and even when prompted by pedagogic principle, as Minnie was at times (she had "definite ideas about bringing up children"), they shared directly in the learning process itself. Thus, Lillian remembered being taken by her mother to hear Ingersoll and Beecher speak and to hear Patti sing; and she also remembered reading aloud to her mother from "a rather lurid New York City periodical" as well as from newspapers and the world's great literature. Equally important, none of the adult members of the Wald family was authoritarian and none was a severe disciplinarian. Lillian remembered being punished only once, and her mother felt immediate and continuing remorse for the slap.[5]

If their pedagogic style added to the inherent appeal of the significant adults in Wald's early life, circumstances further magnified the degree of their influence. During Lillian's childhood, the Walds lived in at least three different cities. At some point after moving to Rochester, they bought their own home, but at the beginning they boarded in a rooming house. Rochester became their home, although they struck their roots rather late in Lillian's childhood, and even after they settled there permanently, they continued to travel frequently as company for Max on his numerous business trips. Perhaps for this reason, Lillian Wald does not appear to have had a circle of friends with whom she grew up. In addition, her family does not seem to have been part of a religious congregation. Their background was Jewish, yet there is no evidence that religious practices were an important part of their life. Moreover, R. L. Duffus's claim that they were "more German than Jewish in their culture . . . with a deep vein of Hebraic poetry and idealism," may indicate that religion was not really important in their ethnic affiliation. However that may be, the point here is that there was little in Lillian Wald's early experience to mediate her exposure to the grown-ups within her family, which was in any case frequent and intense.[6]

Lillian Wald acquired a great deal from emulating her mother, and also her father, grandfather, and uncle; and she also learned significantly from their attitude toward her. Wald remembered that as a child she had "had no instincts that her parents thought necessary to repress." They did at times curb her activities, but they never shamed her or humiliated her. And the characteristics that can be most directly linked to this aspect of Wald's education, notably the imagination and self-assertion that culminated in a sense of self-trust and self-respect, were solidified in play with her siblings. In itself, the freedom of Wald's early years was conducive to the development of creativity, but this quality was additionally supported by the toys Lillian's parents and Favey and Uncle Samuel chose, as well as by the love of drama and stories that was common to all four. The cooperative dramatic play that resulted may not have been part of Minnie Wald's notion of education, but her tolerance for it gave Lillian frequent opportunities for self-expression.[7]

The play usually involved acting out adult roles. One day in Favey's playhouse, for example, Lillian's favoriate doll became sick. Although she was nursed assiduously, she died anyway and was given a funeral, with Alfred reading a eulogy and Lillian leading the procession to the grave. The incident and doubtless others unrecorded contributed to a sense of mastery of the "real" world that in turn fostered confidence and self-reliance.

In the incident described above, it was Alfred who read the eulogy. In fact, the leadership role always seemed to fall to Alfred, not just in the playhouse but also in the nursery. It was Alfred, for instance, who organized the weekly newspaper, with Lillian, Julia, and Gus as the staff; and it was Alfred as well who played the major parts in the Wald children's theatrical company. Of her three siblings, Lillian was closest to Alfred. She once compared their relationship to the one between Tom and Maggie Tulliver, the brother and sister hero and heroine of George Eliot's *Mill on the Floss*. Hence, as one of Wald's biographers has noted, "if Wald's memories were accurate," Alfred was the center of her emotional life at this time. "She was content to follow him everywhere asking in return [only] that he love and admire her . . . She looked to him always as someone to adore. Someone who would love and appreciate her.''[8]

Were Wald's memories accurate? Duffus describes an incident in which Lillian grabbed an umbrella from Alfred because he was not sharing it with her. Duffus's point was that Lillian's quick repentance indicated that ''the spoiling hadn't impaired the workings of her conscience,'' although the more germane reading may be that, along with admiration, respect, and affection, Lillian felt at least some rivalry. The relationship is extremely difficult to untangle. Alfred drowned when he was twenty-four. Minnie Wald never recovered, and the loss was traumatic for the entire family. Whatever rivalry had existed may have been forgotten. In any case, the point relevant to Wald's early years is that her relationship with Alfred, for whatever combination and balance of reasons, was still another source of stimulation, one that with the others must be recognized in reconstructing the sources of her considerable initial self-respect. Alfred was admired; Lillian was his favorite sibling, as he was hers. Alfred was the leader; Lillian was often his chosen deputy. Alfred dreamed of being a doctor; Lillian was to become a nurse.[9]

To draw a cause and effect relationship between Lillian Wald's vocational choice and the death of her brother would be as great a mistake, however, as to ignore its possible influence. First, there is no direct evidence to support such a relationship; second, too many other factors obviously played a part. Within the generous, loving, comfortable, supportive, and stimulating world that was her family, Lillian became a strong, happy, curious child, a child who assumed, having known nothing else, that the world at large was like the world she knew. The experience made for an easy transition to the outside world, as evidenced by Lillian's academic and social accomplishments at Miss Cruttenden's School. Yet it also seems to have nurtured expectations that could not be met within the school. And it was these, one suspects, that stood at the root of Wald's application to Vassar as well as much that would follow.

According to a prospectus from the time Wald was there, the purpose of Miss Cruttenden's School was ''to make scholarly women and womanly scholars, in all thoroughness, genuineness, nobility, earnestness, and simplicity.'' The curriculum included, in addition to the usual elementary subjects, geography, history,

French, German, Latin, trigonometry, astronomy, physics, and chemistry. It was a relatively rich course of study for a girls' school of that era, but one that was neither sufficiently difficult nor sufficiently challenging to engage Wald for very long. She had mastered enough of it by the age of sixteen to be academically eligible for Vassar, and having done so, she apparently found little to hold her at Miss Cruttenden's.[10]

Wald never spoke of any special friends or teachers from the school; she never mentioned an interest in a particular subject. Most likely at the time she was not really bored, she simply wanted more challenge than Miss Cruttenden's could provide. At home life had been exciting. At Miss Cruttenden's life was pleasant. In school Lillian was often the center of attention and very popular. As another graduate reminded Wald many years later, "We, the 'little girls' . . . thought you the most beautiful girl we had ever seen." She and others loved to cluster around Lillian and hear from her every detail of the parties she went to. Receiving attention was not a new experience for Lillian, though. She had learned to expect it. Peer admiration, therefore, did not mitigate the fact that for her life at Miss Cruttenden's was tame, uneventful, and lacking in adventure; it was a far cry from the life she had imagined through Favey's stories, had acted out in play with her siblings, and to some extent had known already through travel, going to concerts and plays, reading a "lurid" periodical, and so on. To go to Vassar, still an unusual, slightly radical undertaking, was undoubtedly more in line with what Lillian had anticipated in life.[11]

It is important to note that the Walds did not urge their daughter to go to college. They expected and wanted her to choose a life like the one her older sister chose when she married Charles P. Barry, a member of an old Rochester family, and advanced schooling was unnecessary for that. Characteristically, however, they did not forbid the Vassar application, nor did they stand in Lillian's way later on, when she applied to nursing school. They voiced objections, but they gave in in both instances. Consequently, they reinforced, yet again, the message they had conveyed from the first: that they were interested in Lillian's welfare but respectful of her wishes, her judgment, her "instincts"— respectful of her. The outcome, Lillian's subsequent course, was surprising to them, but in retrospect it is logical given the nature of their trust and the pattern of Lillian's childhood.

The self-confidence and wish for independence and challenge implicit in Lillian Wald's Vassar application were not manifested again, at least in terms of life choices, for six years. Even then, the catalyst was chance. When Julia had her first child, Lillian was sent for a nurse. She claimed that she had never met a professional nurse before and that her decision to apply to nursing school was an immediate reaction to that one brief meeting, the result of "an irresistible impulse." The claim would seem to be accurate.[12]

During the six years following President McCracken's decision that Lillian was too young for Vassar, "she wore the elegant clothes her mother provided for her and entered the life of the 'stylish young lady' with the unspoken purpose of meeting a man and marrying." She was not looking for a career. If she had been, she could have become a teacher or tried her hand at writing. Or, since Rochester did have a nursing school at the time, she could have chosen that line of work earlier than she did. Instead, she finished at Miss Cruttenden's, went to parties, visited friends in Louisville and other places, and dabbled in the world of work, taking a job for a time as a correspondent for the Broadstreet Company. If she had not encountered a professional nurse, who knows what might have happened. But she did, and the vocational choice that was made suddenly—in a flash—and with more determination than forethought or careful consideration, marked a real turning point in her life as well as in her education.[13]

Many of the immediate influences on Wald's decision are clear. The Bellevue graduate who nursed Julia was one; an increasing sense of aimlessness was another; and Alfred's death, which brought with it loneliness, added family duties, and perhaps a wish to carry out what he could no longer do, was probably still another. At the time she applied to New York Hospital, Wald claimed that she was eager to find challenging work and had already decided that nursing was a vocation she was suited for and would enjoy. Thus, it was her self-confidence, combined with her ability to seize on an idea, to see in it what she wanted, and then to act on it with the will necessary to mold it to her wishes, that enabled her to capitalize on the coincidental and brief meeting that brought awareness of nursing and its appeal to her. Both qualities had been developed during Wald's early education; both would remain central throughout her life. Indeed, a large part of the agenda for Wald's education from nursing school on would be the tempering and channeling of these characteristics with the knowledge necessary to the work she would choose.[14]

After 1889, when Wald left Rochester for New York City, her family played less of a direct role in her education. Still, the influence of the example set by the adult members of the Wald family, as well as the values, attitudes, beliefs, interests, and abilities that had been molded in interaction with adult and sibling family members alike would always remain important. After 1889, as before, Wald was an active participant in her own education, shaping the knowledge she would acquire as much it shaped her. And in this, the "instincts" nurtured by her family would be the constant point of reference.

In the fall of 1889, when Wald began her training at New York Hospital, the field of nursing was still in the process of being professionalized. Menial duties were a nurse's daily routine even at New York Hospital, which was one of the first American institutions officially to accept Florence Nightingale's conviction that nursing was an art requiring advanced theoretical and practical training. Thus, as another graduate remembered, when Wald was a student, "hours were long and work was very hard . . . Besides the care of patients, there was much cleaning of wards, washing of dishes and polishing of brasses." In addition, nurses were given little leeway for the expression of independent judgment. Rules were rigid and touched every area of their functioning. Doctors prescribed: Wald was once chided for encouraging a patient to laugh before she had been ordered to do so. The charge that at this time many doctors saw nurses as being little different from domestic servants would remain a fair one for some years to come.[15]

Considering that Wald saw the nursing role as an important one, it seems clear that the potentially negative lessons implicit in the duties and status of a student nurse had relatively little impact on her, while those associated with the sense of professional pride that was also emerging at this time had a great effect. Except for the time immediately following the completion of her course, when she stayed on at New York Hospital to help Irene Sutliffe, the superintendent of nurses, prepare for the new class, Wald never worked in a hospital. She chose instead to establish at Henry Street an institutional base from which she and other nurses could carry out the professional aspects of a nurse's job without being involved with the less professional. Had she accepted the type of identity implicit in the typical physician's attitude, it is more than likely that her career would have been quite different. One therefore must ask what made it possible for her to learn so selectively.[16]

Before she arrived at the hospital (and she claimed never to have seen a hospital before then), Lillian Wald had decided that nursing was serious, important, congenial, and challenging work. Many of her fellow student nurses shared her conviction. They worked hard but they also found "great enjoyment and happy content during those years." Later the comradery that emerged from their sense of pride and pioneering (the first American hospital-based training course had opened only sixteen years before Wald began at New York Hospital) would promote the linkage many of them drew between the professional organization of nursing and the general advancement of women; during nursing school days, however, their comradery supported identification with a positive, "professional" image of their potential that was well ahead of the status actually associated with the jobs they were given.[17]

Two books contributed to their adherence to this image and were also significant in helping Wald distinguish between nursing as embodied in the New York Hospital regime and nursing as possible under other circumstances. The first was Florence Nightingale's *Notes on Nursing: What It Is and What It Is Not* (1859), a recommended text in most hospital-affiliated nursing schools at the time. In essence, the book argued that disease was a healthy reaction: a "reparative process" caused by a problem in the external environment, a "want of fresh air, or light, or of warmth, or of cleanliness, or of punctuality and the care in administration of diet." According to Nightingale, therefore, the nurse's job was "to act as nature's assistant," by observing the patient's symptoms so that the specific causes of the illness could be isolated and remedied, and by creating for the patient those conditions which would enable nature to do its work. The second book, which was Darcré Craven's *A Guide to District Nursing* (1863), also standard fare in American nursing schools at the time and an important source for many of Wald's early articles on nursing, was equally clear in the elevated responsibilities it assigned to the nurse. Craven argued that district nursing was suitable to "gentlewomen" because their "tact, discretion, and 'good breeding' " would help them introduce sanitary reforms without insulting their patients and their patients' families. Furthermore, to Craven, "district nursing represented civilization at its highest knocking at the door of civilization at its lowest . . . District nursing would teach the poor and the ignorant how to live properly and hygienically."[18]

Wald's emphasis at Henry Street on searching out and ameliorating the environmental causes of disease and her repeated description of the nurse's function as that of an educator and propagandist who would "interpret" each extreme of society to the other clearly reflect the influence of both books. They were among the resources upon which Wald drew to develop a role as suitable to her interests, talents, and expectations as hospital nursing was unsuitable. To fashion such a role, however, Wald needed more than theoretical knowledge and peer support for the possibilities inherent in the nursing profession. She also had to learn to see herself within the profession. And this Irene Sutliffe helped her to do.[19]

Sutliffe, who was herself an 1880 graduate of New York Hospital, was described by Wald as "a woman touched with a genius for sympathy." From the first she had cause to recommend that Wald find her vocation elsewhere. During her initial tour of the hospital, Lillian gasped at the sight of a boy whose legs were in traction. Two days into her training, without authorization, Lillian fed an old man who had been isolated in a padded cell while recovering from delirium tremens. And even though she knew that all student nurses were meant to work in the operating room at the beginning of their time in the hospital, Lillian put off her initiation for as long as possible.[20]

Sutliffe's reaction to each of these incidents was firm. She pointed out that the boy was not suffering, that he was, in fact, a leader on the ward; she explained why the old man was isolated and that Lillian's unconsidered action had caused problems for the cook; and she sent Lillian to the operating room to help a patient for whom she had been caring. But Sutliffe's reactions are noteworthy also for the confidence they evidenced in Lillian's potential. Even after the incident with the old man, Sutliffe never suggested that Lillian leave the school or that she could not learn the attitudes necessary to withstand the less pleasant aspects of hospital life. Quite to the contrary: in discussing the old man, Sutliffe apparently stated that she understood how Lillian had felt, and though she made it clear that she considered Lillian's action irregular, and assumed that it would not be repeated, she closed the conversation by saying: "I personally am glad that you fed that old drunk." Thus, by simultaneously offering Lillian acceptance and refusing to condone inappropriate behavior, she confirmed Lillian's sense that she had the ability to become a nurse and taught her that serious work necessitated serious effort and training. As a result, she elevated Lillian's conception of the profession at the same time that she reassured her that she would be able to meet its demands.[21]

That Sutliffe was able to do this for Wald is interesting. One of the most intriguing and difficult questions that may be raised in an educational biography has to do with the conditions that mediate the effects of explicit teaching as well as the impact of other kinds of experience. Unfortunately, one can never discern all that was involved, although in this instance it is clear that Sutliffe's pedagogical style, which was similar to that of Lillian Wald's family, was crucial.

Through positive rather than negative reinforcement, Sutliffe supported Lillian's existing strengths. Through guidance and example rather than imposition, she taught Lillian the meaning and appeal of the nursing role. And with this as a motivation for learning, she then gave Lillian the freedom to learn from her own experience, even after a time adding to her responsibilities the supervision of an entire ward. Wald tended to see the educative significance of her time at nursing school in terms of a lesson in "discipline." That she did acquire discipline in the sense of professional competence is clear. Yet discipline as the will to direct one's effort to the successful accomplishment of a specific goal, Wald had acquired earlier, as evidenced, for example, by her academic accomplishments at Miss Cruttenden's. What Sutliffe did for Wald, therefore, was to help her add to the general traits she already possessed the knowledge and behaviors necessary to the role she had chosen. And in so doing, Irene Sutliffe made Lillian Wald a nurse.

Nursing skills were invaluable in the work to which Lillian Wald would ultimately devote her life. But at the time she left nursing school, in March of 1891, Wald was still a very long way from 265 Henry Street and the settlement she opened there in

1895. Many of the circumstances that help one understand how Wald ended up on the Lower East Side had relatively little to do with education. Wald's first job, for example, at the Juvenile Asylum on 176th Street, was simply unsatisfactory. It did give her experience in advocacy: to force a dentist to give a child the treatment she thought necessary, Wald used the threat of her own dentist. It did establish an enduring disenchantment with institutionally based child care. And it did make clear that she had yet to find congenial work. Nevertheless, it is difficult to read the experience as having been an important one in terms of Wald's personal or professional growth. Similarly, the time Wald subsequently spent at the Women's Medical College of the New York Infirmary, where she went to supplement her "theoretical instruction, which was casual and inconsequential in the hospital classes" she had attended, does not appear to have had much impact on her vocational choice.[22]

The years between Wald's graduation and her decision to move to the Lower East Side in March of 1893 resembled those between the Vassar rejection and the New York Hospital application. Wald wanted something more and something different from what she could find in traditional nursing jobs, and she was willing to wait, neither rejecting nursing altogether nor compromising her hopes and expectations, until suddenly, she was offered a brief, chance encounter that once again clarified her direction. As Wald described the experience, "a sick woman in a squalid rear tenement, so wretched and so pitiful that, in all the years since, I have not seen anything more appealing, determined me, within half an hour, to live on the East Side," there to do what she could, through nursing, to mitigate the suffering she had discovered.[23]

The sudden flash of insight was remarkably like the one that had inspired the nursing school application. It clearly reveals the traits of mind and the interests that had been developed earlier in Wald's life, which, as here, continued to shape her education. Behind it one can see not only the extraordinarily acute imagination that had been nurtured by the freedom and stimulation of Wald's early education but also the self-confidence that had been born in childhood acceptance, trust, and mastery, and considerably reinforced by subsequent experience. In it, too, one can see the continuing "appeal" to Wald not simply of human need, but of human need that appeared to her to be susceptible to direct, immediate human intervention: human need of a different magnitude but still similar to that she had seen relieved by the Bellevue nurse who had taken care of her sister. Minnie Wald had always relieved whatever distress she encountered. The "appeal" Lillian Wald found in the East Side tenement drew on this, as it did also on her determination to find a way to put into practice the Nightingale and Craven conception of nursing she had studied at New York Hospital. Wald's instant reaction, then, was a compound of many things. At the time, she was as ignorant of conditions on the Lower East Side as she had been of hospitals and nursing in 1889, but determination, further learning, clear convictions, and luck once again made a success of an uninformed decision.

Soon after her momentous decision, Wald shared her plan with Mary Brewster, a nursing school friend: "we were to live in the neighborhood as nurses, identify ourselves with it socially, and, in brief, contribute to it our citizenship." The plan, as Wald later recognized, was the basis for her entire career. In its evolution and elaboration over the years one can find much that was distinctly educative in nature.[24]

The abilities that Wald already had, contributed to the development of her plan. Her quick insight, for example, often enabled her to read into a problem a concrete solution as yet untried by other settlements or still unapplied on the Lower East Side. By observing a group of unemployed men angered by the fact that they had no place to meet, she "instinctively" realized, for example, that a "social hall" other than the saloon was desperately needed. The realization led eventually to the construction of Clinton Hall, which provided low-cost meeting rooms for the whole community. Wald's medical knowledge further increased the range of problems she could recognize and attack, and obviously was the source for the school lunch and school nurse programs that were initially sponsored by the Henry Street Settlement and later taken over by the Board of Education. Thus, the abilities Wald brought to her work served continuously as educative skills.[25]

Over the years Wald's plan was defined more by the programs she established than by abstract philosophy. And it was primarily her established abilities, her educative skills, that made it possible for her to learn, among other things, one initial and crucially important thing: that she could not nurse without becoming involved with the total physical and social environment of the neighborhood. Had she not been able to learn this, many sources of knowledge that were important in the development of Henry Street's program would have remained unknown or disregarded. Obviously, therefore, the way Wald discovered that nursing from "the settlement point of view" was what she wanted to do needs to be scrutinized with care.[26]

Wald's first contacts on the Lower East Side were with settlement workers. Charles B. Stover and Edward King, to whom Wald went for advice in finding an apartment, were both residents at the University Settlement. They quickly made it clear to Wald that she would find understanding and acceptance within their ranks. Stover and King walked with Wald throughout the area and, as they explained the neighborhood, signaled to her (primarily because they showed her the "red light district") "their belief in the sincerity of the girl walking beside them." More important, when Stover said, "why don't you live with those girls at 95 Rivington Street," by which he meant Jane Robbins and the other women who had established the College Settlement there in 1889, he clearly implied that they too would appreciate her plan. They did. Several days later Wald and Brewster were invited to lunch at the settlement. During July and August of 1893, they became " 'residents' in stimulating comradeship with serious women, who were also the fortunate possessors of a saving sense of humor." Thus, partly by chance, Wald immediately was placed within a group that she liked and found interesting and helpful. The nature of her acquaintance was an important influence in defining the direction in which she would take her scheme.[27]

That said, one point must be clear. Lillian Wald seems to have learned best from her own concrete experience. As a result, the views of her newfound colleagues did not obviate the need for independent observation. It is telling, for example, that Jane Robbins, a doctor who was a leading figure in the College Settlement at the time Wald and Brewster lived there, had already found out that on the Lower East Side one could not deal with medical problems unless one also became involved in housing, public education, labor organization, and so on. For when Wald and Brewster left the College Settlement in September of 1893 to move to their own quarters on the top floor of a tenement at 27 Jefferson Street, Wald still claimed that "our work is not identical with the work of the College Settlement," which was "chiefly club work." Henry

Street's mission was never identical with that of the College Settlement. Henry Street was unique among settlements in its emphasis on nursing. But the point remains that Wald did not evidence a real understanding of the relationship between nursing and "club work" (let alone that settlement work was more than "club work") until she had had the chance to find out, on her own, what Robbins and others already knew. Apparently, therefore, it was what Wald learned independently during her first two winters as a nurse on Jefferson Street that allowed her to incorporate the experience of women like Robbins into her point of view.[28]

During the winter of 1893-94, the full effects of the business depression that left over forty thousand New York City families without income became obvious to the two nurses. In caring for the sick they could not help discovering that starvation and total destitution were increasingly common. Medical care often had to be supplemented by the distribution of food, clothing, and money for firewood. In addition, full treatment frequently required finding places outside the neighborhood where convalescence would be possible. And for those who were employed, it sometimes also necessitated finding a different job, one in which the environmental factors that had contributed to the illness would not be present. Under the pressure of circumstances, therefore, Wald became involved in relief work and quickly realized that she could not adequately nurse the sick according to the Nightingale conception of disease unless she was also willing to attend to their non-medical needs.[29]

Having arrived on the Lower East Side with little knowledge of its population and with virtually no experience with people who were poor, Wald discovered during that winter that her neighbors were proud, regardless of need, capable of extraordinary generosity to others in like condition, and often scrupulously faithful to religious custom and belief. Wald's reports to Jacob Schiff and his mother-in-law, Mrs. Solomon Loeb, who were the principal financial backers of her work, show surprise as well as pleasure in the resiliency she found all around her. Writing in November of 1893, she said, for example, "the more intimately we know these poor Russian Jews the more frequently are we rewarded with unexpected gleams of attractiveness." Her reports from this era exhibit a then rather typical sense of superiority. But her ability to empathize with the people of what was still for her a new and foreign world did enable her to develop a counterbalancing sense of respect for the individuals she met and the groups from which they came.[30]

The years immediately following Wald's move to the Lower East Side were profoundly educative. In the insight Wald gained into her neighbors and their problems, one can see the origins of the multifaceted program the settlement would develop as both direct sponsor and advocate. Having in a sense caught up with the men and women who had preceded her to the Lower East Side, Wald was able to draw freely from her continuing conversations with residents of the College Settlement and the University Settlement, as well as from talks with people like Jacob Riis, the muckraking newsman and author, who became her close friend. Over the years the knowledge she gained from them, and later on from frequent meetings of settlement residents and social reformers, as well as from careful reading of magazines like *Charities*, *The Commons*, and *The Survey*, enlarged her understanding of settlement work and provided her with invaluable information. Many of the programs she developed during her first ten years on the Lower East Side were close replicas of ones that had been established successfully elsewhere. When a delegation of boys called on Wald in 1895, for example, she immediately took their advances as evidence of their need for a club, in this case the American Heroes' Club, Henry Street's first, which she herself led. Her understanding and response to them were ready because in the extreme need of that first winter "the settlement point of view" had become relevant to her.[31]

The respect Wald acquired during her two years on Jefferson Street for the people of the neighborhood also added to her effectiveness, because it opened her to another source of knowledge. On the most obvious level, Wald's appreciation for her neighbors taught her that foreign cultures and their representatives were not inferior and that, though different in language and custom, they were similar in many essential values. This attitude promoted Wald's interest in the life around her as well as her ability to understand it. Beyond this, the respect Wald developed for the people among whom she had chosen to live increased her capacity to listen. The increment this added to her presumption of honesty and good will, a presumption taken over from her mother, led to a tendency to see the problem presented as legitimate. Had her experience led her to the opposite conclusion, Wald might have dismissed a great deal of what she instead investigated. Finally, the knowledge Wald acquired confirmed her belief in the environmental causes of disease. Without such validation for what initially had been a theoretical and secondhand point of view, she might not have decided that a nurse must be an investigator, teacher, and advocate as well as a medical assistant.

During her first years on the Lower East Side, the reactions Wald elicited, the coincidence of vision she brought out in the people around her, also had a significant impact on the design of her plan. For if Wald needed to learn about the Lower East Side in order to become effective as a settlement resident, she also needed to learn to see herself in that role. Thus, because both Wald's neighbors and her fellow reformers quickly saw her as more than a nurse, their approach to her fostered her changing conception of her work. As had been true in nursing school, however, one person played an especially prominent part in transforming Wald's occupational self-image.

Of the "many fine personalities who influenced and guided us from the first few weeks of residence in the friendly college settlement through the many years that have followed," Wald wrote later, two were particularly important. Mrs. McRae, the devoted, loving, and motherly janitoress of the Jefferson Street tenement, and Josephine Shaw Lowell. Mrs. McRae's function was essentially one of emotional support. As Wald put it, "she covered us with her protecting love and was no small influence in holding us to sanity." Mrs. Lowell's function, on the other hand, was essentially educative. As she was to Maud Nathan, Josephine Shaw Lowell was a mentor to Lillian Wald.[32]

During the winter of 1893-94, Lowell coordinated and administered the Lower East Side relief work supported by New York City churches, synagogues, philanthropic groups, and individuals. In her effort, she called on Wald often, asking not only for her assistance but also for her opinion and cosignature on letters to the newspapers describing the situation. In a memorial address for Lowell, Wald described what she had done for her: "inexperienced as I was, and unaccustomed to thinking of troubles so grave and great, she treated me like a comrade . . . in the responsibility and service of the winter. I think because she was so simple about it, one took it in the same way and talked freely without self-consciousness, or perhaps it was her deeply thought-out plan to encourage the beginner by dignifying her.'' Jacob Riis, who knew both women well, once remarked, in describing the trust that Wald was able to engender among the people of the Lower East Side, that ''no woman, since Josephine Shaw Lowell, has been able to do what she has done.'' The two women may have been similar in their innate capacity for sympathy, but Wald's view of herself, as well as her abilities, was tutored profoundedly by Josephine Shaw Lowell. Indeed, Lowell was to Wald at this time what Sutliffe had been earlier. She shared her knowledge and point of view; she served as a model for what Wald could be; she enhanced Wald's prestige in the eyes of other philanthropists and reformers; and by the simple fact that she sought out and accepted Wald's views, she helped her recognize her own potential. What is more, the kind of ''discipline'' Wald could see in Lowell, who was a master of efficient organization, was no less necessary to her success in the role she was now assuming than it had been earlier as she was becoming a nurse.[33]

The educational components most important to the initial development of Lillian Wald's impulsively realized plan, then, were three: first, her own abilities, her educative skills; second, her neighbors on the Lower East Side; and third, the men and women with whom she worked, particularly Josephine Shaw Lowell. Jacob Schiff, however, who financed Wald's and Brewster's work during their first two years, who bought the house at 265 Henry Street, and who remained one of the settlement's largest donors, also had a great influence on Wald, and at no time more so than during Henry Street's early years. Wald could not have developed the programs she did if she had not been able to bring in large amounts of money. And since it was Schiff more than anyone else who taught her how to do this, he too had a hand in defining her plan.

Jacob Schiff was a wealthy German-Jewish immigrant. By the time he met Wald in the 1890s, he was a senior partner of Kuhn, Loeb and Co., one of the major banking firms of the day, and prominent in established German-Jewish circles. Beginning as it did in the depression year of 1893, his willingness to support Wald was in itself educative. Schiff could have given the money he earmarked for Wald's work to any number of other good causes, as Wald no doubt knew. His support, in addition to confirming

Wald's conviction that her work was worthwhile, therefore proved to her that she would be able to solicit for it the necessary financial support.[34]

Schiff was a man of definite convictions, imposing authority, and quick temper. He insisted that Wald keep careful, detailed records of her daily rounds. He urged her to follow his example and remember her "uptown" friends on birthdays, anniversaries, and so on. In asking for money, he counseled her to phrase her appeals in language familiar to the wealthy. Thus, she spoke most often of an "opportunity for service" or the "privilege" of helping, and many of her requests were indirect, leaving ample room for donors to recognize on their own the chance of "service" that she was offering. Finally, in requiring of Wald a degree (or tone) of deference, by virtue of his own more conservative social and political views, Schiff helped Wald learn to style her statements according to the moods and persuasions of her backers. This should not imply that Wald compromised her views in order to please her supporters, but rather that the ability she developed for communicating with them allowed her to create understanding for her work and its social significance. Schiff, therefore, was Wald's tutor in fund raising and administration. She had the necessary personal qualities before they met—the energy, the enthusiasm, the charm, the personal magnetism. But it was Schiff's insight into the people to whom she would have to direct her financial appeals and his knowledge of efficient business operation that turned these qualities into specific skills.[35]

As a result of Schiff's financial generosity a new ingredient was added to Wald's education. In 1895, Schiff bought the house at 265 Henry Street to make room for more nurses. And from then on, Wald (Mary Brewster was forced to retire from the venture at this time because of a nervous breakdown) attracted an extraordinary group of people to live and work at the settlement. The nurses were mostly young women looking for opportunities similar to those Wald herself wanted, and the group that was called the "laity" was a mix of young, middle-class women inspired by Wald's personality and work and of already convinced reformers who found Henry Street a pleasant place in which to pursue their own concerns. All, though differently, influenced Wald's thought and added still further to the sense of competence and authority that Lowell and Schiff nurtured in their own special ways. From

1895 forward, the Henry Street "family" had a major influence in shaping Lillian Wald's career.[36]

Among the nurses who were residents at Henry Street at this time, Lavinia Dock was one of the most important in terms of Wald's education. Like Wald, Dock was the product of a cultivated, comfortable childhood, hospital trained (she graduated from the Bellevue Training School in 1886), and a zealous fighter for the further professionalization of nurses. Although few people could have been more dissimilar in temperament, Dock and Wald were close friends for more than forty years. Dock adored Wald, and vice versa. Affection, as well as recognition of Wald's unusual potential for public influence, led Dock to offer Wald assistance with her writing (which was often accepted) and in other ways to attempt to influence the "dearest Lady's" activities and thinking.[37]

Dock was also an ardent feminist and a committed suffragist. After Tammany's victory in the 1903 mayoralty election, she wrote from Europe as soon as she heard of "the awful calamity" to beg for news. Her letter illustrates her point of view. "How can you all keep on from day to day—it seems to me such a sickening testimonial to the deep-rooted corruption of men that it almost destroys faith in the possibility of their doing any better—Is there any hope for the future . . . How will everything be affected . . . I am convinced there will be no salvation for municipal politics until the women get their own votes." And a second letter, written twenty-three days later, following Wald's reply to the first, went on to point out that "we will never have municipal good government until women vote . . . This trying to get good things done by persuading men to do them is degrading to us—effeminizes men—and has no effective result." Now, Wald never became a militant feminist. Before the 1920s, she even talked of woman's special aptitudes within the home. Yet she did become a suffragist; criticized Woodrow Wilson in 1912 because his otherwise admirable platform did not contain a plank supporting the vote for women; belonged to many feminist organizations; and subscribed to the belief that the enfranchisement of women would promote acceptance of humanitarian reforms. Thus, Dock's persistent, enduring, and systematic counseling does seem to have had an important influence on her views.[38]

Others of the Henry Street "family" also contributed to Lillian Wald's education. Lavinia Dock was important but so too among others were Ysabella Waters, Helene McDowell, Annie W. Goodrich, and especially perhaps Florence Kelley, the general secretary of the Consumers' League, who lived at Henry Street for many years. In fact, I have discussed Lavinia Dock here primarily because she is illustrative of a category: those among Wald's closest colleagues who were most significant for their influence on her thought. Through collegial exchange at meals, joint projects, and more purposeful efforts to swing her to their point of view, the women in this category pushed Wald to be, on the whole, more feminist and less conservative than she might have been otherwise. Alice and Irene Lewisohn, by contrast, exemplify a second, subsequently significant, category of influential colleagues. Like Dock in her group, the Lewisohn sisters in their group were among the most important women, and also like Dock they are discussed here because they represent a category: the younger women among Wald's comrades (Rita Wallach Morgenthau, Helen Arthur, and Mabel Hyde Kittredge would belong in this group) who idolized her, sought her attention and affection, and lavished theirs on her.[39]

When Alice and Irene Lewisohn were introduced to Lillian Wald by their father, Leonard Lewisohn, an avid Wald admirer and Henry Street contributor, they had already learned to see her as "a woman of miracles." Alice remembered that during their first meeting she had had the feeling that "once in her presence every other consideration vanished." The settlement group as a whole and the neighbors who flowed in and out made an impression on the two sisters that evening, but it was "the Leading Lady [who] was felt here, there, everywhere . . . sowing, grafting, pruning, joyously happy . . . [in her] garden of human sympathy."[40]

The Lewisohns' admiration grew with the years as their attachment deepened. To the settlement they contributed their theatrical talents. They taught drama classes, organized the famous Henry Street festivals, and in 1915 established the quasi-independent Neighborhood Playhouse. To Wald they gave continuing devotion. They made large financial contributions; they sought her advice and counsel; they expressed concern for her personal welfare; and they constantly acknowledged the significance of her role in their own education. As a result, the Lewisohns fostered Wald's understanding of her personal magnetism and nurtured her recognition of its import to the settlement's effectiveness, particularly in its effort to "interpret" the people of its neighborhood to those of other worlds. Through their discipleship, the Lewisohns made Wald more conscious of her extraordinary appeal to others. Of course, the Lewisohns and other women in their group also added at times to Wald's substantive knowledge, just as women like Dock nurtured Wald's acceptance of her role as "Leading Lady." In fact, the influence of the two groups converged in support of Wald's movement toward public prominence.[41]

The Henry Street "family," especially during the early years, had one further effect on Wald's education. Beyond what the residents and nonresident staff taught Wald as individuals, their life together provided an atmosphere that was conducive to her own, continuing self-education. Life at Henry Street was strenuous, exciting, and varied. Conflict among residents was rare. Devotion to common cause and to Wald made for cooperation without suppressing the uniqueness of individual personality. If, therefore, one leaves aside the obvious differences, it becomes apparent that life within the Henry Street "family" was similar to life within the family in which Lillian Wald had grown up. The parallel, nurtured no doubt by Wald herself, supported the strengths that had emerged earlier—the imagination, the generosity, and so on—and again led Wald to expect the world outside to resemble the world within. When Wald had first discovered the squalor and poverty of the Lower East Side she had been convinced that "if people knew things . . . such horrors would cease to exist." Over the years she became more sophisticated, though never cynical, and always at heart convinced that through education, conditions would change. Within her settlement "family" and among her supporters, there was knowledge and there was a determination to change "things." Thus, a great deal of what Wald did was an effort to extend this equation between knowledge and reform to society at large. The expectations born within her family of origin and reinforced within her "family" of choice pushed her to acquire the skills necessary to this effort.[42]

Outside of her settlement "family" there were many reformers who contributed to Wald's development as a settlement leader, among whom Jane Addams was perhaps uniquely important. Hull House opened four years before Henry Street. When Addams first visited Henry Street in the fall of 1898, she had already become, as she put it in a letter to her sister, "the grandmother of American Settlements." Her visit, according to Wald, "stirred the household deeply," and left Wald herself "struggling between a longing to weep and a longing to say in more articulate language . . . how much, how very much realizing you is to me." Addams's recognition carried with it a stamp of official approval. Her increasing reliance on Wald as a colleague to whom she could turn for advice and assistance added to Wald's stature. The two quickly became close friends: friends who could write briefly without long explanation; friends who asked each other for small favors; friends who seemed intuitively to sense the similarities of their responsibilities. Still, Addams was to Wald, throughout their adult lives, a model and an inspiration as well as a friend and colleague. "Beloved Lady," Wald wrote in a typical letter to Addams, "I long to see you and [to] refresh my soul with your wisdom." Yet Wald did not always agree with Addams; she could not always give what Addams asked; and their careers differed more than is apparent at first glance. Addams, for example, being philosophical by nature, easily became *the* spokeswoman for "the settlement point of view." Indeed, as Allen Davis has argued in his biography of Addams, she purposefully cultivated the role of "heroine." Wald, by contrast, though often seen in much the same way, did not want to be placed on a pedestal and tended to be more pragmatic. Dinner table conversation was a medium suited to her style of persuasion more than lecturing or writing, although she also did these often and well. Nonetheless, Wald looked up to Addams and was able to understand her in ways that others could not. Knowing Addams this way—"realizing her"—Wald knew better what she also wanted to do.[43]

Ten years after Lillian Wald moved to the Lower East Side, Henry Street was incorporated. Jacob Schiff opposed the action and was uneasy about the institutional growth that had preceded it. In Wald's ability to overcome Schiff's reluctance and to persuade him to continue his affiliation as a board member, as well as in her confidence that the growth in program and in size were manageable and necessary, one can see a prodigious change. Wald was no longer simply a nurse who wanted to live and work among her neighbors on the Lower East Side; she was now a nurse who was also the leader of a staff of over one hundred people, the manager of seven settlement centers, eighteen nursing depots, and a budget well in excess of $15,000 a year. She was also a woman of increasing outside affiliations, whose name and support and advice were eagerly sought by nursing groups, social reformers, and politicians. A simple scheme had been transformed into a complex organization. It could not have happened if Wald had not been able to learn as quickly and easily as she did, or if she had not found an environment so rich in human "appeal" and congenial spirits. Education was an important part of what made Lillian Wald an effective and well-loved "Leading Lady."[44]

With the change in the nature of Wald's responsibilities came a change in daily routine. Wald's contact with her neighbors became less frequent. More of her time went into administration and fund raising. She continued to work closely with the Henry Street staff, but by 1914 she had had to delegate so much daily supervision that a complex diagram of organization was necessary. The change, not surprisingly, had an effect on Wald's education.[45]

First, during the years after 1903 there was a diminution in pace and in intensity. When Wald moved to the Lower East Side, she literally entered a new world. She had located a neighborhood but she knew little about it. Each day brought new discoveries; each phase of her work as it unfolded demanded new skills. By 1903 her work was clearly defined and her role essentially set. The skills that were still new in 1893—nursing, fund raising, administration, writing, public speaking—were by then well established. The various elements of Wald's role would shift in relative importance over time, and her skills would be further refined for many years; but there was little further dramatic change. Less was totally new. What was learned could be integrated without such fundamental effect.

Second, after 1903 Wald's education changed in source. With distance between herself and her neighbors and staff, she focused less exclusively on the neighborhood, more on the nation. As a result public events and broad social issues took on greater significance. They became a major source of her education. This is not to say that Wald did not continue to learn from other people. She did. It is simply to say that as a result of the experience of the last ten years, she knew the small and the local well enough to see them in a larger picture.

The substance of Lillian Wald's education after 1903 is difficult to describe and impossible to summarize. She was always pragmatic and problem oriented. At times, therefore, she was inconsistent in the stands she took. She also chose to work for many organizations rather than a few. And although she tended to avoid becoming involved with organizations other than Henry Street on the day-to-day committee level, she did assume this kind of role in some organizations and for some causes. Hence, the effects of Wald's education after 1903 cannot be seen in a clear pattern that can be traced through the chronological sequence of her interests and activities. They can only be seen as they were manifested, in a slow, cumulative broadening of focus.

Rather than investigating the needs of only one family, after 1903 Wald was likely to study an entire trade. In 1906, for example, she was a member of the Pushcart Commission established by Mayor George McClellan; in 1908-1909, she was a member of the state commission whose report on the conditions, welfare, and industrial opportunities of aliens in the state of New York led to the creation of a State Board of Industries and Immigration. Rather than focus primarily on the solution of immediate problems, she now often worked for more sweeping reforms. Wald's support for the establishment of agencies like the Children's Bureau illustrates, for example, that she now saw the problems of children not only as a series of complex, interrelated problems that were national in scope, but also as an issue that could be used to lobby for a change in national priorities. And Wald's activities during World War I, especially her leadership of the American Union against Militarism, a group set up to urge caution and restraint, not only in government armament policies but also in the limitation of internal civil rights and other, similar war-related policies, indicate that her vision had come to encompass a clearer, more articulate sense of the place of her work in relation to fundamental moral and ethical concerns. In 1916, she argued, for example, that "Militarism is an evil growth which threatens our industrial democracy, our political institutions, our educational ideals and our international relationships . . . It threatens the great, constructive, upbuilding, life-saving social work."[46]

The United States's entry into World War I deeply dismayed Wald. "I feel it down to my toes. I feel it in every fibre of my body," she explained to Ysabella Waters in August of 1917, and then continued: "Ever since I have been conscious of my part in life I have felt consecrated to the saving of human life, the promotion of happiness and the expansion of good will among people, and every expression of hatred and of the dissolution of friendly relations between people fairly paralyzes me." Wald's attitude toward the war clearly shows the clarity with which she was now able to express her purpose in life. That purpose had originated from life within her family. Nursing school and Henry Street transformed it into concrete interests and added the skills and knowledge necessary to pursue these. And direct engagement with national problems in turn regeneralized these interests. The period of intense schooling that for Wald spanned the years from 1889 to 1903 was like a funnel, directing and shaping and making effective her capacity to act on the "instincts" she had learned so well as a child. It was the period after 1903 that made Wald famous, but it was the education she had received before that time that enabled her to do all that she did thereafter.[47]

The enlargement of Wald's perspective that occurred with the changes in her education after 1903 is nowhere more clear than in the two books she wrote about Henry Street. The first, *The House on Henry Street*, was published in 1915; the second, *Windows on Henry Street*, in 1934. Both describe the settlement's program; both express Wald's point of view. But the first is an attempt to explain Henry Street per se and the second an effort to use Henry Street as an example by which to explain settlements in general. Thus, at the opening of *Windows on Henry Street*, Wald stated that she would describe Henry Street's post-1915 activities in "an attempt to show the place of a settlement in the movements of the day." The book was written, she said, as an antidote to the "limited comprehension" evident in popular literature and in the hope "that I may have the good fortune to encourage people—particularly young people—to participate more widely than they do in the affairs of the going world, with no selfish gain in view beyond increased ability to discuss intelligently and to inquire seriously."[48]

Behind this statement one can see what Wald herself had alluded to in a letter written in 1913: "I do not believe that the Settlement's influence or importance is lessened when it establishes on a more permanent basis the organized activities that it initiated . . . we have been freed . . . for new visions, or for bringing before the public moral issues that are bound to arise until we reach the milennium . . . I am no less busy than I was then, but the form of my social interests has changed. Even if we should abolish poverty, education for the mind and the body will still be needed.'' In a sense, the letter is uncharacteristic. Wald was never a moralist in the narrow sense. She was always less concerned with ''the milennium'' than with the here and now. What she obviously meant, therefore, was that slowly but increasingly after 1903 she had learned to address the root causes of the problems with which she was concerned as well as their specific manifestations. Nursing and settlement work had educated her sufficiently so that she could move beyond a professional, local, small-scale response. Wald's enlarged capacity, in pedagogic form, was at the heart of her purpose in *Windows on Henry Street*.[49]

A broadened focus, an authoritative tone, and didactic goals may not be unusual in old age. In Wald's case, however, each of these elements, especially the last, indicates the continuing vitality of the assumption that had led her years before to exclaim: ''if people knew things . . . such horrors would cease to exist.'' And the persistence of this assumption helps to explain how Wald was able to maintain her direction as she changed and the world changed: as she moved through World War I, when she was subjected to considerable and rather vicious criticism in the press as a result of her pacifism; as she remained optimistic and active thereafter; and as she endured a slow and painful physical decline. Beyond this, Wald's enduring belief that knowledge would bring whatever social change was necessary ''until we reach the milennium'' indicates that, to the end, the attitudes that had been so generally and strongly implanted during her early education—the ones Wald had learned well enough to call ''instincts''—were still intact. The belief that all people would be generous if they knew of need, that all people could be as happy as she had been if they too lived in a peaceable, caring, interesting world, and that she could do something to create that kind of world were ones that were acquired early, sustained through time, and never forgotten. What Wald had learned from her family and within her family established a legacy that remained with her to the end. And it was this legacy, shaped, refined, and solidified by the more specific knowledge, skill, and understanding that Wald acquired from her schooling, formal and otherwise, that was the substance of her education and the source for her point of view and work from childhood through old age.[50]

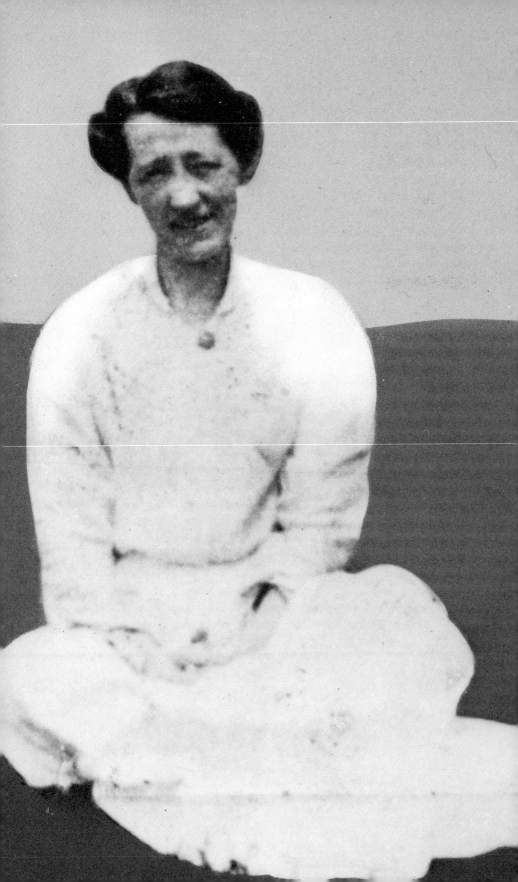

4

Leonora O'Reilly
1870-1927

LEONORA O'REILLY was born in New York City on February 16, 1870. Her father and brother died within two years of her birth. Having lost the grocery store that she and her husband had recently opened, Leonora's mother, Winifred Rooney O'Reilly, was forced to return to the needle trades to support herself and her daughter. When she could find work, Winifred O'Reilly left Leonora at home during the day, in the charge of a neighbor or simply on her own in the street. When she did not have work, Mrs. O'Reilly and her daughter went hungry. At times, Leonora had to wear "a woman's shawl and a man's hat" instead of a coat during even the coldest months of winter. Though she did go to public school for a time, economic circumstances forced Leonora to find a job as soon as she was able. In her early teens, she was already at work in a collar factory, having learned to sew by helping her mother with the clothing she brought home to finish in the evening. In a sense, therefore, Leonora O'Reilly became a garment worker as soon as she was physically able to hold a needle.[1]

Extraordinary though it may seem in light of the circumstances in which she grew up, Leonora O'Reilly became one of the most articulate, well-informed, and influential social reformers of the progressive generation. She did not hold public office; she did not found an extant institution; she did not write a book. But her ability to explain the labor movement to people from all walks of life, at large public gatherings, at street corner meetings, and in private conversations made her an important figure in the lives of many of her contemporaries. It was for this reason that O'Reilly was once described as "the leading working woman" of her time.[2]

In part, O'Reilly became a powerfully persuasive advocate for social reform because poverty, child labor, and hunger were not abstract conditions for her. As a result, she could portray the need for social change more personally than many reformers could. It was not just intimate acquaintance with hardship, however, that made Leonora O'Reilly such an effective proponent of social change. It was also the nature of her education. From birth, O'Reilly was "schooled" in the belief that through organization and education the social and economic realities of her world would be transformed. Her mother could not give her economic security, but she could teach her all that she knew. Winifred O'Reilly was an unusual person, a woman of great dignity, humor, self-respect, and hope, and Leonora's educational biography must begin with her.

Winifred O'Reilly had arrived in the United States in the late 1840s. She had known poverty from the first, although as a child she had also known pride in craftsmanship. She had learned to sew as an incidental part of her job as an errand girl in a dressmaker's shop. And as she once told Leonora's friend Alice Henry, she had "liked those years"; having been taught first to make sleeves, and then the whole dress, she had felt "very proud indeed of the accomplishment." The lesson was important. Mrs. O'Reilly could distinguish between work and working conditions more easily than people who had done only piece work in a factory could. The "passion for trade unionism" that grew from this knowledge may have been somewhat romantic, but it was this that made it possible for Winifred O'Reilly and her daughter to surmount the harsh realities in which they lived.[3]

Mrs. O'Reilly's verve and spirit testify to the fact that her life had not defeated her. Her experience had taught that there was inherent equality between the rich and the poor as well as an injustice that the labor movement might correct. As she remembered it, for example, she and the Seligman brothers had begun work in the same trade at the same time. She had made the flannel shirts that the Seligmans had sold; Civil War contracts had made them rich;

they had been able to give up peddling to become bankers, while she had remained where she had begun. According to Winifred O'Reilly, something was amiss, and it was the responsibility of honest, hard-working people like herself to set things right.[4]

In itself, Winifred O'Reilly's attitude toward life set an example of strength and determination for her daughter. Even beyond this, however, her "passion for trade unionism" gave her aspirations to pass on to Leonora. The labor movement, Winifred O'Reilly believed, would create a society in which dignity and decency and work would be commodities shared equally by all. Consequently, her primary goal in life was to help Leonora become a good working woman and an intelligent trade unionist. Through education, the best she could offer, Winifred O'Reilly hoped to give her only surviving child a place in the movement that she expected to change the world. Furthermore, because her late husband, like so many other men in the printing trade, had been "a good union man," by teaching Leonora about the labor movement, Mrs. O'Reilly could also transmit the ideals of the father Leonora did not remember.[5]

Except when Mrs. O'Reilly was at work, Leonora, as a little girl, was her mother's constant companion, and in spirit she became much like her. To Winifred O'Reilly one must attribute Leonora's verve and vivacity as well as her initial interest in labor. By asking Leonora's help with the sewing she did at home, Winifred O'Reilly also trained her daughter in the skills of a trade. By reading to her and taking her to meetings and lectures at public forums like Cooper Union, she gave her an appreciation of the written word, whetted her appetite for ideas, and exposed her to the power of eloquent rhetoric. And because Mrs. O'Reilly listened to her daughter and tried to take her wishes into account, she encouraged her self-assertion. Once she even gave up a job as a live-in cook because Leonora was not happy and wanted a home of her own. Finally, by the very fact of caring enough to devote herself entirely to giving Leonora the best home and best education possible, Mrs. O'Reilly nurtured in her daughter a sense of personal promise and an enduring loyalty to cause.[6]

Leonora's devotion to her mother, and her mother's to her, would become legendary to many of the women who were Leonora's colleagues later on. More to the point, Mrs. O'Reilly's steadfast allegiance to the labor movement, as well as her unremitting affection for Leonora and her total attachment to her, made Leonora's education their continuing and mutual quest. Even though the factual record of Leonora's early life is somewhat sparse, the educative significance of her mother's personality and convictions is clear. Though economically impoverished, Winifred O'Reilly had the wherewithal to cultivate the intellect, the drive, and the wry Celtic wit for which her daughter would be known. She taught Leonora a good deal. It was what Leonora learned from her mother that made it possible for her to educate herself and also to attract the men and women who helped her to do this. Having found through her mother a clear sense of purpose early in life, Leonora was able to teach herself more than many people can. And because she could learn so well on her own, and was obviously determined to do so, other people were eager to offer her their knowledge and skill.

By the time she was sixteen, for example, O'Reilly had been inducted into the Knights of Labor. Her sponsor was John Baptist Hubert, a French machinist, whom she called Uncle B. Unfortunately, little is known about this man, although his letters indicate that his efforts with Leonora were designed to underscore and extend all that her mother had already taught.

Uncle B urged Leonora to study French, to improve her grammar, and in all ways to strive "to see things in a clearer light." Mrs. O'Reilly, he believed, had made Leonora unusually "able to feel that the working people is crushed by the existing state of society." If she would become his "fellow-ess Knight of Labor," Uncle B counseled, therefore, he and his friends could help her achieve even greater understanding. Soon after Leonora joined the Knights and was taught "the grip" and "the secret pass-word," Uncle B made good on his promise. He wrote: "My Dear Pet Nora . . . Whenever you see my friend Mr. Joseph Banes . . . I want you to call him near you . . . and to tell him that you are my *Pet—Elenora O'Reilly* and that I want him and Mr. Drury to push you in the Labor Movement and to send you to 'the School of Instruction.'" Leonora apparently took Uncle B's advice. Victor Drury, an Italian furniture maker and friend of Mazzini, whom Leonora also called Uncle, became such a close friend that during the last years of his life he lived with Leonora and her mother.[7]

What Leonora actually gained from these men is difficult to know. But since their convictions were more systematic than Mrs.

O'Reilly's, their tutelage was probably a source for Leonora's increasingly coherent point of view. However that may be, Uncle B's and Uncle D's recognition and affection were certainly educative. Up to this point, Leonora had had little outside confirmation for the potential her mother had seen. At the least, therefore, to have found leaders in the labor movement eager to train her substantiated this aspect of her mother's teaching.[8]

At approximately the same time that Leonora joined the Knights of Labor (1886), she began to attend meetings of the Comte Synthetic Circle. And here, too, the qualities Winifred O'Reilly had helped her daughter develop, particularly her keen intellect, which was apparent to all who knew her, made it possible for Leonora to find the kind of opportunities she and her mother wished.

The Synthetic Circle had no explicit connection to the labor movement. Rather it was a kind of mutual education society, a discussion group, that had grown out of a series of lectures about "Comte's Positivist Religion of Humanity." Its leader was Edward King, the same man who with Charles Stover several years later took Lillian Wald on her tour of the Lower East Side. By trade, King was a printer, although Samuel Gompers once claimed that "he was a man of such broad information that he was at home in any circle." However that may be, King's acquaintance with many different kinds of literature made it possible for the Synthetic Circle to read and discuss everything from the classics to Herbert Spencer and to exchange views on topics ranging from Stoic philosophy to the pros and cons of marriage versus free love. Through the Synthetic Circle, therefore, Leonora O'Reilly was able to increase her familiarity with books and ideas. Because she had had so little formal schooling, the group provided an especially important supplement to her previous education.[9]

The Synthetic Circle offered Leonora O'Reilly even more than what was in essence a kind of liberal (collegiate) education. According to one of the group's original members, "King preached and inspired *self-mastery* . . . 'There may be an excuse some time to bluff others,' he used to say, 'but beware of deceiving your own self.' " Heretofore, even if Leonora had not read "the cardinal principles of Auguste Comte," which she would muse on in her diary for the rest of her life, she had been exposed to much that was implicit in Comte. Uncle B and Uncle D, for example, even at this time, were telling her repeatedly that ''ignorance, ignorance is the great enemy.'' Edward King, following Comte, also believed that life was education, and that self-education was one's contribution to ''Humanity's Progress.'' Nonetheless, the notion that one had a duty to one's self that was separate from, though complementary to, one's duty to cause was not an idea that had been emphatically presented to O'Reilly elsewhere or before. Over the years, the ''clearer light'' Uncle B had prophesied would lead Leonora to act as few working women could do. Her loyalties were not always clear to others or even to herself, but King's insistence on total honesty to one's self helped Leonora find her way. She was a bright person, whose quick mind was frequently admired. And Edward King, building on what Winifred O'Reilly, Uncle B, and Uncle D, as well as Leonora herself, had already established, taught Leonora how to use this to study her own convictions above and beyond all else.[10]

O'Reilly remained a member of the Comte Synthetic Circle for forty-one years. After Edward King's death in 1922, she became the group's leader. By that time she and King and King's wife were very close friends and Leonora had become King's intellectual peer. In the Synthetic Circle, O'Reilly had a kind of intellectual family to which she could turn for ideas and discussion and with whom she almost always measured ''Humanity's Progress'' at a New Year's celebration. The group helped her discover that the cause to which she had been dedicated by her mother was very much her own. Leonora may never have doubted this, but King's motto—''beware of deceiving your own self''—did call for the kind of self-scrutiny that would have promoted a more articulate awareness of this.

The Synthetic Circle was rather typical of the kind of study group that flourished on the Lower East Side at this time. In the 1880s and 1890s, that section of New York was filled with young people who were searching for truth, for new ethics, for ways to find a better life. The atmosphere in those days was charged with intellectual inquiry, as well as with both optimism and doubt. Consequently, as Morris R. Cohen, the philosopher, has pointed out, the sense of searching that was so common among people like Cohen, O'Reilly, and Mary Ryshpan, O'Reilly's friend who became Cohen's wife, caused them constantly to gather not just in quasi-formal organizations like the Comte Synthetic Circle, but also more informally. The intellectual environment in which Leonora and her friends came of age was invigorating. It made the stimulation Leonora had found with her mother at places like Cooper Union a part of her daily life. The urgency she felt about her own education, the commitment she brought to her efforts to make the world a more humane, enlightened, and just place, and the faith that allowed her to believe that such a world might be realized through persuasion and reform were nurtured by the people with whom she walked to work and spent the evening, all the while talking, arguing, and worrying ideas. Leonora O'Reilly grew up among men and women for whom education was entertainment, and this had a profound effect on her taste and her interests as well as on her politics.[11]

The kind of cooperative exploration that Morris Cohen recognized in the Synthetic Circle was not limited to philosophizing. As one can see in the Working Women's Society, the group whose report on conditions in large department stores taught Maud Nathan so much, the same spirit also led to social activism. And the Working Women's Society, which O'Reilly helped to organize, is significant here because it illustrates the way in which Leonora was able to synthesize the various components of her education.

The Working Women's Society was formed around the time Leonora joined the Knights of Labor. Its strategy seems to have come directly from the Knights' program. Unlike the American Federation of Labor, the Knights sought to improve working conditions by arousing the public's conscience and thereby gaining support for the legislative measures in which they placed their ultimate hope. The Working Women's Society did just this. The women met to share information, gathered additional facts, got these to Josephine Shaw Lowell, with her help brought their report to the attention of the public, and ultimately with the help of the Consumer's League and the Social Reform Club guided the Mercantile Inspection Act of 1896 through the New York state legislature. Clearly, therefore, even though there is insufficient evidence to argue that O'Reilly purposefully used the Working Women's Society to test the approach to reform that Uncle B, Uncle D, and others were teaching her, its plan of action argues a connection. Similarly, because O'Reilly was one of the founders of the Working Women's Society, it is safe to assume that she was also trying out her ability to be what her mother and so many others thought she could be—a leader.[12]

Leonora O'Reilly's early life was difficult, but she was able to find rich educational opportunities in the people she met, and she was able to use what they taught her to educative ends. Through the Working Women's Society, she once again found someone to whom she could turn for instruction, advice, and, in this case, more concrete forms of assistance. It was at the Working Women's Society that Leonora O'Reilly met Louise S. W. Perkins, Josephine Shaw Lowell's Bostonian friend, who became her mentor.

Louise Perkins, like Josephine Shaw Lowell, was a kind of advisor to the Working Women's Society. Most likely, her first contact with O'Reilly was rather limited in purpose. Within a short time, however, she became a part of every aspect of O'Reilly's life. Partly because Perkins recognized O'Reilly's unusual ability, especially perhaps her intellectual curiosity, and partly also because she believed O'Reilly was fighting "the world's battles," for approximately ten years Perkins devoted considerable energy and money to O'Reilly's education. Her goal, as she explained it to Leonora, was "to help and perfect" her "capacity for service." Like all of her earlier teachers, therefore, Louise Perkins was drawn to O'Reilly because she could see great potential in her; more than O'Reilly's other teachers, however, Louise Perkins was able to expand the avenues through which Leonora could "serve."[13]

Perkins herself remains a rather elusive figure. She lived in Concord, Massachusetts and summered in Annisquam. A "Miss Rodgers" and a "Miss Fisher" were her constant companions. She was obviously wealthy, well-educated, and well-connected to people who could help her newfound protégée. She had a great appreciation for art, was steeped in Transcendentalism, and sympathetic to the doctrines of the Ethical Culture Society. She was also determined in her efforts with O'Reilly, although acute enough to realize that she could counsel and assist but not impose.[14]

At the outset, O'Reilly was probably suspicious of Perkins. She had grown up feeling distrust and contempt for "gentlemen" and "ladies." Later on she described herself as "one whose thinking had been along lines directly opposed to taking anything—not even their sunny smiles from the rich." As a result, Perkins's first lesson had to be that she could be trusted, although at the time she may not have recognized the need to establish the sincerity of her motives. In any case, for O'Reilly to take advantage of the advice and opportunities Perkins offered, she did have to develop confidence in Perkins. And she was able to do this because Perkins was forthright in her expressions of concern for the problems O'Reilly knew so intimately as well as honest in her avowal of her own subjective need to be involved with the solution of these, and also because Perkins's view of what O'Reilly could be was compatible with those of the teachers whom Leonora could trust more readily. Thus, as she became able to understand Perkins and Perkins's interest in her, O'Reilly also became able to accept Perkins's dreams for her and, along with those, a great deal more.[15]

According to O'Reilly's diary, Perkins believed that "the reformer's place and work . . . is . . . first to know himself, become conscious of how much of the larger life he himself has been able to grasp, and then go forth and teach it wherever his voice can be heard." Edward King would have said much the same. Uncle B, Uncle D, and Mrs. O'Reilly also would have concurred, even if nothing in their experience had urged them to describe a role apart from its relevance to the labor movement. As would be true of the relationship in general, therefore, Perkins's views confirmed what was already established at the same time that they extended and broadened O'Reilly's "capacity for service." Louise Perkins did not make Leonora O'Reilly a social reformer. But since her notion of social reform was close enough to the mission that Leonora had already assumed, she was able to do for her exactly what she had promised to do.[16]

Few people could have found a more devoted and generous "Guardian Angel" or "Older Sister" than O'Reilly found in Perkins; and few people could have found a more apt and eager "Little Sister" than Perkins found in O'Reilly. The confidence, respect, and affection that grew up between them, despite the discrepancies in their backgrounds, made it possible for Perkins to advise freely and for O'Reilly to accept her help. In 1894, for example, when O'Reilly was made forewoman of the shirtwaist shop in which she worked, Perkins wrote immediately to point out the promotion's advantages. "I have thought so much of the good you can do as head of the shop. You can make it into real mission work of the noble kind . . . If you can stand as a middle man of righteousness, faithful and just to the interests of all, you can not only help your own shop, but set a higher standard for the place or position everywhere." As she always would do, Perkins at times reminded O'Reilly that she must not allow the job at hand to interfere with the further development of her "own soul and its strivings to see the biggest right." Thus, she urged O'Reilly to read, and suggested and gave the books she thought valuable. She arranged for O'Reilly to spend vacations with her in Concord or Annisquam, where she could study in peace, discuss the "essence of life," and simply enjoy what O'Reilly called the "dear little nest," which she described in her diary so that "in some dark hour of a city life [I may] read it over and be reassured of what life may be if one only lives up to her highest thoughts."[17]

As O'Reilly's mentor, Perkins was constantly on the lookout for larger and better opportunities for her. Thus, for example in September of 1894, she arranged for O'Reilly to meet Felix Adler, the leader of the Ethical Culture Society. And it was probably Adler who brought O'Reilly into the Social Reform Club, which first gathered on his suggestion two months after he and O'Reilly met. According to one member, the Social Reform Club joined together "all those prominent in 'Social Service' work." O'Reilly's membership in this club is worth considering, therefore, for in her reaction to what she found to be a rather trying experience, one gets some sense of the hurdles she had to surmount in order to work with and to feel a part of this group.[18]

To participate in the Social Reform Club was not easy for O'Reilly. Even though she had learned to feel comfortable with Louise Perkins, amidst the likes of Felix Adler, Josephine Shaw Lowell, Charles Stover, Lillian Wald, and Maud Nathan, O'Reilly still felt out of place. Soon after the club convened, she wrote in her diary: "As the membership stands at the present I am the only woman wage-earner; that is: a woman who works at a common trade . . . There are many women in the club who work for wages, but they keep telling me all the time that I am the only real representative working-woman; in other words I am the only factory girl." To be a "factory girl" was not a mark of inferiority to Leonora. Indeed, while her fellow club members were telling her that this was what she was, she herself may have been thinking: beware Leonora, you are becoming a "lady." After all, it was that status that was distasteful to her, even if when she was among women who seemed to embody it, she was acutely aware of the limitations of her background. After one club meeting, she wrote, for example: "once in a while there is a discussion in which the working woman's point of view has to be given [and] my Sister members of the S.R.C. insist on my taking the trouble to torture the rest of the members, with my eloquence and my factory made logic." Obviously, therefore, it was difficult for a "factory girl" to associate with and learn from people who represented a status she disliked and resented; and to feel that such people, despite their status, had something to offer was even more confusing. As the years went by, O'Reilly came to be at home with this group. Yet before this would happen, she had to grow into a reformer who could trust her own "eloquence" and "logic" more than she did as a young woman.[19]

Louise Perkins did not abandon Leonora once she was admitted to the Social Reform Club. In fact, she worried continually that "the shop," plus the Social Reform Club, the Comte Synthetic Circle, systematic reading, a physical culture class at the YWCA, and another class in business training would be too much for Leonora. She had reason to worry: "the shop" alone was too much for many people, and Leonora's health was always precarious. Increasingly, too, Leonora herself craved "relief." As a result, when Perkins raised enough money among her friends to pay Leonora's salary for a year, so that she could go to work for Lillian Wald at the Henry Street Settlement, Leonora eagerly accepted. Perkins hoped, as always, that the year would allow Leonora "to perfect her power to work and to increase her value in a large and true way." For as she wrote to Lillian Wald, and probably also to Grace Dodge, Josephine Shaw Lowell, and the other women who contributed to O'Reilly's support, she firmly believed that Leonora O'Reilly "had a message to deliver, and should be enabled to deliver it."[20]

During her time at Henry Street, O'Reilly investigated sweatshops with Lavinia Dock, ran a club for young boys, and was put in charge of an experimental cooperative workshop. In the workshop she trained girls to become expert seamstresses, and not surprisingly, she did this in the way she knew best. As had been true for her mother and herself, Leonora taught her students to make the whole garment rather than just a piece. But O'Reilly's workshop was not a success. It had been designed to prove that women's shirtwaists could be made under the best conditions with no loss in profit, and the shirtwaists it produced were too good to be placed in the standardized market. O'Reilly's first attempt to enact in a formal sense the role Perkins had encouraged—to be a teacher—was short-lived, therefore, although the experience was valuable nonetheless. The girls whom Leonora trained adored her and mastered all that she taught. O'Reilly was a good teacher, and at Henry Street she was given the chance to see this.[21]

O'Reilly's diary entries during this period frequently mentioned how much she enjoyed life within "the family." She did not live at the settlement, but she and her mother spent many evenings there, and Winifred O'Reilly's stories about Henry George and her readings from Mazzini were apparently an inspiration to all who heard them. Like Louise Perkins, therefore, who also admired Leonora's mother, the women at Henry Street offered Leonora total acceptance. At the Social Reform Club she had initially felt out of place; at the settlement she felt at home from the start. The experience underscored what she had first learned from her mentor: that women of nonworking-class background could be as sincere and devoted to social change as she was. Moreover, since Lillian Wald, Lavinia Dock, and Helene McDowell, the residents whom Leonora mentioned most often, were in the midst of "the world's battles," rather than on the sidelines, as Perkins seems to have been, their example was even more significant than hers was. Perkins could give what O'Reilly called "ethics lessons"; she could give advice and arrange concrete help; and she was to Leonora a living model of what she had wanted to be at least since she met Edward King: a person who "lives up to the highest thoughts." But since Wald, Dock, and McDowell shared Leonora's immediate world and had considerably more practical experience than Perkins, their colleagueship nurtured the sense of sisterhood that Leonora, among others, would eventually seek to institutionalize in the Women's Trade Union League.[22]

O'Reilly's official association with Henry Street was relatively brief, although her year there stands out as a real turning point in her education. At Henry Street, Leonora O'Reilly was given her first chance to work at a job that was not a "common trade." Previously, she had run a sewing machine; at best she had been a skilled manual worker. She may not have found such work degrading, but it was far easier to see herself as a reformer as she moved into work that allowed her to be a reformer: to "go forth and teach," as Louise Perkins had said a reformer should, not just as an avocation, but also as an occupation. In a sense, therefore, O'Reilly's time at Henry Street was the juncture between the years during which she aspired to be a reformer and those during which she was, in fact, by trade, a reformer.

From approximately 1900 forward, O'Reilly found it increasingly possible to collaborate with reformers from all walks of life. She never totally gave up her almost instinctive suspiciousness of reformers of nonworking-class background. But the broadening of her circle to include people of the kind she had initially distrusted at the Social Reform Club, which expanded the group with whom she could communicate and from whom, in some cases, she could learn, represents a slow and cumulative change in her sense of self. In order to take the desire of "her sister members" to hear her point of view as genuine interest instead of patronizing condescension, O'Reilly had to feel sure of who she was and of what she had to say. By themselves, the assurances of her mother, her "Uncles," and her mentor had not given her sufficient self-confidence to feel this way. Over time, however, their continuing assurances, combined with her growing "eloquence" and "logic" and further opportunities to put into practice the role for which she had been preparing, eventually did give her such confidence. What is more, O'Reilly was growing up. By 1900, she was thirty years old. It was easier to speak out freely and easily among the kind of men and women who belonged to the Social Reform Club as she became a more mature woman.

Soon after her time at Henry Street, O'Reilly went on to Pratt Institute, where she studied psychology and wrote a thesis, entitled "Has Sewing a Right to Be Termed Manual Training?" that left her determined "to master this art of writing." In itself, the step illustrates a wish to solidify the kind of abilities she had enjoyed in herself and the other women she had known at Henry Street. She graduated from Pratt in June of 1900. Afterward, she discovered that since she had not taken the academic course she could not get a job with the Board of Education. She was keenly disappointed. At approximately the same time, she wrote in her diary: "tonight, LO'R's whole soul goes out into the prayer that her life may prove worthy of the trust put in her." Her wish to find a way to use her skills and competence and to demonstrate her worth speaks clearly.[23]

In 1902, following a brief stint as head resident of the Asacog

Settlement in Brooklyn and as a teacher at a summer sewing school run by the Alliance Employment Bureau, O'Reilly joined the faculty of the Manhattan Trade School for Girls, a project initially organized by the women's auxiliary of the Ethical Culture Society. Because of her background, her expertise in the field, and her acquaintance with many of the project's original backers (some of whom were also members of the Social Reform Club), O'Reilly was consulted about the school's initial organization. She may even have written the school's first prospectus, which stated that one could not train "the best type of worker" unless "the worker is interested in her work, sees its relationship to other forms of industry . . . and through intelligent work attains an inspiration for a higher form of life." As it turned out, however, O'Reilly's influence at the trade school was limited. She was made head of the department of machine sewing, yet she was never asked to join the board, as she and some members of the Board of Directors had hoped.[24]

In other ways, too, the experience at the trade school was disillusioning. In 1902, O'Reilly had been so enthusiastic about the school that she had wanted to give "all that I possess or may acquire" to make it a success. But as the school developed over the years, her hopes for it were shattered. O'Reilly had wanted the school to be called the "New York College of Industries for Girls/or Women," and her name for the institution was not adopted. More important, despite her arguments for a program evenly divided between the "intellectual" and the "practical," the curriculum strongly emphasized training in specific skills. In her own department, she included discussions of Aristotle, J. S. Mill, Emerson, and the like, in the hope that these would help students develop a better sense of the meaning and value of their work. Yet the school as a whole did not promote such fare and was primarily concerned with preparing its students for immediate employment, rather than nurturing in them the "intelligent" attitudes O'Reilly considered ultimately more significant. Also, in appointing as its head Mary Schenck Woolman, a Teachers College graduate who was simultaneously a professor there, and in refusing to appoint a representative of the working class to the administration or to the board, the trustees made clear that the school was not to be even partially controlled by the people it sought to help. And this contradicted O'Reilly's strong conviction that the school must express "the *wish* to be in close touch with those whom it seeks to benefit."[25]

While she was at the Manhattan Trade School, O'Reilly also became involved in the formation of the WTUL. And there is no doubt that participation in that organization grounded her criticisms of the school in concrete experience. According to R. L. Duffus (and perhaps also, therefore, Lillian Wald), O'Reilly was "so intense that few dared contradict her." She felt morally obliged to act according to her own convictions. To have ignored the shortcomings of the Manhattan Trade School, as they became increasingly apparent to her, would have been to deceive herself, and this Leonora O'Reilly had learned not to do. Once again, therefore, various aspects of O'Reilly's experience combined to clarify her views and her direction. Her disenchantment with the trade school was heightened by what she learned at the WTUL.[26]

The WTUL was primarily the child of William English Walling and Mary Kenney O'Sullivan. It was established at the AFL convention in Boston in 1903. The idea was Walling's. As a resident of the University Settlement in New York, Walling, who was a millionaire from Kentucky and a student of Thorstein Veblen, had been especially interested in the labor movement. He quickly discovered that women workers were less organized than men, though equally if not more in need of organization, and he saw in the British Women's Trade Union League (founded in 1874) a model that might be usefully replicated in the United States. He therefore joined forces with O'Sullivan, the daughter of Irish immigrants, the organizer of the first women's bookbinder's union in Chicago, and the wife of John F. O'Sullivan, a friend of Samuel Gompers and an influential member of the AFL, to mobilize the people necessary to form a cross-class alliance, controlled by working women. Leonora O'Reilly was on the WTUL's first board and was also the main speaker in November 1903 at the meeting, sponsored by Walling and attended by Lillian Wald, Florence Kelley, and Jane Robbins, among others, that established the New York league. Thus, O'Reilly was not only Walling's "first recruit"; from the very beginning she was one of the league's most influential members.[27]

The WTUL was a logical home for Leonora O'Reilly. Its purposes were to organize women workers into unions, to improve the conditions under which they worked, to educate and train them for leadership in the labor movement, and to offer to its "ally" members—nonworking-class women—an opportunity to further the advancement of labor, as well as their own education. Throughout its history, however, the WTUL was not very successful in organizing unions. Its first efforts in this direction were a disaster. " 'Sociables,' as members called them . . . 'drinking tea and discussing unionism,' " did not work. Nor did the street rallies at which O'Reilly and others preached from soapboxes to women leaving factories. Even concentrating exclusively on "the most exploited of female wage-earners" bore few results. The presumption that unionism would quickly appeal to the most oppressed was unfounded. From 1906 to 1913, therefore, the league concentrated on teaching unorganized women "the combined principles of feminism and unionism" and gaining greater support from male trade unionists, who were at best indifferent and at worst hostile to the organization of women workers.[28]

The problems the WTUL faced as it attempted to help women workers, in addition to increasing O'Reilly's awareness of the divergence between her interests and those of male trade unionists, confirmed the point of view she argued unsuccessfully at the Manhattan Trade School. The league's difficulties in its unionizing campaigns made her even more convinced that workers needed a broad education as a prerequisite to organization: an education that would inspire them with a sense of dignity and encourage them to recognize their identity of interest, whatever their trade or their immediate employment situation. What Uncle B and Uncle D had said was indeed right. "Ignorance"—narrow vision—was "the enemy." For O'Reilly to remain at a school that had opted for immediate results and a limiting conception of vocational education became increasingly difficult. Trade training was not industrial education, and industrial education, O'Reilly wrote in 1904, was the "knocking at the door" of her generation.[29]

O'Reilly's experience within the WTUL also heightened her dissatisfaction with the organizational structure of the Manhattan Trade School. And one incident in particular had this effect. Cross-class cooperation had been a central goal of the WTUL from the first. But to achieve a balance in which working-class women guided their upper-class sisters, many of whom were competent, articulate, and of strong opinion, was more difficult than had been anticipated. Friction developed at many points. Within the New

York League tensions came to a head in 1905 over League plans to publish chapters of *The Long Day*, a book written by Dorothy Richardson, an "ally" type, that described the life of a working girl in New York City. O'Reilly considered the book not only misguided but "rank exploitation of the working women of New York." She tried to persuade the league to repudiate the book, but failed. As a result, she resigned from the league in disgust.[30]

"I may have felt [before] that I had reason to believe I could be of further use to my own people some where else," she wrote to Gertrude Barnum, an "ally" who was the league's general secretary at the time, "but now . . . I know I do not belong." Barnum and others worked hard to convince her to rejoin and were ultimately successful. The struggle added to O'Reilly's determination that working people should control any efforts to solve their problems. But it also reminded her that within the WTUL there was at least the desire on the part of "allies" to listen and to learn from women like herself. Arguments such as the one Barnum presented in the following letter therefore undermined O'Reilly's allegiance to the trade school, perhaps even more than Barnum realized. Barnum wrote: "If you keep getting off of every Com^{te} in which every member does not agree with you in every respect, you will not contribute much to any constructive work . . . You may be right about the Long Day. The last chapter is abominable and we have 'educated' Miss Richardson considerably . . . I should like to have read the Long Day with you. It might have helped make me worthy to espouse the Trade Union Cause, which I sincerely wish to do honestly and democratically and faithfully and well. Fortunately everyone does not abandon us 'allies' as soon as they disagree with us and we [still] may be made useful . . . I have often had to explain to workers your position in the Manhattan Trade School. They have said much the same sort of thing you say of us."[31]

But what was O'Reilly to do? Resign from the trade school? She had to earn a living. To return to "the shop" would hardly magnify her influence; at this point the league could not offer a full-time salary; and most settlement jobs did not pay enough to live on. The tension produced by this dilemma was great. Five months after Barnum's letter, Louise Perkins, who continued to advise and encourage O'Reilly throughout her life, wrote to tell her that she was glad she had been "forced into the complete rest, a Sanitarium gives." O'Reilly had obviously had a breakdown of some kind. The physical and emotional strain of a full-time teaching job as well as work for the league, both of which embroiled O'Reilly in constant conflict with other people and provoked considerable inner turmoil, were just too much. As can happen when one is stretched to the limit, however, O'Reilly seems to have wrung from the experience a more realistic and accepting understanding of herself. Earlier, Mary Drier, an "ally" leader of the league, had set aside an annuity for her, and in 1908 she finally accepted it. Apparently, she now knew what she needed to carry on her work, which indicates how far she had come as a result of the exhausting and turbulent experience of the last eight or ten years.[32]

O'Reilly originally met Mary Drier when she worked at the Asacog Settlement, where Drier, who was one of three daughters of a prosperous Brooklyn family, was on the Board of Directors. She quickly recognized in her the makings of a strong ally. As a result, when the WTUL was organized in 1903, she brought into the league not only Mary Drier, but also her sister, Margaret, who later, after her marriage to Raymond Robins, became president of the National League.[33]

During the early years of her friendship with the Driers, though she knew it was "a kind of madness," because "no people could be kinder or more willing to serve," O'Reilly had felt uneasy in their home. While visiting them in Stonington, Connecticut, for example, she had told her mother that sometimes she was taken over by "the old rebellious spirit." When she thought of "the 'old man' " (Uncle B?) and his "burlap sheets," the contrast in life circumstances was excruciating. It made her feel like "a child of the gutter." O'Reilly did not feel that way in 1908. Between the time she wrote that letter and the time she accepted the annuity, she had changed a great deal.[34]

O'Reilly's willingness to accept Drier's gift shows that she now totally trusted Mary Drier, as Mary Drier trusted her. Had this not been the case, she could not have believed that the legacy was intended to do what Mary Drier claimed: to allow her "to be free to do her work" as she thought best. Beyond this, O'Reilly's acceptance shows that she was now able to take a luxury (a guaranteed income) that was unavailable to most working women. And this she could not have done if she had still felt even the least bit tainted, self-conscious, and disloyal when enjoying unearned and unequal comforts and wealth. Thus, when O'Reilly said yes to Mary Drier's offer, she showed that at least in her own eyes she deserved the freedom the endowment would bring. Her now proven competence entitled her to be able to do her work on the same terms that a woman like Lillian Wald did hers: through the financial generosity of other people.[35]

Leonora was now able to feel this way for many reasons. Perkins, Wald, and her colleagues at the league had all in one way or another helped her to realize the ability Edward King, Uncle B and Uncle D, and so many others had seen first. And her work at the Manhattan Trade School and the WTUL also had a profound effect because it clarified and strengthened her convictions, enhanced the value she could see in her earlier experience, and made her more aware of the necessity for expressing her special point of view. Above all else, however, it was her mother's continuing support, confidence, aspirations, and love that stood behind the transformation evident in Leonora.

Winifred O'Reilly's role in her daughter's education had changed after Uncle B and the others became important. That part of her effort that had involved nurturing the skills and attitudes directly related to Leonora's work was no longer necessary. Others could advance Leonora more than she. Yet without her approval, Leonora would not have accepted Mary Drier's legacy, just as without her constant acceptance and reassurance, she could not have endured the tensions inherent in her changing status. Louise Perkins had known this, which was why she constantly asked about "Mother O'Reilly's" opinions. So too did Mary Drier, who wrote to Mrs. O'Reilly to explain her gift. And Leonora's letter from the Driers' house in Stonington illustrates the nature of her mother's continuing influence. The letter was riddled with reassurances that she would not leave, which indicates that her mother encouraged her ability to see "Dear Beautiful Mary Drier" apart from "the inequality as expressed in the two modes of life." And even the simple fact that Leonora, who was at that moment "a child of the gutter," could sign the letter "but your, Blossom," makes it clear that her mother's attachment in itself continued to urge her on. Mrs. O'Reilly seems never to have doubted that her daughter could be a working woman, and therefore legitimately entitled to be a leader in the labor movement, even if she did not work for a wage. It was Mrs. O'Reilly's vision, refracted through the opinions of Leonora's other teachers as well as the insights she drew from her work, that made Leonora strong enough to realize that she could do her job better if she would take her friend's money.[36]

Having accepted Mary Drier's legacy ($125 a month), O'Reilly resigned from the Manhattan Trade School. She then took to the road, traveling all over the country to organize unions and to advise striking working women. In a sense, she was doing for them what Josephine Shaw Lowell and Louise Perkins had hoped to do for the Working Women's Society. At this time, she was also a constant speaker at suffrage rallies both as a representative of the WTUL and as a member of the New York City Wage Earners' Suffrage League. Between 1909 and 1919 little that was totally new was incorporated into O'Reilly's thought. She continued to believe that social progress—greater economic and political equality—was directly linked to the advancement of labor. She also continued to believe that women could not participate fully in the labor movement unless they were organized, and that a group like the WTUL could be instrumental in bringing this about. Characteristically also, during these years O'Reilly was at times plagued by disillusionment and doubt.

In 1915, for example, following a convention of the New York State Federation of Labor at which the WTUL seems to have been criticized for its "ally" membership and blamed in some way for the AFL's poor record with women workers, O'Reilly told Mary Drier that she had lost all faith in the league and that her "hands were off the Trade Union job in New York." The league's continued existence, she felt, provided male trade unionists with a "scapegoat" and prevented working women from seeing "who it is that is playing foul in the game"—apparently the men. Drier's response to O'Reilly's comments was unusually vehement. She wrote: "what impresses me is that you, of all people, should accept what you think to be the desire of the leaders (alas for the misnomer) in the labor movement in NY [?]—men—. . . and yet here you are . . . saying—'I'll get out of this, because men don't want an outside body like us . . . ' If all women had done, what you propose to do—there never would have been a chance of our ever learning even to read and write . . . the fathers and husbands and brothers . . . did not want an outside interference like a school . . . I for my part feel it worth all the thing there is [*sic*]—to help hold up the hands of . . . the less gifted but equally noble and devoted other sisters. And this I hold to be the function of the League.'' Drier's letter, therefore, by recalling O'Reilly to the purpose they had come to share, reminded her that she could not renounce sisterhood without also renouncing all that she believed, for by this time, O'Reilly no less than Drier had become convinced that women must lead the way toward social progress. Men could not and would not see what had to be done. The exchange is important. It illustrates the subtle, not always consistent rearranging of priorities that took place in O'Reilly's mind during the years she was actively involved in the league.[37]

The political and reformist powers of sisterhood had been clear to O'Reilly at least since the days of the Working Women's Society, although after that time a number of experiences moved gender into a more prominent position in her thought. O'Reilly never married, though she had opportunities to. She lived throughout her life with her mother, and most of her closest adult friends were women. In the letter quoted above, Drier commented that she and Leonora had been ''born'' in 1903, the year the league was founded. To an extent she was right. The league gave institutional form to the aspirations of women like O'Reilly and Drier. Their loyalty to the league and to what it represented gave birth to a profound sense of comradery and common cause. And an increasingly prominent part of that cause was mutual support as both a means to an end and an end in itself. O'Reilly was a central figure in the league. She may have shaped league policy more than it shaped her, but it did shape her, nevertheless.

League members gave O'Reilly constant overt support. They applauded her speeches; they followed the progress of her unionizing campaigns with interest; and they urged her to write for *Life and Labor*, the league's magazine. In a variety of ways, then, they told her, as one member put it, that ''you do have the gift of 'getting across the footlights.' '' Beyond this, league members, especially ''ally'' members, gave O'Reilly the material assistance without which she could not have done what she wanted. They opened their homes to her when she was on the road; they gathered the audiences to whom she spoke; and when she was away from New York City, members of the New York league often looked after her mother. If league members created for O'Reilly a public audience and helped her reach that audience effectively, they also provided her with a constant private audience. They sought her views and

guidance on league policy. They listened sympathetically whenever she wished to share her ideas. Conflict notwithstanding,
"allies" not excepted, the women of the WTUL made it clear to
O'Reilly that they shared her cause. To help *her* speak out, they
believed, was part of their cause. The identity of interest between
them was the business of their daily exchange.[38]

If Mary Drier and the WTUL supported O'Reilly's sense of
sisterhood, the refusal of male trade unionists to acknowledge the
class-related problems of women workers undermined her class
consciousness. Women were eager to hear her; male trade unionists often left when she or another woman was given the podium.
The AFL found money to support striking men, but funds dried
up when women were the pickets. In fact, the AFL could not even
be consistent on whether or not women should receive equal pay
for equal work.[39]

During this period, O'Reilly's thought was also influenced by
the simple fact that she was becoming increasingly self-conscious of
herself as a woman. Her work forced her to think about this, but so
too did public discussion of "the woman." The "sex" question
was constantly in the news at this time. Because O'Reilly loved the
theater and recognized its educative potential, public concerns affected her most acutely through dramatic presentation. "In the
theaters we should continue our studies after all college and university life is passed," she once wrote. "In fact the theater is the
General Classroom in Life's University." It is interesting, therefore, that although O'Reilly, with her mother, went to many
plays, the ones she discussed in her diary tended to reflect questions of gender. Thus, for example, having seen *The Lilley*, she
wrote: "more woman question. When will women understand
and understanding be brave enough to act"; and following *As a
Man Thinks*, she noted: "the tyranny of male over female strongly
put . . . a race question well stated."[40]

More than anything, however, O'Reilly's identification with
other women—woman in general—was heightened by the fact
that for three years she was a mother. At some point in 1907 she
and her mother adopted a baby named Alice. While Alice was
alive, O'Reilly would race home from union meetings to play with
her and to feed her. She delighted in everything Alice did. When
Alice died in January of 1911, she was crushed. By early February
she was back on the picket lines, but on February 8 she noted in

her diary that she had "prepared an article on motherhood"; a few months later, after almost 150 working women were killed in a fire at the Triangle Shirtwaist Factory, she wrote: "Labor Fire Talk— thesis—I must save every child from the coal and the grave"; and during the summer of 1911, she and her mother ran what she called the "Children's Rest Farm or Never-Grow Old Land," a sort of camp for ten children between the ages of three and six. Having discovered in herself the capacity to mother a child, without, significantly, the concurrent opportunity to discover what a child can mean to a man, which might have been a revelation to O'Reilly since she had never really known her own father, the bonds O'Reilly shared with other women became apparent on a new level. Philosophy aside, she discovered that women were not joined only by cause. Women, all women, were united by "their feeling of motherhood of the human race."[41]

This sense of "solidarity" with other women accounts in part for O'Reilly's involvement with the suffrage campaign, from which many working-class women remained aloof. Yet O'Reilly's continuing identification with working women also accounts for her insistence on the need for a separate organization, the New York City Wage Earners' Suffrage League, which she helped to establish in 1911. Most likely, suffrage work in itself changed O'Reilly very little, although it did help to keep "the woman question" at the forefront of her attention and urged her to ponder further the relevance of feminist concerns to those of labor.[42]

In an undated statement on the "Labor Movement and Ballot," O'Reilly wrote: "our first duty as women is to gain equal political rights with men. Equal pay for equal work will soon follow. After which, we must build up our unions to work harmoniously with those of our brothers, and in that way build the bridge over which thoughtful honest toil, and sagacious capital shall walk to the social democracy of the future." At least in this statement, then, O'Reilly gave in to the kind of exaggerated claim that was not uncommon among suffragists at the time: grant women the franchise and all else by way of necessary social change will follow. Moreover, having listened admiringly to Jane Addams while they crossed the Atlantic together on their way to the International Congress of Women at The Hague in 1915, O'Reilly became convinced that women were responsible for the war, simply because they had not prevented it, and that in the future they must find ways "to use power as well as influence" to achieve international peace, understanding, and cooperation. She never gave up her allegiance to the labor movement, but her effort to do all she could for that cause led her to the conclusion that it was female solidarity that would create the kind of world she wanted. Quite appropriately, therefore, her last major public effort was to help Margaret Drier Robins organize the International Conference of Working Women in Washington, D.C., in 1919. Thereafter, her own poor health and her mother's increasing senility forced her to give up most of her activities.[43]

During the last years of her life, O'Reilly became an ardent supporter of Irish independence and of women's education in India. She also gave a course at the New School for Social Research called the "Problems and Progress of Labor." Most of her energy, however, went into caring for her mother, and after that, reading, studying, and writing an outline for a book on the "Theory of the Labor Movement."

O'Reilly had been a reformer, a feminist, and a working woman. She virtually summarized her own education when she wrote: "This price the Gods exact for Song, That we become what we Sing—I should say that is the price the Gods exact for all good work—That you become what you do." But she should have added—if you think. For it was, in the end, Leonora O'Reilly's ability to think, critically, clearly, and insistently, that made it possible for her not only to convince others of the need to create a different and better social order, but also, on her own and for herself, to pursue always the "clearer light." O'Reilly was educated by her mother, her "Uncles," her mentor, her friends, and her colleagues; she learned profoundly from books, theater, work, and talk. As the twenty-five volumes of her diary indicate, however, all that she was told or discovered was continuously synthesized, modified, counteracted, or otherwise restructured by an uninterrupted dialogue with herself. If, therefore, Leonora O'Reilly was as lucky in the teachers she found as she was unlucky in the economic circumstances in which she grew up, she was especially fortunate in her ability to think.[44]

5

Rose Schneiderman
1882-1972

ROSE SCHNEIDERMAN spent the first eight years of her life in Russian Poland. She came to the United States with her family in 1890. During her childhood she was subjected to extreme deprivation, and in surviving, acquired the tenacity and self-reliance that account in part for her subsequent accomplishment. Rose Schneiderman was also lucky. As a young woman she found a number of people who were able to teach her how she might achieve the kind of life she wanted. She never had all of the opportunities she wished for, but her educational biography tells a good deal about how she became ''an outstanding light in the field of labor.''[1]

Schneiderman's educational biography begins in the village of Saven, where she was born. Her father, Samuel Schneiderman, was a tailor and her mother, Deborah Rothman Schneiderman, was the daughter of a tailor. Their life was one of meager subsistence. Even with his wife's help, Samuel Schneiderman did not prosper. As a result, before Rose was eight, Samuel Schneiderman had moved his family first to the city of Khelm and then from Khelm to New York. Two years later he was dead. His wife, who was pregnant at the time and still unable to speak English, was left with three children, no job, and no money. The United Hebrew Charities sent food every few days; Deborah Schneiderman took in sewing and a boarder. Nevertheless, by the time Rose was ten, she and her four-year-old brother, Charlie, were in an orphanage run by the Hebrew Sheltering Guardian Society, and Harry, her six-year-old brother, was at the Hebrew Orphan Asylum on 138th Street.[2]

In placing Rose, Charlie, and Harry in orphanages and her new baby with a sister, Deborah Schneiderman was not giving up her children. She sent them away because she could not work and they could not go to school if the family remained together. After Jane, the new baby, was weaned, Rose had had to stay at home taking care of her so her mother could go out to work. If Deborah Schneiderman had not wanted Rose to go to school this might have been all right. As it was, however, Deborah Schneiderman believed it would serve Rose's best interests to place her in an institution.

Rose knew this and accepted it—eventually. In 1967, when she wrote her autobiography, *All for One*, she explained the situation exactly as I have. In 1905, however, when she wrote an autobiographical sketch for *The Independent*, she told a somewhat different story. She never mentioned that she had been in an orphanage and said instead that "when the other children were sent away mother was able to send me back to school . . . till I had reached the Sixth Grammar Grade." Could it be, then, that this account is correct and that Schneiderman was never "sent away"? Not very likely. For one thing, in the story for *The Independent* Schneiderman admitted to other gaps in memory. She stated, for example, that she had "no memory" of life in Russian Poland. Yet sixty-two years later she had a number of rather exact memories that appear to be credible. Furthermore, it seems entirely plausible that Schneiderman had to forget in order to survive the horror of the experience and of the years immediately preceding it. If one assumes, therefore, that the account in *All for One* is more accurate, the questions to ask of Schneiderman's childhood are: first, how did she learn to cope with the traumas she faced so early in life, and, second, what effect did this have on her subsequent experience.[3]

For an answer to the first question, one must look to Schneiderman's parents, both of whom were strong and determined people. Her mother, for example, had never been able to go to school, but had "taught herself to read the prayer book so she could go to synagogue . . . and recite the prayers." In Russia, she had also "managed somehow" to feed and clothe her family on only three rubles a week. While pregnant with Rose, Deborah Schneiderman had even interceded with army officials to secure the military exemption to which her husband was entitled as an only son, which he would have been denied if she had not intervened. Apparently, then, Deborah Schneiderman was not an ineffective person, even if she was temporarily overwhelmed when her husband died. From *All for One* it is also obvious that Rose admired her mother. "When Mother said 'come,' you went," she explained. "When Mother made up her mind, things happened." Thus, in her own character, as shown in her ability to deal with the problems she encountered, Rose would indicate that her strength of will, which resembled her mother's, had come at least in part from watching and copying her.[4]

Samuel Schneiderman also transmitted strength to his daughter, albeit of a different kind. When Rose said that "Father was inclined to be satisfied with his lot as long as he could read books and have friends about him," she did not mean that this man who was so obviously ambitious for his family was complacent; rather she meant that her father was a man who could find pleasure in books and in people, a man who could be happy despite his lot. Samuel Schneiderman enlivened his daughter's life by his own capacity for enjoyment. By reading to his family from *The Arabian Nights* and joining the men of the neighborhood in amateur theatricals, Samuel Schneiderman brought light to diurnal routine and added entertainment and joy to a grimly serious life. By example, then, Samuel Schneiderman taught his daughter to look for and accept whatever pleasures she could find. More important, perhaps, because it gave Rose a goal, Samuel Schneiderman made it clear to his daughter that formal education was supremely important.[5]

Both of Rose Schneiderman's parents wanted their children to be educated as much as they wanted anything in life, but it was Samuel Schneiderman's efforts as well as Rose's special attachment to him that made her parents' aspiration hers as well. Samuel Schneiderman helped Rose learn to read and write. He also walked her to school every morning once they settled in New York. Finally, and this clearly had a profound effect, he pointed out to Rose that she could become a teacher if she studied very hard, which was what Rose later claimed she wanted to do "more than anything in the world." Rose once said of her father that, "like

Mother, he was not demonstrative, but he shared his love of books with us, reading to us a great deal and helping me with my lessons. In a way it was natural that I should feel closer to him than to Mother. She had a habit of teasing . . . She would praise me to others but never to my face. Father, on the other hand, always encouraged me openly." Considering all this, as well as Rose's comment that she "couldn't accept the fact of Father's death . . . I was so very fond of him," it is not surprising that Samuel Schneiderman's dream became a driving force in his daughter's education.[6]

The qualities one can trace to Rose's early interaction with her parents are the ones that seem to have helped her most during her time in the orphanage. And logic would argue that it was the nature of Rose's experience in that institution that made these qualities so pronounced.

The matrons at the orphanage to which Rose was sent were strict and cruel. Girls who were disobedient were beaten or locked in closets for up to twenty-four hours. All of them had to wear "most unbecoming" uniforms and on entering they had to have their hair cut, which Rose hated most of all. "The shame of that experience is very real even now," she wrote as an old woman. "To say it was humiliating is to put it mildly." At the orphanage there was little room or time to play. The girls were marched on line wherever they went. Most of them slept in an "enormous dormitory" and their only private possessions were the trunks provided for their dolls and books. Since Deborah Schneiderman "could not afford to provide . . . anything," however, Rose did not even have such a trunk.[7]

Along with these horrors, Rose also remembered that "nothing has ever tasted quite so good . . . [as the] bread and butter covered with sugar" that she was given by one of the matrons. She claimed, in addition, that the hymns the girls sang in synagogue on Friday evening and Saturday morning made the week "endurable"; that she had had a "good teacher" at the public school she attended and had been able to make up for the schooling she had missed; and finally, that she had escaped most of the punishments inflicted on other girls because she had been obedient. Apparently, the orphanage brought to the fore the strength of will, the ability to focus on small pleasures, and the overriding wish to do well in school that Rose had acquired earlier in her life.[8]

Rose's time in the orphanage was relatively short. She was

there for a little less than one year. When her mother unexpectedly came to reclaim her and take her back downtown to the Lower East Side, she was "quite depressed." As she explained it, "everything looked so drab and dismal . . . I almost wished I was back in the orphanage." To get through the year she had had to adapt. Had she been there longer, who knows what would have happened. But if, as she asserted, her life before the orphanage had made her "more of an adult (in behavior, at least) than many children," even a year in that setting had severed her from the little bits of security, freedom, irresponsibility, and play she had known. To endure the orphanage Rose had focused on the immediate: following the rules, doing well at school, singing the hymns, eating the bread and butter with sugar. To have thought of the past would have been to evoke a contrast that might have been unbearable. So at least for a time, Rose forgot "the small, one-room house, newly white-washed and with a sanded floor," that had been her home in Saven; the thrill of finding a cousin to play with, a "big school," and even a circus when her family had moved to Khelm; and also, perhaps, the new clothes, the "abundance of food," and "more important . . . [the] sense of safety and hope" that she later recalled in describing her family's first Passover in New York. To an extent, Rose's childhood was later reclaimed. But having been separated from it suddenly, totally, and at a young age took its toll. Rose knew how to survive better than she knew how to play. She would always wish for the carelessness she had lost, but she never would achieve it to the degree she would have liked.[9]

To get along at the orphanage, Rose had had to learn to size up a situation to determine how best she could negotiate her way through it. And having done this, she then had had to develop the extraordinary self-discipline and self-denial the situation demanded. Her strength had been put to the test and was increased considerably in the process. Samuel Schneiderman's confidence had not been misplaced. His encouragement, his faith that Rose could study hard and thereby become a teacher, helped her call forth the attentiveness that she was forced to exercise in every aspect of orphanage life. Without this she could not have been so obedient and studious, nor could she have found comfort in the small pleasures that had made life "endurable." The trauma of Rose's early life taught her to attend to the business at hand with unusual vigor and stamina. It also made her both more and less fearful than people who had been through less. Rose Schneiderman knew how easily and unexpectedly tragedy could come and how totally devastating it could be. Yet having proven her ability to make the most of a terrible situation, she also knew she could take care of herself and survive.

After the orphanage Rose spent two years caring for her baby sister and going to school. She "loved school and studied hard." She finished nine grades in four years. When her mother lost her job, however, Rose herself had to go to work. Her first job was as a cash girl at Hearn's Department Store. For a sixty-four hour week, she earned $2.16. Her second job was as a check girl at another department store, Ridley's on Grand Street. The hours were the same; the salary this time was $2.25 a week. After three years, with only a 50¢ increase in her weekly wage, Rose was fed up. She convinced a neighbor who worked as a lining maker in a cap factory to get her a job in her shop and teach her the trade. Within a month she was earning $6.00 a week.[10]

When Rose first went to work she had no intention of discontinuing her schooling. After one month at night school, however, she decided that it was not worth the time. Her teacher was more concerned with gaining attendance than with learning and Rose was impatient with the jokes and stories that were his stock in trade. In *All for One* she claimed that "to my great joy I found there were other ways of acquiring knowledge." She read in Yiddish to her mother, first Bible stories, then more "current books," as well as *Abdenblatt* serials: Zola's "J'accuse," and stories about Henry VIII, Anne Boleyn, and Thomas à Becket. In addition, she read novels in English to herself, and with a friend from Ridley's joined the "Lady Manchester Club" at a nearby settlement, where she "learned something about parliamentary procedure." All of the above is undoubtedly true, but Rose probably realized that "there were other ways of acquiring knowledge" after the fact and not at this time. Formal schooling was what she had wanted. It must have been a bitter experience first to give up day school and then to discover that night school was a sham. The purposefulness evident in Rose's employment record indicates, therefore, that she had had to put her dream out of mind at least for the moment and accept the inevitable. She wanted schooling as she had wanted her father to live and her family to remain intact. Because it was again necessary, however, she focused on the immediate.[11]

For Rose Schneiderman, perhaps more than for most people, it was the circumstances of life that educated. This should not imply that Schneiderman was a passive person, not at all; nor should it imply that her earlier experience did not mediate the meaning of what life presented to her. Circumstances were immensely important to Rose Schneiderman's education simply because there were few people to whom she could turn for help or advice. Had Rose had a mother or father who could have guided her at this time, her education might have been quite different. Since her mother was no more experienced than she, however, she had to go it alone. And she learned what she could through observation.

Rose worked hard at her job and quickly became a sample maker. The promotion did not increase her wages, but it guaranteed that she would not be laid off during the slack season when many other workers were let go. The increment skill could add to one's job security did not escape her. Rose had learned to read the reality around her with unusual discernment. In it she discovered that what her father had said about school was true in other situations as well: set your mind to the task and you will reach your goal. In the same way, by simply attending closely to what she could see happening around her, Rose discovered how to get along in her trade. Cap makers in that day had to provide their own sewing machines and thread. When Rose lost her first machine in a fire, she replaced it with one bought on the installment plan. She had learned the hard way, but learned nonetheless, that a machine not yet paid for was insured by the store that had sold it, as one that was owned outright was not. There were ways one could hedge against loss and Rose found these out as best she could.[12]

Even though Deborah Schneiderman could not serve as a teacher in the ways that Winifred O'Reilly could, Rose's relationship with her mother was not unimportant to her education. Deborah Schneiderman was a model of strength and endurance. Beyond this, however, because she was such a forceful person, her personality and her attempts to exercise parental authority created something of a tug-of-war between herself and her daughter, which provoked self-assertiveness and independence in Rose.

Rose did not always see things the way her mother did. She was younger; she had little memory of Russia; and she adapted to life on the Lower East Side more quickly. Thus, for example, although Rose and her mother had agreed that she should leave school and get a job when she was still only thirteen, Deborah Schneiderman was upset when Rose left her job at Ridley's. Being a check girl at Ridley's was more "genteel" than being a cap maker, she believed, and gentility, probably for its value on the marriage market, was something Deborah Schneiderman wanted for Rose. Rose too wanted to get married but she had learned to be realistic. As a result, she was more immediately concerned with earning the money her family so desperately needed. Soon after Rose left Ridley's, she also began to withhold some money from the wages she gave her mother. Deborah Schneiderman protested that "a dutiful daughter" did not behave that way. Rose did not agree. She wanted to have prettier clothes. She was learning to gauge what she needed for herself. Her mother's admonitions were losing power as she got to know more about the world around her.[13]

It took Rose some time to achieve full independence. After she withheld the money from her salary, she went with her mother to Montreal for a year even though she did not want to. Her mother had told her to come, and she could not say no. Still, the process of separation was in motion and it moved along fast. Rose knew she could stand on her own. She also knew that it was she who fed her mother, not vice versa. Thus, she had only to learn to assert her freedom to make it an accomplished fact. If Deborah Schneiderman had been able to support Rose through school or if she had been able to "school" her herself, things would have been very different indeed. Rose's life was more difficult because her mother could give her so little, but the fact that Rose had to care for herself and her family helped her learn to do so early and well. As her brother Charlie once put it, from this time on Rose played a "mother-like" role in the Schneiderman family. To do so was demanding. It was not just the orphanage that robbed Rose Schneiderman of her childhood. To give her sister candy and a doll, and all three of her siblings more schooling than she had had, Rose had to grow up very fast.[14]

Partly because she needed and wanted support from adults other than her mother, Rose cultivated whomever she could find. She made friends with the older saleswomen at Ridley's and borrowed their books. She went to the woman next door to learn to sew. And when she lived in Montreal, she attached herself to a neighboring family who introduced her to music and interested her in politics. As she remembered it, however, her adolescence was "far from happy." In a sense, Rose had been unhappy and alone ever since she had lost the parent who showed his affection, the parent who did not call her "dinyeh" (round as a pumpkin). Deborah Schneiderman was very upset when Rose became involved in the labor movement. "She kept saying I'd never get married because I was too busy—a prophecy which came true." Yet Deborah Schneiderman's attitude was "the only cloud in the picture" once Rose did find a union, for as she herself put it, "all of a sudden I was not lonely anymore."[15]

Rose discovered the labor movement through a woman named Bessie Braut, who joined the factory where she worked in 1903. According to Rose, Bessie Braut "was radical and progressive, and she stimulated thoughts which were already in our minds before she came." No one needed to tell Rose that working conditions were hard. No one needed to tell her that she was working to make "the bosses" rich. Nor did anyone need to give her the daring necessary to work for change: she knew that she could count on herself. But someone did need to tell her what organizing might accomplish. The principle of solidarity—all for one—was not part of Rose Schneiderman's inheritance. It was through conversations with Bessie Braut, therefore, that she became aware that a union could provide the security and power she wanted, needed, and did not have.[16]

Bessie Braut's "lessons" seem to have included essentially three points: first, that the men in the trade were a little better off than the women because they were organized; second, that the benefits the men were able to get were not absorbed by "the bosses" but by the women (each half-cent deduction in their pay was a half-cent raise for the men); and third, that the women could and must form their own local. Bessie Braut's analysis made sense to Rose. Soon after meeting her, she and two other women went to the local office of the United Cloth Hat and Cap Makers' Union to ask for help. They were told to come back when they had twenty-five signatures from women in several different factories. Within days they returned and in late January of 1903, Local 23 of the United Cloth Hat and Cap Makers' was chartered with Rose as secretary. She had organized her first union.[17]

Rose Schneiderman's life changed markedly. Before 1903 Rose had found few activities that were exciting. She liked to read and she enjoyed going to the theater with her mother when they could get free tickets. In comparison with the heated debate at union meetings, however, such activities were bland. Before joining the union Rose had spent Saturday nights going to dances with Anne Cyprus, her friend from Ridley's. She liked to dance, although she found the boys she met "loud and dull" and said that their "small talk" was not her "line." As a delegate from her union to the Central Labor Union of New York, she met a very different group: men (and a few women) of passionate conviction who appeared masterful and commanding, as the boys at the dances did not. Furthermore, as one of the leading figures in her local, Rose was treated as an adult. The other women came to her with their problems and she in turn went to the employers. The men in charge of the union also called on her for help. In the spring of 1903, for example, Maurice Mikol, the secretary-treasurer of the national organization, asked Rose to speak to a group of women strikebreakers in Bayonne, New Jersey. She did and later wrote of the experience: "I was scared stiff . . . When I was called on to speak, my knees turned to putty. I doubt whether I lasted more than five minutes and I don't believe I deserved the enthusiastic applause they gave me. But even if it was undeserved, it felt good."[18]

Rose's efforts for the union found a different reception than she was used to at home. To fulfill her duty to the union, Rose was expected and encouraged to be forceful, to say what she believed, and to act as she thought best. The demands placed on her by her new role were far more to her liking, far more appropriate to her temperament, and far more consistent with her experience to date than Deborah Schneiderman's were. In a sense, the labor movement gave Rose the kind of support her father had given her, and it had a similar effect. By adding excitement, it made Rose's life more fun; by offering her companionship, it made it less lonely; and by openly applauding her effort, it made Rose eager to strive, not because she had to, to survive, but because she wanted to, to reach a goal. The labor movement brought back some of the light that had gone out when Samuel Schneiderman died. It gave Rose purpose and it inspired her sense of dignity.

The last point is especially significant. Samuel Schneiderman had taught Rose the value of schooling, and schooling had helped her get through the year in the orphanage and had given her pleasure during the years immediately following. Still, a sense of purpose and even some success had not made Rose fully invulnerable to shame and humiliation. "Being poor was the worst part of growing up," she once said. It had made her feel "ashamed" to invite anyone into her house. Apparently, she had taken her family's poverty as a sign of inferiority, as outward evidence of God's disfavor. Poverty was no less visible and no less of a stigma than being forced to accept the uniform and cropped hair that had set the orphan apart from her unorphaned public school peers. As a result, though she wished for close friendship, Rose could not even let her comrade from Ridley's, Anne Cyprus, into her house. She spent a lot of time at Anne's house, but she could not endanger the friendship by allowing Anne to discover who she, Rose Schneiderman, really was. Feeling as degraded as the tenement building in which she lived, Rose had kept a distance between herself and the people who might have made her life less lonely. The point of view she learned in the labor movement was a revelation that over time fundamentally changed Rose Schneiderman's sense of self.[19]

After she joined the union, Rose was still poor, although she now understood her poverty in a new way. Poverty was the result of an unjust system. It was not punishment—public disgrace—for her family's inherent lack of worth. When Rose said that once Local 23 was chartered she was "not lonely anymore," she meant primarily that she no longer had to hide her poverty from other people. And this realization added tremendously to her ability to seek effectively for what she wanted. What Rose learned from the labor movement transformed the meaning of what she had survived. Her situation was a problem others shared. The notion of comradery so fundamental to labor philosophy was even more educative for Rose than the actual fact of association. Her description of "the real meaning of trade unionism" and of what she had learned from her union makes the point: "It is so much more than getting that loaf of bread, buttered or not. To me it is the spirit of trade unionism that is most important, the service of fellowship, the feeling that the hurt of one is the concern of all and that the work of the individual benefits all. I came to see that poverty is not ordained by Heaven, that we could help ourselves, that we could bring about a decent standard of living for all and work-hours that would leave time for intellectual and spiritual growth."[20]

After Rose joined the United Cloth Hat and Cap Makers' Union, she discovered the Lower East Side as she had not done before. She found the Manhattan Liberal Club and "wouldn't have missed a meeting for anything." Listening to the speakers she heard there taught her to speak English properly. Around the same time she also heard Florence Kelley talk about factory conditions in Illinois. She was "shocked." The problems she faced were indeed widespread. On Sunday mornings at Bryant Hall she found a minister named Hugh Pentecost lecturing on current events. Hearing him once made her hunger for more. "I simply had to go and hear him every week, despite Mother's efforts to dissuade me." She was not afraid, as Deborah Schneiderman was, that Pentecost would convert her to Christianity. What Rose got out of all the talk she heard is far less important than her attitude. Learning to speak English correctly was vital to her career. Yet her eagerness for ideas and for discussion had an even more significant effect on both her career and her education. Rose was beginning to be able to mine a wider field for what it might offer because her notion of relevance was expanding beyond the here and now of daily survival. The sense of comradery she had found in the labor movement was lightening her load. She could now afford to explore as she had not done before, and in doing so she found the Women's Trade Union League, which she later claimed was "the most important influence" in her life.[21]

Rose went to her first WTUL meeting in 1904, soon after the New York league was first gathered. She went despite the fact that she "had reservations about the organization because of its membership." She just did not think that "men and women who were not wage-earners themselves understood the problems that workers faced." What is important here, however, is that Rose was still willing to go to the meeting. A friend of hers, who was also a friend of Leonora O'Reilly's, said it could be worthwhile, and Rose went to see if she was right. The meeting seemed strange. There was "very little business transacted . . . no reports of any kind and when it adjourned everyone danced the Virginia Reel." Skeptical but-still undecided, Rose agreed to follow her friend's advice and join the league. As it turned out a strike in her trade prevented her from doing so at that time. But her intention still indicates that she was now willing to go beyond first impressions to pursue something the value of which was not instantly apparent. Had Rose's entry into the labor movement been a less positive experience, she might have attended to the here and now of her daily life even more closely than she had before. Instead that experience encouraged her to branch out.[22]

Schneiderman's curiosity should not be overdrawn, however. She was always a direct, no-nonsense type, and rather utilitarian in her approach to life. Her interests may have been expanding, but she was willing to join the league because it seemed somewhat promising and she was smart enough not to reject too quickly an organization that might prove worthwhile. It is important to consider, therefore, what made the league seem even vaguely appealing to Rose. For the way in which she made this decision reveals a good deal about what Rose wanted in life and how she determined what would and would not serve her ends, which in turn directly reflect on her education up to this point.

At the first WTUL meeting Rose attended, she was immediately drawn to Leonora O'Reilly. She had heard of O'Reilly before the meeting and knew that she was regarded as a working woman whose views could be trusted. What is more, Rose noticed that O'Reilly was "tall and willowy and most attractive" and that she seemed to sense Rose's reaction to the meeting. Rose claimed that O'Reilly had "winked" at her as she danced past during the enchanting but baffling Virginia Reel, which led her to the conclusion that "she must have realized the impression I was getting." O'Reilly, then, intrigued Rose, and so did Margaret Drier Robins when she sought Rose out at her union's strike headquarters in the winter of 1905. As Rose remembered it, Robins appeared to her as "not only beautiful, but understanding. She wanted to know all about the strike and the women connected with it." She also wanted to help. She offered to get the union favorable publicity and carried through on her promise. Presumably, therefore, when Rose joined the WTUL at the end of the strike, she did so for two reasons: she liked the women who were connected with the league and they seemed to like her. Rose had been before and always would be attracted to ideas and organizations through the people involved. She was not ideological. The publicity the league got for Rose's union was also important, however. Rose was pragmatic. She was most interested in immediate possibility and concrete results. She had an almost intuitive ability to separate the romantic from the practical, and though she might flirt with the first, she gave her real devotion only to the second.[23]

Rose Schneiderman's education, despite her wish for schooling, had not offered her many opportunities to engage with ideas. The loneliness of her early life had also left her hungry for friendship, affection, and understanding. Finally, having been forced to fend for herself and, to a large extent, to educate herself in the skills and occupational hazards of a trade, in the English language, and in the mores of American society, Rose had learned to assess carefully and accurately what would and would not serve her ends. She was neither crass nor cynical, but the nature of her previous experience had taught her how to be sensible. All of this is evident in the way in which Rose scrutinized the WTUL and then, having made a judgment, decided to join.

In light of this, Schneiderman's long involvement with the league makes sense. Many working-class women would have nothing to do with the organization. Others gave up on it because of the class and ethnic conflicts that were endemic to its history. But if these tensions troubled Schneiderman, as they did especially during the first ten years of her membership, they did not prevent her from holding firm to her initial commitment. Thus, Rose's determination and discrimination—her ability to attend to what she wanted—allowed her to stick with an organization that was for her generally more appealing and useful than not. Rose Schneiderman found many of her closest friends and most significant jobs through the WTUL. She joined the organization in 1905 and stayed with it (except for the brief period I shall discuss below) until its demise. The national league, over which Rose presided for almost twenty-five years, went out of existence in 1950; the New York league, five years later.[24]

Once into the league, Rose began to work closely with three of its leaders, Leonora O'Reilly, Margaret Drier Robins, and Mary Drier, each of whom had qualities she admired. O'Reilly was already a recognized figure in the labor movement. She was forceful, articulate, and seasoned in the trade union world. Her intellect was easily recognized and her ability to persuade apparent to all. Furthermore, since O'Reilly had had to leave school to go to work at an early age, she was living proof that a working woman could become an intellectual. Margaret Drier Robins was quite different.

She had all the graces Rose wanted. She was "beautiful," dynamic, "understanding," and stylish. She invited Rose to her wedding, which was held in "a house where everything was beautiful," a house the likes of which Rose had never even imagined. To Rose, Margaret Drier Robins represented what a woman could achieve as a woman. And Mary Drier? Mary Drier was also beautiful, Rose claimed, and even more than her sister a "spiritual inspiration." She was patient, tolerant, totally devoted to the working woman's cause, and "one of the most generous people" Rose ever encountered. Thus, Margaret Drier Robins had the feminine qualities Rose wanted, Mary Drier, the spiritual, and Leonora O'Reilly, the intellectual, although each in different degrees had them all.[25]

Rose Schneiderman was an acute observer. She could not become "tall and willowy," but she could notice and copy the details of a person's style. As a result, she learned profoundly from exposure to the three women who together served as her mentors. Rose, for example, had become a good speaker even before she joined the league. She became even better thereafter. Her speeches were witty, ironic, and at times powerfully angry. Practice helped her develop this art, but so too did watching and listening to Leonora O'Reilly when they shared a podium or went on speaking tours together. Rose had always paid considerable attention to her physical appearance, as her earlier conflict with her mother over the money she wanted to keep for clothes illustrates. And she became even more self-conscious about this and more fashionable as she learned from Margaret Drier Robins's example. Finally, descriptions of Rose also reflect Mary Drier. Rose could get very angry and she could lose her temper, although she did become a "forgiving soul and so generous" that she seemed to her friends always to give even more trust and acceptance than they deserved. Mary Drier was that way. It was she who arranged Rose's first vacation: two weeks in the country with herself and the O'Reillys. It was she who claimed to understand, even though she really did not, when Rose once felt she had to leave a league job. It seems, therefore, that Rose tried hard to be the saint that she thought Mary Drier was.[26]

To tease out distinct, separate lines of influence should give emphasis to the special qualities of each of these women, which may indicate why the composite of their example was so appealing to Rose. Together O'Reilly, Robins, and Drier stood for a strong and assertive but attractive and gentle feminine ideal. As one can see from the simple fact that Schneiderman became an effective, direct, and rather chic woman, she learned much from her three friends that helped her style the characteristics she shared with her mother according to her own tastes and inclinations and the fashions of her day.

The significance of O'Reilly, Robins, and Drier in Rose Schneiderman's education cannot be understated. Before she joined the WTUL, Rose had had few role models beyond her mother, whose capacity in this regard was quite limited. What is more, before she joined the WTUL, Rose had found few people who were as interested in developing her abilities as these three women were. And since the three also had the wherewithal to help Rose, their influence was profound.

O'Reilly, Robins, and Drier educated Rose, not only through the power of their example, but also through purposeful and to an extent coordinated instruction. The WTUL needed working-class women, especially ones who had had organizing experience, as Rose had had. Moreover, because Rose could speak Yiddish she was able to reach out to workers with whom most members of the league could not even converse. Consequently, after Schneiderman joined the league, her mentors moved her along fast. She was made a vice president of the New York league in 1906, a part-time organizer for the East Side in 1908, and a full-time organizer in 1909. O'Reilly, Robins, and Drier did not offer Rose these jobs for altruistic reasons. They needed her and recognized her potential. And as a result, they helped Rose see that she had special talents. In fact, O'Reilly, Robins, and Drier, for their own good as well as hers, intentionally made Rose aware of this.

"Dearest Rose," Margaret Drier Robins wrote in a typical letter, "go out among your fellow workers, speak to them on any street corner, fire them with your spirit and you will help give birth to the new world emerging." Not all women could do this, they said. But as O'Reilly once put it—and all three women reminded Rose of this constantly—Rose was "specially fitted to build up an organization." Beyond this, O'Reilly, Robins, and Drier also explained to Rose that she could reach upper-class as well as working-class women. "That 'vision splendid' is yours Röschen," Robins told her. "It is because I remember your great gift of interpretation that I am so eager for you to be our interpreter to the great unknowing and unthinking world."[27]

To a woman who had had little recognition and affection, such praise and confidence must have been terribly compelling. O'Reilly, Robins, and Drier were letting Rose in on what they cared about most. They were saying, "We love you dearly and trust you utterly." In short, they were telling her that she, Rose Schneiderman, had the capacity to do great things. Rose believed them. Later she even used their language to explain her accomplishments. She once said, for example, "I have always been a rather mild human being and have depended largely on my ability to interpret and persuade people in order to get results." What is especially interesting, however, because it is this that really made the three women's teaching so effective, is that their view of what Rose could do meshed with what she had always wanted to do. O'Reilly, Robins, and Drier could not give Rose a formal classroom, but they did explain to her that the league's purpose and the first purpose of the whole labor movement was education. Thus, if she would make their work her life's work, as they were giving her the opportunity to do, she could at last be the teacher she wanted to be "more than anything in the world."[28]

When Rose took the job as a full-time organizer for the league, she had to give up all hope of finishing school. An organizer's life was too demanding and too unpredictable to allow her to attend regularly scheduled classes. Rose knew this and recognized the choice as "a great decision." Yet she took the job, not only because "at last I knew my heart was in the trade-union movement," but also because O'Reilly, Robins, and Drier had made her see that in the trade union movement she could be a teacher as she probably could not be anywhere else. Rose was realistic. She might have preferred to be a schoolteacher. But she knew that the chances of becoming a schoolteacher were diminishing with time. As she had always done, she accepted the inevitable, only this time it was not so hard to do. O'Reilly, Robins, and Drier had transformed her dream so she could achieve it within the real world in which she lived.[29]

At the time Rose became a full-time organizer, things looked promising for the league. In November of 1909, thousands of shirtwaist makers went out on strike. The "Uprising of the 20,000," as the strike was called, was one of the largest and longest in East Side history. It also marked the heyday of cross-class cooperation within the league. Prominent society women—Anne Morgan (J. P. Morgan's daughter), Mrs. O. H. P. Belmont, Mrs. Henry Morgenthau, Sr.—joined the picket lines and raised bail money for arrested strikers; and working women joined the league in unprecedented numbers. Fairly soon after the strike, however, it became apparent to many members of the league that the walkout had not been as successful as they had hoped it would be, either in terms of creating enduring loyalties among workers to their unions and to the league, or in terms of significantly improving working conditions and wages throughout the industry. For this reason, among others, the league decided to put its first efforts in the future into the shop by shop organization of "American" workers (mostly uptown, English-speaking, skilled seamstresses), rather than into continuing support for strikes among the predominantly Jewish East Side workers with whom Schneiderman was working. In December of 1912, therefore, Schneiderman resigned as the league's East Side organizer (although she continued to work for the league). And two years later, following a presidential election in which she was defeated by Melinda Scott, the league's organizer for "American" workers, in a vote that followed class lines, she left the league entirely. She returned to the WTUL in 1918, but for the next few years she worked for the National American Woman Suffrage Association and for the International Ladies' Garment Workers' Union. Although her jobs during these years were outside the WTUL, her work still illustrates how far the teaching of O'Reilly, Robins, and Drier had taken her.[30]

When Rose resigned from the league, she did not consider returning to a cap factory. For obvious reasons this was unappealing, and she apparently recognized that she had marketable skills in other lines of work. She remained a dues-paying member of her union until she retired in 1949, but after 1912 she was no longer a cap maker. It is also interesting that Schneiderman's choice of jobs at this point was based less on the causes involved than on the nature of the work. She was a convinced suffragist as well as a trade unionist. Yet she was also a socialist and might well have gone to work as an organizer for the Socialist party if she had been offered that kind of work. In other words, what she seems to have wanted most was the chance to go on giving speeches, talking to individuals, and otherwise doing what she could to "interpret" conditions to "the great unknowing and unthinking world." By 1912 Rose Schneiderman was a "teacher." Through systematic, sustained, and self-conscious effort, O'Reilly, Robins, and Drier made Rose Schneiderman an example of the educative power of the WTUL. Had Schneiderman been a less astute person or less susceptible to what her mentors had to offer, this might not have been the case. As it was, however, if the WTUL was not *the* most important influence in Schneiderman's life, it certainly was the most important educative influence in shaping her career.[31]

After 1912 Rose Schneiderman was fairly set in what she believed and what she wanted to do, and so far as one can tell, she was changed little by her suffrage work. The arguments she used at the rallies she addressed throughout the Midwest rested on observations that she had made earlier: that women must fight for their own rights; that they needed political power to achieve better working conditions; and that woman's nature would make women the kind of socially concerned citizens the world so desperately needed. To dramatize the value of suffrage, Rose had to articulate what she had noted earlier, which may have made her even more convinced than she had been that women with political power could improve industrial conditions and "increase wages, compel shorter hours of work, and check the white slave trade." But since Rose had believed all of this before, campaigning for the vote did not fundamentally modify her point of view. And the same can be said of her job as an organizer and business agent for the ILGWU. The experience was lonely and disheartening. The men in charge of the union failed to provide Rose with adequate support. But their attitude, however galling, could not have been a total surprise to a woman who, by this time, was well aware of the political realities of the labor movement. Thus, Rose's sojourn away from the league confirmed her feminism and her allegiance to the cause of working women, and, because it offered a contrast, it may also have restored her loyalties to the league.[32]

Over time, however, in response to the climate in which she lived, Schneiderman's view did shift and her work did change. Her career was marked by a clear upward progression in terms of the jobs and offices she held inside and outside the league as well as by continuing growth in skill and knowledge. By the 1920s, the cap maker of the early 1900s was representing the National Women's

Trade Union League at international conferences, running for the U. S. Senate on the Farmer-Labor party line, and organizing the Bryn Mawr Summer School for Working Women. By the 1930s she was president of the NWTUL, an honorary vice president of what had become the United Hatters', Cap, and Millinery Workers' Union, and a government official. As she had always been able to do, Rose could adapt to the challenges she was offered and learn from them what might be useful for her ends. Still, the point remains that Schneiderman's education after 1912 was an elaboration on themes established earlier, as the following examples will illustrate.

In the 1930s the labor movement found a strong ally in the federal government, and Schneiderman's views reflected the change in government policy. Strikes might be useful to secure immediate small-scale advances, she believed, but she placed her first hope in the government's power to legislate and enforce measures that would have effect beyond a single factory or trade. As a logical corollary to this, she also thought that labor leaders like herself should concentrate on advising government officials— educating them. Rose always said that Leonora O'Reilly had been her tutor in "revolutionary labor philosophy." What did she mean? O'Reilly believed that through education working people would acquire the self-respect and historical perspective necessary to demand and to achieve a more equitable and humane social order. Schneiderman, by contrast, looked primarily to the government to bring about the reforms she advocated. Yet Schneiderman's convictions, particularly her faith in the sufficiency of moderate social change and her belief in industrial regulation as a means for ultimately achieving more comprehensive economic and social betterment, were entirely consistent with O'Reilly's point of view. Not all progressives became liberals, as Schneiderman did. But liberalism was a logical outgrowth of progressivism, and in Schneiderman's case, liberalism was an extension of what she had learned from O'Reilly. Some of her friends became party-line socialists and communists. Had her experience in the years after 1912 been different, she might have gone that way too. Instead, however, her thought continued in the direction in which it had been going ever since she met O'Reilly and learned from her the philosophy by which she interpreted subsequent events and her relationship to them.[33]

Schneiderman's goals for herself also remained remarkably consistent over the years. And this becomes clear when one considers what she most valued about her friendship with Franklin and Eleanor Roosevelt and the jobs that resulted from it. Rose met Eleanor Roosevelt through the WTUL, an organization Eleanor joined in the early 1920s. During the winter of 1921 Eleanor turned to Rose in her effort to find people who could bring her recently paralyzed husband information that might rekindle his enthusiasm for politics. An initial Sunday night supper was followed by meetings in New York City, Hyde Park, and Campobello. FDR liked "Rosie," and as Frances Perkins has pointed out, Rose and her league friend Maud Schwartz "made a good many things clear to Franklin Roosevelt that he would hardly have known in any other way." As a result, according to Perkins, Roosevelt "appeared to have a real understanding of the trade union movement," and Rose Schneiderman became one of his trusted advisers. Roosevelt appointed Schneiderman to the Labor Advisory Board of the NRA, from which it was an easy step, especially with his backing and Eleanor's, to being secretary of the New York State Department of Labor, a post she held from 1937 to 1944. Furthermore, Roosevelt read, noted, and often acted upon whatever passages of Rose's letters Eleanor had transcribed for him to see.[34]

Schneiderman's relationship with the Roosevelts illustrates her skill as a learner. It did not take her long to recognize how to reach FDR. She was quickly able to see how she might tell him what he had to know in a fashion that he could understand. She also realized early that one could often accomplish more via Eleanor than directly. One even suspects that some of her letters to Eleanor were written so they could be easily excerpted for Franklin. Rose's ability to analyze and adapt to situations served her well throughout her life, although the point here is, not what allowed her to accomplish what she did, but what these accomplishments meant to her.[35]

One of Rose's friends once remarked while staying with the Roosevelts in the White House: "Imagine me, Feigele Shapiro, sleeping in Lincoln's bed." Rose felt exactly the same way. The Roosevelts' interest impressed her and pleased her tremendously. Virtually every White House invitation she received was saved. In a general way, then, the relationship simply meant having come a long way from the village in Russian Poland where she was born. Yet Schneiderman's relationship with the Roosevelts was even more important to her because she saw in it the fulfillment of her lifelong dream. When Eleanor Roosevelt, a woman whom she totally admired, stood up at an AFL-CIO convention and, according to Rose, "said to the audience that I had taught her all she knew about trade unionism," Rose felt that she had been vindicated. "It was one of the very proud moments of my life," she remembered.[36]

Before she met Leonora O'Reilly, Margaret Drier Robins, and Mary Drier, Rose had had to put her wish to be a teacher aside. But after joining the league she avowed that dream and thereby found greater satisfaction in life. O'Reilly, Robins, and Drier had taught Rose Schneiderman that she was a teacher, one who could strive to teach anyone, even the President of the United States and his wife. She taught effectively and with great result. She had a significant influence on what the New Deal did for working women and men. Rose Schneiderman's friendship with the Roosevelts gave her the power that a great teacher can have. And she was very, very proud of what her student, "the Chief," had done.

As an old woman, Rose Schneiderman could look back on her life with considerable satisfaction. Yet when she did so to write her autobiography, she must have been reminded of what she had not achieved, as well as of what she had achieved. Although she wrote the book herself, she felt compelled to ask a free-lance writer to polish her prose. Attentive though she might be on her own, she could not surmount the limitations of her education. Rose Schneiderman could tell her own story, but since she had never gotten the schooling she wanted, she had to ask for help when she wanted to write it down.[37]

It is also rather sad to note that in *All for One* Rose said at least twice that her mother had prophesied that her job would keep her from marrying, and that her mother's prediction had indeed come true. She made it clear in *All for One* that she had had romantic flirtations with men throughout her life, although she had been too absorbed in her work and perhaps too realistic about marriage itself to find someone to whom she could really be devoted. Years earlier she probably had not cared. Marriage was not very fashionable among the women who were her colleagues and friends. And Rose knew that marriage was no solution to the problems that were her cause. "If you think you will be a grand lady after you leave the factory and are married," she used to tell other women, "you are sadly mistaken, for you will have to work yourself to death." No doubt Rose had believed this and still did at eighty-five, when *All for One* was published. She knew the reality of many working women's lives. But she also knew, at least at the end, that she had had to work hard and in some ways had little to show for it. When with her usual realism she signed herself into the old-age home where she died a few years later, she may well have wondered whether marriage might not have made her life a little less lonely.[38]

By attending to her business, Rose Schneiderman had almost surmounted the loneliness she hated. In a way, too, she had achieved what she set out to do. Schneiderman's education made it possible for her to teach, even if her life did not allow her to secure the training that would have permitted her to become the kind of teacher she had originally wanted to be. Living as she had, however, Rose Schneiderman was lonely again when her ability to be active came to an end. Rose concluded her autobiography by saying, "I know that nothing is impossible in this country of ours." Her capacity to focus on what she had achieved was a sign of the tenacity that marked all aspects of her life. And it was that same quality—tenacity—that kept Rose hoping that in the future women like herself would not have to work so hard and give up so much to become what they wanted to be.[39]

6

The Education of
a Generation

THE LIFE CIRCUMSTANCES into which Grace Dodge, Maud Nathan, Lillian Wald, Leonora O'Reilly, and Rose Schneiderman were born were fundamentally different. So too in many ways were their lives and even more so their personalities. Nonetheless, all became prominent social reformers of relatively similar persuasion. The coincidence is intriguing and raises a number of questions. What led these women into careers in social reform? What enabled them to achieve as they did? And how were the similarities in their experience influenced by the culture and the economic and social structures that defined the world of the progressive generation? In short, what can one learn about the history of women's education from the educational biographies of five progressive social reformers?

To begin, think back to the childhood experiences of the five women. The variables were numerous. The families from which they came differed in size, relative roles of parents, connections with kin. Educational opportunities beyond those available through familial relationships also differed tremendously in kind and in quantity. So too did the goals, values, and normative expectations to which each woman was exposed in a multitude of different ways. With one crucial exception, therefore, the early education of these women was more dissimilar than not, the exception being the existence in each case of powerful and centrally important parental pedagogy.

The substance of this pedagogy varied significantly because it reflected parental personality as well as the family's social, economic, and cultural location. But genuine parental attachment was always at its core. At least one of the parents of all five women was vitally invested in his or her daughter's development, and in each instance, this attachment was grounded in the parents' ability to see in their daughter something of themselves or something of their own, often unrealized, hopes. Thus, to William Dodge, Grace was a child who would grow into a devout "steward of God"; to Annie Florance Nathan, Maud embodied the nascent attributes of a beautiful, "cultured," and sought-after lady; in her parents, Lillian Wald inspired hopes for the continuation of a comfortable, secure, happy, and traditional middle-class life; to Winifred O'Reilly, Leonora was always a good trade unionist; and to Samuel Schneiderman, Rose was a potential teacher.

Deeply felt parental attachment provided a foundation for each woman's sense of self-esteem. And in the transmission of this sense of worth there were also several common elements. Parental aspirations were invariably linked to clear, specific, incremental tasks, behaviors, attitudes, and the like. Goals were immediate and comprehensible. As children Grace Dodge, Maud Nathan, Lillian Wald, Leonora O'Reilly, and Rose Schneiderman knew what was expected of them to win parental approval, and they were given ample opportunities to gain parental acknowledgement because in each case there was relatively frequent, often didactic contact with parents. William Dodge included regular time with his children in his busy schedule, wrote to them frequently when away, and designed his stories and letters to be instructive; Annie Florance Nathan participated in many aspects of her children's daily life, as did all of the adults of the Wald family, and in both cases explanations of religious ritual, social decorum, family history, and current events were part of the mix; Mrs. O'Reilly and Samuel Schneiderman were with their children whenever possible, and they too taught insistently, offering the opportunity to learn through example as well as through verbal exchange.

Daily contact, then, provided an arena for constant teaching and frequent reinforcement, and learning resulted and was as fundamental in effect as it was because each woman wanted to please her parent(s). Many things contributed to this, but in particular, on the part of the women, the ability necessary to accomplish much of what was asked, and, on the part of the parents, a generally nurturant attitude. Some of the women were subjected to harsh punishments and severe criticism. Annie Florance Nathan, for example, could be condemning and unreasonable and Maud remembered being intentionally humiliated at times. Occasional breaches notwithstanding, more often than not parental teaching was conveyed via gentle persuasion, encouragement, and example, and it was frequently nothing more than an incidental part of daily routines.

How, for example, did Winifred O'Reilly commit Leonora to the labor movement? Very simply: by talking of her own interest, by taking her along to meetings, and by encouraging her independent movement in this direction. How did Samuel Schneiderman teach Rose the value of schooling? By helping her with her homework, by personally escorting her to school, and by constantly expressing his hopes and convictions. The style of William Dodge's parenting was much the same. William Dodge was probably disappointed by Grace's clumsiness as a child, by her unhappiness at Miss Porter's School, and even by her ultimate assertion that she would work rather than marry. Throughout, however, he accepted his daughter as she was, supported the strengths that were evident, and attempted to influence through suggestion and guidance rather than argument, recrimination, or continuing insistence. Whenever Annie Florance Nathan gave in to an outburst of temper, apology and reunion followed swiftly. And praise, encouragement, and, most effective of all, the sharing of intimacies were the more usual forms of exchange. Finally, as Lillian Wald herself explained, her parents taught so gently that their pedagogy was hardly felt at all. Being generally loving, likeable, companionable, and accepting, as well as concerned, clear, and definite in their own convictions, the parent(s) of these women brought out in their daughters emotional attachments that matched their own, and with these, a return on their investment that took the form of a desire to learn and to please and acceptance of at least the essential qualities of the self-image their parents offered.

Parent-child relationships never exist in a vacuum, and in the lives of these women they were affected by and in turn affected other relationships and experiences. Again, there is one discernible pattern in common. For each woman parental pedagogy both mitigated and enhanced all other early educative influences. Leonora O'Reilly, for instance, went to work in a sweatshop at the age of eleven. The initial outlook she had learned from her mother moderated the impact of the debilitating lessons implicit in the experience. So did her mother's continuing efforts, which helped to keep her focused on finding a way to change conditions rather than surrendering to them or simply attempting to escape from them. Similarly, Grace Dodge might have given in totally to the meaning her siblings attached to her awkwardness and size had it not been for her father's recognition of other attributes. And Rose Schneiderman might not have survived the time in the orphanage if both of her parents' previous teaching had not given schooling vital, positive connotations and established the strength to endure extreme isolation and loneliness.

Parental pedagogy also magnified positive experiences. Thus, the events surrounding Maud Nathan's wedding took on greater significance because Nathan saw them as a celebration of her mother's hopes and efforts. Likewise, Uncle B's teaching had symbolic meaning for Leonora O'Reilly, as well as practical value, because it represented a milestone on the path her mother had drawn. Finally, in some instances, parental pedagogy simply made the mastery of specific tasks easier. Having been led to expect success, Lillian Wald excelled easily outside of the home, particularly in all aspects of life at Miss Cruttenden's School. Having already received training in organization and management as her father's helper at home, Grace Dodge was an unusually effective assistant to Dwight Moody and Louisa Lee Schuyler.

One could go on, although by now the point may be clear. In a variety of ways, parental pedagogy orchestrated the impact of nonparental teaching. Other teachers—peers, siblings, friends, employers, tutors, schoolteachers—often had an important effect, but the meaning attached to the perceptions, knowledge, and skills thus acquired tended to be drawn from parental teaching. In short, because it established the core to which other encounters were connected, parental pedagogy shaped and colored the rest of each woman's early experience. Furthermore, however important the more specific lessons provided by school, church, labor organization, choral society, newspaper, or whatever, none was as critical to the continuing education of Dodge, Nathan, Wald, O'Reilly, and Schneiderman as the central common outcome of parental teaching.

The nature of this outcome becomes clear when one returns to the key elements of parental pedagogy mentioned above. Parental attachment transmitted an initial sense of self-esteem. To this, frequent attention and nurture added considerably by virtue of the fact that both conveyed interest, appreciation, affection, and trust. And the chance to validate and enlarge emerging strengths through experience that demonstrated actual competence served a similar function. Dodge's household tasks reinforced and extended parental teaching, as did Nathan's accomplishments in the high school and social world of Green Bay, Wald's activities at home and at school, O'Reilly's involvement in the Knights of Labor, the Synthetic Circle, and the Working Women's Society, and Schneiderman's progress at school. A clear cycle emerged in each case. Confidence promoted a willingness to experiment; success called forth additional effort; mastery renewed parental aspirations. As a result, over time, each woman's potential for growth was enlarged. Above all else, therefore, parental pedagogy nurtured a disposition for continuing education that was added to and combined with the innate capacities with which each woman had been born.

This disposition included several distinct elements. One was an achievement orientation: the wish to accomplish plus the capacity to strive with persistence. Another was an aptitude for discrimination or the ability to be selective, focused, or purposefully and willfully attentive. And still another was a tendency toward self-direction, guided by acute interpersonal intuition. These qualities did not necessitate movement beyond traditional roles or outside of the domestic sphere. Nor were they an unmixed blessing. Dodge, Nathan, Wald, O'Reilly, and Schneiderman drove themselves hard. Leisure was difficult for them. Each was burdened with an inner sense of responsibility. What is more, the general capacity that resulted from the interaction of these qualities was not necessarily what the parents of these women had sought to establish. For one thing, parental intentions were quite specific; for another,

The Education of a Generation

much that parents did to produce this capacity was unselfconscious and spontaneous. However that may be, the point is that in every case, parental pedagogy helped to make possible what was to follow.

That the parents of these women should have played such a similar role in their early education is interesting. Each of the women came from a different segment of late nineteenth-century American society. Yet the behavior of their parents was fundamentally alike. Why? How can one account for such a striking resemblance in the early education of five women who grew up in totally different objective circumstances? Most likely, the answer has to do with domesticity. For if attitudes loosely associated with the domesticity ethic were influential in Dodge's, Nathan's, and Wald's experience, the kind of conditions that originally gave rise to this ethic seem to have played a part in O'Reilly's and Schneiderman's experience.

The connection is most apparent, perhaps, in Grace Dodge's education, where, in her father's concept of the paternal role, one can see the marks of the "soft" evangelical Protestantism that gave rise to a large and varied literature in which arguments for affectionate parental nurture in the raising of children were often presented. William Dodge obviously believed that a father must teach, and do so insistently, but he also believed that a father must teach gently and for purposes beyond the child's eternal salvation. Had he lived earlier or been of a more conservative or a different religious persuasion, his views might have gone in another direction. One wonders, for instance, if they might not have resembled those held by Lyman Beecher, whose relationship with his daughter Catharine was more rigidly didactic, more demanding, and less accepting than William Dodge's with Grace. That aside, in his expectations for Grace, William Dodge also expressed the belief that women had specific primary duties toward their families. Even as a child, Grace was expected to relieve her semiinvalid mother of as many of her responsibilities as possible. It so happens that "the family claim" appealed to Grace Dodge. But that is not the point; rather the point is that if William Dodge had not believed that such responsibilities were educative, he might have decided that it was inappropriate or unwise to allow Grace to take on as much as she did, a decision which would have changed her experience and

143

most likely diminished his direct influence. "Home-work" shaped Grace Dodge profoundly, and in this, acting as her mother's substitute and therefore her father's helpmate was central.[1]

Similar presumptions appear to have been at work in the upbringing of Maud Nathan and Lillian Wald. Annie Florance Nathan, for example, would not allow Maud to work outside the home, despite the fact that their family needed money and Green Bay custom attached few stigmas to the employment of young women. She also would not allow Maud to go to college. Advanced formal schooling, she believed, was unnecessary for women, and personal maternal guidance and protection, vital. As a result, Annie Florance Nathan regulated Maud's choice of outside activities and friends, and maintained a continuous intimate dialogue that rested at least as much on her own need for attention and sympathy as it did on Maud's need for counsel. Minnie Wald's behavior and opinions were much the same. She was the director of Lillian's education to a far greater extent than her husband, partly because she believed it was her job to educate her children. She and her husband allowed Lillian to leave home, but they had not intended for her to do so, except when she married, and they were not pleased when she did. One surmises, in fact, from the reading demanded of Lillian during her mother's frequent migraine headaches, that Minnie Wald, like Annie Florance Nathan and even William Dodge, believed that service to one's mother, which usually also provided opportunities for intimate personal exchange, was the most important part of a young girl's training.

The exact sources of these views are impossible to reconstruct. Dodge probably read examples of the domesticity and child-rearing literature that was so closely aligned with his family's religious tradition; Annie Florance Nathan and Minnie Wald may not have, although the newspapers Lillian read to her mother probably contained serialized versions of the genre. Whatever the origin of their views, one thing is clear: Annie Florance Nathan and Minnie Wald, no less than William Dodge, acted as parents in terms of a number of notions that had popular cultural currency at the time. As domestic reformers would have urged, all of them believed that the family should be the emotional and social center of one's life; that the home should be a sanctuary and a school; and that a parent, especially a mother (at least for a girl), should be a teacher and a guardian and to an extent a friend. Implicit in these ideas, of course, was also the notion that the world was threatening and dangerous and that young women were vulnerable; and underlying the whole construct was the unquestioned assumption that the sexes operated in different "spheres" and that the education of a woman should be designed to make her attractive on the marriage market and successful in the home that would follow—in short, that the education of a woman should prepare her for the domestic vocation that would surely be hers.[2]

These attitudes not only influenced parenting, they especially supported the kind of parental pedagogy evident in the education of Dodge, Nathan, and Wald. One need not go through a complete review to point out the influence. Suffice it to say that Victorian culture promoted a self-conscious and didactic, though gentle and intimate, view of a parent's responsibilities toward a daughter, directly through prescription, as well as indirectly through the patterns of social organization that followed from its concern with delineating the public and the private, the domestic and the foreign, the moral and the immoral. And this milieu shaped the behavior of Dodge's, Nathan's, and Wald's parents.[3]

A totally different orientation was involved in the education of Leonora O'Reilly and Rose Schneiderman. Here the desire to help their children find a better life provided impetus for the parents' teaching. In her "passion for trade unionism" Winifred O'Reilly found pride and hope. To teach Leonora the precepts that followed from this—the dignity of skilled manual labor, the importance of working-class solidarity—was not only natural, it was also the only way she knew to give her daughter's life meaning and purpose. The O'Reillys' life tended to merge with life in what Leonora later called "the old neighborhood." Even as a very young child, Leonora sometimes was simply left in the street when her mother went to work. Within this world there was little to make the O'Reillys special. Status as a skilled worker, and, even more, recognition within the labor movement, especially within the Knights of Labor, which was select and secretive, would have been likely to bring distinction. Mrs. O'Reilly's pedagogy was inevitably influenced by her desire to feel distinctive, as it was also by the fact that economic circumstances made her unable to offer much beyond what she could provide directly (sewing instruction, for example) or free of charge (labor meetings, political rallies). Even schooling was beyond her means once Leonora was able to go to work.

In Rose Schneiderman's case, more diffuse mobility aspirations were the catalyst. Samuel Schneiderman believed in the promise of America. He believed that in the United States, with effort and luck, one could achieve the most exalted position. In the United States a Jewish woman could become a teacher. The expectation reflected traditional values and it predated the Schneidermans' arrival in New York. But the relatively easy availability of free schooling plus the chance for social and economic mobility through a career in teaching may have shaped Samuel Schneiderman's hopes for Rose even before the idea of immigration was firmly established.

In the early education of O'Reilly and Schneiderman, then, one can see again cultural patterns that were central within the groups to which they belonged. Winifred O'Reilly's brand of broad, romantic trade union philosophy was hardly unusual in the 1870s. Many workers needed and used a perspective like hers to cope with the sense of powerlessness and disorientation that accompanied industrial growth. After all, this was the era when the Knights of Labor were in their heyday, and their philosophy served many like Winifred O'Reilly who never actually belonged to the organization. The form that Samuel Schneiderman's aspirations took was equally widespread among his fellow East European Jewish immigrants. And here again, purpose shaped by a synthesis of inherited values and actual and presumed opportunity served a clear function, sustaining hope, rationalizing hardship, and generally providing guidance in an unfamiliar world.[4]

What is even more interesting, however, is that such different cultural patterns as the ones represented here, in Dodge's, Nathan's, and Wald's education as well as in O'Reilly's and Schneiderman's, should have molded parental behavior into a common form. To explain the convergence is far beyond my purpose, although it would seem to argue that as the world expanded in immediate experience—via immigration, greater distance between employer and employee, and so on—as well as in secondhand perceptions, personal relationships intensified, at least in subjective meaning and value, with direct effect on parent-child relationships, and particularly on parent-child education. This phenomenon may have affected different groups at different times, and it did not always lead to the kind of explicit prescription evident in the domesticity literature, but once felt, it does seem to have had a fundamentally similar effect on familial education. That is conjecture, though, and what is not is that very different cultural patterns influenced the parents of women from a wide spectrum of American society to invest heavily and personally in the education of their daughters.

If parents were the commonly significant agents of early education for Dodge, Nathan, Wald, O'Reilly, and Schneiderman, mentors were the common vehicle for vocational education. All five women had at least one such mentor: for Grace Dodge, this was Louisa Lee Schuyler; for Maud Nathan and Lillian Wald, Josephine Shaw Lowell; for Leonora O'Reilly, Louise Perkins; and for Rose Schneiderman, Leonora O'Reilly, Mary Drier, and Margaret Drier Robins.

Each mentor performed three functions, and it was the combination of these three functions that defined the mentors' special role vis-à-vis other important teachers. The first function was instruction. Here, Leonora O'Reilly's relationship with Louise Perkins is especially illustrative. When they were together, Perkins gave O'Reilly "lectures" on ethics, history, and aesthetics, many of which O'Reilly later transcribed into her diary. She also took O'Reilly on tours of the Boston museums and other points of historical and cultural interest. When they were apart, Perkins wrote to O'Reilly constantly, offering advice, suggesting reading, and commenting on the news contained in O'Reilly's latest reports. In addition to teaching, mentors directed their protégées to other sources of education: to people who might offer them further instruction or vocational opportunities and to jobs that might provide a chance to practice the role they envisioned for them. Thus, Perkins introduced O'Reilly to Felix Adler, and O'Reilly, Drier, and Robins offered Schneiderman the jobs that allowed her to make labor organization her primary work. Finally, mentors also served as role models. Josephine Shaw Lowell, for example, in turning to Lillian Wald for help with the East Side relief work during the depression winter of 1893, offered her ample opportunities to observe her style. And Wald's admiration for Lowell's ability to combine sympathy, efficiency, and dignity, as well as the similarities that emerged as her own style developed, indicate that she learned greatly from the exposure.

The relative importance of each of these functions varied from one relationship to another, as did the mentor's significance within the overall configuration that defined each woman's vocational education. Josephine Shaw Lowell's impact on Lillian Wald's career was far less profound, for example, than it was on Maud Nathan's. By the time Wald met Lowell she had already had a good deal of "schooling" for the role she was developing. She had been to nursing school, identified her "neighborhood," and talked with others engaged in similar work. When Nathan's apprenticeship began, however, she was little more than a raw recruit. Still, the factors that combined to make these mentor relationships educative were similar in every case.

Timing was always important. Thus, for example, when Wald met Lowell she was looking for ways to relate to her neighbors beyond those traditionally associated with her established professional role. She had also already learned by this time that relief would have to be part of her job. Had she met Lowell earlier, the example she offered would have been irrelevant; had she met Lowell later her influence would also have been less formative. In each case, then, mentors were able to educate because they provided instruction, opportunities, and examples before the women were clear in vocation, but after the possibility for the kind of vocation they represented had been established. To illustrate the point once again, it is hard to imagine that Maud Nathan would have sought out Lowell while still totally engaged by housekeeping and social life; and it is equally hard to imagine that she would have adopted her as she did if she had already found a sufficient niche.

Personality match was another necessary condition. Similarities in temperament, interest, or some other aspect of identity existed on both sides of each equation. Louisa Lee Schuyler, like Grace Dodge, was deeply religious and the two women came from the same stratum of New York society; Josephine Shaw Lowell's sense of "noblesse oblige" resembled Maud Nathan's, as her inherent sense of humanity resembled Lillian Wald's; Leonora O'Reilly was philosophic by nature, as was Louise Perkins; and in Leonora O'Reilly, Rose Schneiderman could see something of her own background, as in the Drier sisters she could see the poise, beauty, and femininity she prized, at least as a dream, in herself.

A third factor was compatibility of purpose, on the one side, the wish to teach, and on the other, the desire to learn. Obviously, this was related to timing and personality match. Less obviously, it was also related to the nature of each mentor's vocation and the range of occupational choices open to her protégée.

To go beyond a domestic vocation, a life devoted to the fulfillment of traditional female roles, women needed to gain access to work. They could do this in one of three ways or through some combination of the three. They could create work for themselves; they could compete for whatever jobs were open to them on the basis of their skills or credentials; or they could find a sponsor who could offer them employment. The first option was the most difficult. It demanded a degree of financial independence and extraordinary strength and imagination. The second option was the most limited. The jobs open to women through competition tended to be household related or unskilled; those that offered greater challenge—professions like law and medicine or fields that were becoming professions like teaching and nursing—required at least some advanced schooling, and in the case of law and medicine, were few in number. To find work through sponsorship, however, required only that one obtain an established, willing, and acceptable backer.[5]

The problem, of course, was to find such a backer. Not surprisingly, Dodge, Nathan, Wald, O'Reilly, and Schneiderman found theirs within the voluntary social service and reform organizations. For several reasons such organizations were the most likely place for women of this generation to find mentors. First, because cross-sex vocational sponsorship was unusual, and because women were sufficiently established within benevolent groups to offer employment to others, the opportunities for sponsorship were greater there than anywhere else. Second, because of their voluntary nature, the structure of these organizations required that their leaders constantly recruit new members if they were to continue, let alone expand, their work, as the increasing need for their services and a growing concern for social justice and social control were pushing them to do at this time. Thus, the advantages of the sponsorship mode of vocational access for young women meshed with the occupational needs of career-established women social reformers to make "social work" a logical career choice for many progressive women. Beyond this, however, because women needed a sense of calling to justify their commitment if they were to relinquish a domestic vocation for a career outside of the home, the stated purposes of the voluntary benevolent associations added to the appeal of what a Louisa Lee Schuyler or a Josephine Shaw Lowell could offer as a mentor. And this too influenced the vocational direction of many women.[6]

Dodge, Nathan, Wald, O'Reilly, and Schneiderman, whether religious or not, all came of age with rather clear, prescriptive notions of how the world ought to be. In some cases, Grace Dodge's for one, Leonora O'Reilly's for another, these notions were clearly articulated, coherent patterns of belief. In others, they were nothing more than often unstated, rather unsystematic sets of assumptions. Lillian Wald, for instance, just "knew" that people should have dignity and happiness, and Rose Schneiderman, that everyone should have a fair chance. In still other cases, Maud Nathan's, for example, these notions were a combination of religious precepts and other more general values, specifically here a synthesis of Judaism, the egalitarian ethic Nathan associated with a frontier community like Green Bay, and the more aristocratic credo of upper-class New York. To an extent for all five women, these ethical prescriptions were derived from parental beliefs and values, having been purposely taught or simply absorbed. That aside, if such religious or ethical concerns did not determine that "social work" need become a career—in fact, it was mentor relationships that helped these women discover how best they might translate such ethical constructs into a life's work—they did add to the attraction of the career exemplified by each woman's mentor.

Finally, the value nineteenth-century American society placed on close relationships among women also supported the vocational function served by the mentor relationships so important to these women. Idealized conceptions of female friendship were still widespread at this time, and reflected a degree of actual sexual segregation as well as presumed differences in male and female sensibilities. To entrust oneself to the guidance of an older woman not only was acceptable, it was praiseworthy; and to pattern oneself after an older woman required only the kind of educational acumen that girls were expected and trained to have. Furthermore, at least with-

in middle-class circles, a mentor relationship was a logical extension of the intimacy between mother and daughter that was
thought to be so central during childhood. Much, then, stood behind the mentor relationships that were so important in the vocational education of these women.[7]

The education of Grace Dodge, Maud Nathan, Lillian Wald,
Leonora O'Reilly, and Rose Schneiderman did not end once vocation was initially established. It continued at least through the
years of active involvement in work. Unlike the education that had
preceded it, however, the adult education of the five tended to be
more refining in effect than definitional. The changes wrought
clarified identity and sharpened direction, but the fundamental
design of both were to a large extent preexistent. Comparatively
speaking, the adult education of these women was also more self-
directed than what had come earlier. The skills established and
knowledge acquired were largely self-taught, through a combination of observation, investigation, and experimentation that was
made educative by the self-conscious effort to become more effective in all aspects of vocational role. And since the daily routines of
each woman's life varied considerably, the outcomes of the education associated with these also varied. Even as adults, however,
Dodge, Nathan, Wald, O'Reilly, and Schneiderman had at least
one educative experience in common. During their adult years
female colleagues played a significant role in each woman's continuing education.

From their colleagues, Dodge, Nathan, Wald, O'Reilly, and
Schneiderman acquired information and advice as well as feedback
and reaction. From their colleagues, Dodge, Nathan, Wald,
O'Reilly, and Schneiderman received emotional support and concrete help, which, if not educative in themselves, certainly enhanced the educative potential of other kinds of interaction. And
through exchange with their colleagues, Dodge, Nathan, Wald,
O'Reilly, and Schneiderman developed an outlook on life that was
crucial not only to their work, but also to the meaning they were
able to see in their lives. Colleagues, then, were the common
denominator in this phase of the five women's education, as mentors and parents had been earlier.

In part, other women became especially important in the
adult education of Grace Dodge, Maud Nathan, Lillian Wald,
Leonora O'Reilly, and Rose Schneiderman because of the single-

sex character of the organizations in which they tended to work. All of them belonged to organizations that included both sexes: organizations like the Social Reform Club, the Ethical Culture Society, the People's Institute, and, later, the National Association for the Advancement of Colored People. All of them at one time or another worked with men in specific political or issue campaigns: Seth Low's (1901) mayoralty race, for instance, or the fight waged jointly by the Working Women's Society, the Consumers' League, and the Social Reform Club to secure passage of the Mercantile Inspection Act of 1896. Nevertheless, the organizations with which the five women were most closely associated generally either barred entrance to men or attracted mostly women. In the early years, there were no male residents allowed at Henry Street; one of the founders of the Women's Trade Union League was a man, William English Walling, but there were no male organizers, and women dominated the membership overwhelmingly; the same was true of the Consumers' League, even though on a national level its first president was a man; and the gender-related nature of the working girls' clubs and the YWCA speaks for itself.

On its own, however, the preponderance of women among the people with whom Dodge, Nathan, Wald, O'Reilly, and Schneiderman worked does not explain the special influence of female colleagues. To understand the pedagogic significance of sororal teaching for all of these women, one must consider the ways in which their experience as adults affected their beliefs and values, their most fundamental perceptions.

Work, cause, social change became extraordinarily important to these women. For all of them, work was the dominant activity of adult life. Consequently, all five women tended to seek personal relationships that would support their work and tried to avoid ones that might interfere with it; and, like so many other women social reformers, four of the five chose not to marry. The fear that marriage would conflict with their careers was very real to them. It was this apprehension, for example, that seems to have stood between Leonora O'Reilly and George McGregor, a man with whom O'Reilly had a long-standing, close relationship. The following letter written by McGregor makes this clear: "I want to know more about the Trade School . . . Yes, Nora, I see that you belong there. I see others could not possibly get along without you. I said: 'I want you.' Understand me, dear heart, . . . not in the sense of ownership or possession. *I ask nothing you will not freely give.* Not a pebble would I put in your path. You would be free to come and go—no restraints—no questionings—simple comradeship—truth —trust. I yearn for this. Nothing else is worthwhile."[8]

In O'Reilly's reluctance to marry, one can also see some of the other concerns that often made close same-sex friendships more appealing to women social reformers than heterosexual ones: for example, a realistic general appraisal of marriage's consequences for a woman's independence, regardless of initial intent, which would have been clear to O'Reilly through observation of the demands put on her close friend Mary Ryshpan after she married Morris R. Cohen; or the presumption described by another friend in a tortured letter announcing her pregnancy, that marriage meant children (because "in the male, the sex feeling seems as strong as life itself. It will not be eradicated") and that to bring children into "this awful world we live in . . . was simply unthinkable"; or even the feeling expressed by O'Reilly's close friend Mary Drier that between women there could be friendship and love uncomplicated by marriage's fearful associations and based on "the sense of utter freedom . . . that could never be destroyed." Alternatives aside, emotional attachment was a logical corollary to continuous daily exchange as well as to the common cause women social reformers frequently found with each other.[9]

If joint interest, daily contact, and a propensity to trust other women contributed to the pronounced educative influence of female colleagues, so too did the fact that men often resisted the reforms these women sought. Maud Nathan, like so many women of this generation, attributed her conversion to suffragism to legislators' indifference and opposition to questions of special relevance to women. And Mary Drier, echoing the sentiments of many members of the WTUL, claimed that "the attitude of labor men to the working women has changed me from being an ardent supporter of labor to a somewhat rabid supporter of women,—to feel that the enfranchisement of women and especially of my working sisters is the supreme issue." Preestablished notions concerning male sensibilities (or lack thereof), as well as the fact that men held power in the government and labor unions, may have made their opposition more visible, easier to notice. Still, actual conflict with men was a common experience.[10]

In contrast to this, women like Dodge, Nathan, Wald,

O'Reilly, and Schneiderman frequently discovered through their work that women from different social classes shared common goals and could often develop real comradery. O'Reilly's and Schneiderman's relationship with the Driers shows this, as does O'Reilly's relationship with Grace Dodge. A great deal stood between O'Reilly and Dodge. They had grown up in totally different worlds. O'Reilly was fiery and temperamental; Dodge, quiet and calm. Church-based religion was as alien to O'Reilly as socialist economics was to Dodge. Nonetheless, if Dodge's contributions to O'Reilly's financial support (when she was at Henry Street) created a bond between them, their relationship rested on much more than this. "I feel that while we do not see each other often, our friendship means a great deal, and that we can stay in touch in many phases of our work among young women," Dodge wrote to O'Reilly in 1908. Answering a letter from O'Reilly in 1912, she wrote again, "You are, indeed, 'my Miss O'Reilly,' for I admire you and your work so much. I wish that we could meet often, for it would be a pleasure to hear of all your interests." Winifred O'Reilly, who liked many of her daughter's more labor-oriented friends, did not understand what Leonora saw in Grace Dodge. To her, Dodge was only a "typical society woman" with an "English finished voice." Having participated in Leonora's experience only indirectly, she could not see in Grace Dodge or her work the similarity of purpose upon which Leonora's attachment was based.[11]

As job-related interests made possible associations and friendships that went beyond the confines of kin, neighborhood, ethnic group, religious congregation, or social class, then, women social reformers such as Leonora O'Reilly and Grace Dodge were able to find "kindred spirits" among women from all walks of life. And over time, their friendships nurtured a sense of community that suffused all aspects of their thought. In the similarities of mind or consciousness that took root in this sense of community, one can see the effects of the experience these five women and others of their generation had in common, as well as the lines of influence among them.[12]

This consciousness, which may be called social feminism (it included the kind of prosuffrage position associated with that term), matured over the years in rough correlation with the chronological, developmental, and educational growth of the women who shared it. It was born with the realization of common purpose. It was born when the women were young, when they were looking for meaning, attachment, identity. It was solidified with full commitment to work, with the recognition that choices had been made and direction set. The issue at this point was no longer with what and with whom they would affiliate, but how best they might realize themselves, each other, and their mutual goals. And finally, it was placed within history and seen as the generational consciousness that it was, when clear, definite, firm convictions tested by experience led to a sense of authority and the integration that can come with age. In its fully developed state, this consciousness can be summarized as follows.[13]

Men and women were different. Women were unique in their ability to bear children. With this capacity came an "inborn . . . mother instinct." The instinct gave special perceptual powers. It heightened sensitivity to basic human needs. Men, not sharing in this sensitivity, tended to be blind to interests beyond their own. And since they had controlled political and economic power, human needs had been neglected. Now able to recognize this, women of this generation had had to join cause. Influence within the domestic sphere was no longer sufficient. The deplorable state of the world demanded that women find new, more direct channels of influence, ones that would check male power and rectify its effects. Within the consciousness that Dodge, Nathan, Wald, O'Reilly, and Schneiderman shared, therefore, social reform was a natural concern to women, one that was directly aligned with female tradition, really nothing more than the form into which woman's work had evolved as a result of the interplay of the historical forces that had shaped contemporary life. Social feminism was social reform as a gender-related mission, a mission causatively linked to women's sexual identity. The comparison between "the women of 1915" and "The Men of Forty-Eight" that Leonora O'Reilly drew in her report on the International Congress of Women at The Hague is illustrative. She said: "Even those magnificent men—men are mannificent [*sic*], and yet they are only men, and this is said with no meaning or anything against them, they have one piece of work to do and we have another—even those magnificent men of forty-eight did not realize that they were only half of the human unit which is to do the work of the world, and it has taken all the women and all the fight the women have carried on since that time for an opportunity to get educated, for an opportunity to go in and express themselves, here, there and every-where, that brought about that meeting in Holland, where the women carried on the torch of the men of forty-eight just a little bit farther. And women can do this, with their feeling of mother-hood of the human race—not my child and thy child, but all children everywhere our children.''[14]

The consciousness that grew up among Dodge, Nathan, Wald, O'Reilly, Schneiderman, and others of their contemporaries served a clear function. It helped each of them explain her invest-ment in the problems that defined her work. In the consciousness, for example, Grace Dodge could find a means of identification with working girls, as well as an explanation for the belief that she could draw something from her own experience that would be of value to them. From the consciousness, Leonora O'Reilly and Rose Schneiderman could draw a logic to support allegiance to middle-class women as well as to working-class women, which was imperative if the connection between feminism and trade union-ism that guided so much of their work was to make sense. To Maud Nathan, however, who never relinquished traditional roles or a class-bound life, such a consciousness may have been less impor-tant. Nonetheless, a social feminist consciousness supported her involvement in what she called ''civic'' as opposed to ''commu-nal'' problems and provided a rationale for her suffragism. Finally, for Lillian Wald, who was an officially certified professional, the consciousness was of least use. Nursing skills were sufficient justifi-cation for much that she did. But for her, too, although the ac-crued knowledge of years of settlement work served also, the con-sciousness made participation in politics or in international peace campaigns more supportable.[15]

Social feminism made sense to Dodge, Nathan, Wald, O'Reilly, and Schneiderman partly because it reflected their com-mon need for vocational legitimation: their wish to objectify per-sonal interest and self-defined career demands. But if social femi-nism served a function that is clear in retrospect, this does not mean that it was consciously created to fulfill this need. It would be a mistake to see this consciousness as a purposefully wrought, essentially contrived, and artificial construct. To Grace Dodge, Maud Nathan, Lillian Wald, Leonora O'Reilly, and Rose Schneid-erman social feminism was ''reality.'' For each of them, its central tenets were related to personal goals and beliefs, to precise occupational roles, and to whatever additional "credentials" each of them possessed. Furthermore, over the years, the assumptions inherent in social feminism became less pronounced in some of their minds. Rose Schneiderman, for example, lived until 1972 and her thought reflected the influence of the New Deal era. It must be remembered, therefore, that between individuals there can never be exact coincidence of mind. Each woman's consciousness, though similar to that of the others, was still unique. For all of them, however, social feminism became a way of seeing and understanding. For all of them, social feminism defined the world and its workings as well as their place in it. It was an integral part of each of them. It was an entirely logical interpretation of the experience they shared.

Having worked and in some cases lived within a world that was predominantly female, having shared with other women common cause and close friendship, and having frequently encountered the exact opposite in men, it was rather easy to derive the linkages that gave coherence to this consciousness. Some women seem to have done this rather autonomously, for example, Leonora O'Reilly, who was by far the most intellectual of the five. For O'Reilly, music, theater, even the small happenings of daily life stimulated searching self-reflection. So did literature. O'Reilly read widely and knew works as divergent as Edward Bellamy's *Looking Backward*, Thomas Carlyle's *History of the French Revolution*, and Lester Frank Ward's *Dynamic Sociology*. Furthermore, her diary served to focus her thought, as evidenced by her many long philosophical musings and even an outline for a book on "the theory of the labor movement." Like the others, during her mature years O'Reilly had tutors other than herself. Like the others, then, she was influenced by the thinking of her peers. In her case, however, their thought probably confirmed connections she drew independently, rather than triggering their formation in the first place.

However that may be, there is reason to believe that O'Reilly herself, as well as a small number of other especially influential women, Florence Kelley, for instance, had a part in creating the similarities of mind that the consciousness represented. In a poem she wrote soon after O'Reilly's death, Mary Drier said:

You held the torch aloft when we were young
For us to follow gallantly.
Whate'er we did or not, you held the torch.
Your passionate faith and fervor drew us on
And your true eloquence our spirits fired.
You taught us never, never to despair . . .

You dreamer of dreams, seer of visions,
Saw the new world, fellowship divine
Replace the old dares see it, hope it, teach it
and believe . . .

And Mary Drier's acknowledgement was far from unique in the indebtedness it described. Rose Schneiderman also proudly admitted that Leonora O'Reilly had taught her all she knew of "revolutionary labor philosophy." Grace Dodge, Lillian Wald, and Maud Nathan paid no such public tribute, although all three knew O'Reilly, respected her, and more than likely incorporated some of her views into their own thinking.[16]

The case for O'Reilly's persuasiveness, also the more general argument that women like O'Reilly and Kelley were the midwives for the consciousness of many of their colleagues and peers, need not rest on direct acknowledgement, however. The fact that O'Reilly and Kelley expressed their views widely, frequently, clearly, and with great potential for credibility also indicates that their perceptions may have been unusually formative in effect.

O'Reilly and "Sister Kelley," as she was often called, were both irreverent and indignant by temperament, strong and autonomous in their convictions, and exceptionally articulate. Both women could call on knowledge culled from relatively long and unusual experience. O'Reilly, of course, had been involved in the labor movement for most of her life; Kelley had been a friend of Frederick Engels, knew the American socialist world intimately, was trained as a lawyer, and not only had been married but also had divorced her husband and taken on the complete support of their three children. Thus, a combination of personal charisma and long experience gave authority to the views of both women. O'Reilly may have been less influential than Kelley, who lived at both Hull House and Henry Street and had a marked impact on both organizations as well as their leaders. Nevertheless, if Kelley's effect as a public speaker, as a participant in meetings, and as a casual companion was electrifying, so too was O'Reilly's.[17]

To argue for influence is not to argue for imposition. No doubt Dodge, Nathan, Wald, and Schneiderman drew the typical social feminist linkages between gender and mission for themselves. After all, such connections were verifiably true within their experience and no less subjectively necessary for them than for O'Reilly and Kelley. But familiarity with the thought and the example of women of such strong opinions did make it easier to see these connections. And so, too, though differently, did Jane Addams.

Grace Dodge, Maud Nathan, Lillian Wald, Leonora O'Reilly, and Rose Schneiderman all knew Jane Addams. Her direct effect upon some of them, particularly Lillian Wald, was profound. After Addams's first visit to Henry Street, Wald wrote to her that "it may be of some little service to you that one small group has a deeper desire than ever to press its service into and for a fairer society for having touched you. It isn't at all said as it should be but turn your perceptions here and know that we want to be *good* and like children look up to you for guidance." Generally speaking, however, Addams's influence was greatest in indirect form. As a writer, Addams had an extraordinary talent for drawing general precepts from her own experience and for presenting these in a style that was both immediate and general. Because her articles and books were easy to read with assent, the meaning she saw in her life and work could be readily synthesized with the meaning other women saw in their own efforts. Many women (and men) of her generation venerated Jane Addams as a heroine, almost a saint. To them, she literally symbolized the highest form of feminine wisdom and selfless humanitarianism. Thus, her thought, her example, and the popularity she brought, at least for a time, to all that she represented, not only embodied the social feminist consciousness, but also helped to create a climate of opinion that provided a healthy growth medium for the kind of thought it expressed.[18]

The consciousness that was the central common outcome of the adult education of Dodge, Nathan, Wald, O'Reilly, and Schneiderman was related to much besides their shared experience and mutual influence. But to go beyond Addams in tracing its nonimmediate sources would add little to the point I hope I have made. And that is, that self-education and sororal education were the common central forms of adult education for each of the five women.

By now the essential similarities between the adult education, the vocational education, and the childhood or early education of these women should be apparent. All were characterized by intense, often intimate, educationally significant personal relationships. All had far more to do with the provisioning of interpersonal orientations than with the development of specific substantive knowledge. Grace Dodge, Maud Nathan, Lillian Wald, Leonora O'Reilly, and Rose Schneiderman gained their most significant education from the people they encountered outside institutions primarily designed to educate. And people—their problems and their relationships to one another—were also the central curriculum of their education. In part, the nature of these women's education was determined by objective circumstances. In part too, however, it was determined by the kind of educative abilities that were nurtured and sustained throughout their lives. Thus, the "educative style" that was both a source for and an outcome of the commonalities noted above is also important to consider.

Educative style is the way in which an individual "engages in, moves through, and combines" the various experiences from which his or her education is derived. It is not only the way in which an individual learns, but also the way in which he or she approaches experience, scans it for meaning, and then incorporates that meaning into what is already known. No two individuals can have an identical educative style. Among a number of individuals, however, there can be similar tendencies, and among these women there were at least three such tendencies.[19]

Dodge, Nathan, Wald, O'Reilly, and Schneiderman were inclined to be utilitarian in their outlook on life. They observed, talked, listened, read, wrote, and pondered with antennae directed toward the applied value of information: its tangible, practical significance. Ideas became interesting to them as they were related to the problems with which they were concerned. Dodge, Nathan, Wald, O'Reilly, and Schneiderman were rarely given to idle curiosity. Indeed, they were especially astute in their ability to transform abstract knowledge into the kind of empirical insight that could inform their actions. Their approach to learning was more goal oriented than playful. Their educative style was more intelligent than intellectual.[20]

Dodge, Nathan, Wald, O'Reilly, and Schneiderman also tended to project their thought toward the outside world and away from themselves. They did not like to probe their own motivations. And when they sought self-knowledge, they did so most incisively and most comfortably if such knowledge could bring greater understanding of other people. Consequently, they were more attracted to the social than to the personal, and they tried constantly to understand individuals, including themselves, in terms of their relationship to a group. These women were more altruistic than egotistic. They recognized the compatible and the symmetrical more readily than the reverse. They noticed identities more than differences, unity more than disunity, and harmony more than dissonance.

Dodge, Nathan, Wald, O'Reilly, and Schneiderman also relied heavily on intuitive insight as a means of discovery. Their assessment of a situation was more often based on their sense of things than on systematic, "objective" information. Their own experience rather than the accumulated knowledge of others tended to guide their judgments, and they were able to draw on this knowledge—their experience—quickly, unselfconsciously, and with considerable confidence. They found deliberate reasoning and formal logic more difficult and less useful. In sum, their educative style was utilitarian and intuitive, and it was guided for the most part by what one might call social intelligence.

Obviously, the educative style described here fits Leonora O'Reilly, but it fits her less well, less fully than it does Grace Dodge, Maud Nathan, Lillian Wald, and Rose Schneiderman. More than Dodge, Nathan, Wald, and Schneiderman, O'Reilly sought and enjoyed ideas for their intrinsic worth as well as their social utility. She could be and was more self-reflective than the other four. And she was significantly more capable of deliberate, sustained, and objective reasoning than they were, although she was equally if not more adept at intuitive projection. In other words, O'Reilly's educative style was instructed by a social intelligence at the same time that it was also influenced by the ability to speculate freely and broadly. It included a wider range of skills than the educative style of Dodge, Nathan, Wald, and Schneiderman. Even though the difference between O'Reilly's educative style and that of Dodge, Nathan, Wald, and Schneiderman was only one of degree, it is still important to mention because it indicates that O'Reilly's education was less constricted than the other women's in terms of the behavioral restraints that she was taught.

Good manners, ladylike conduct, and general obedience were not postures that were emphasized in O'Reilly's upbringing. What was emphasized was that she could and must advance the cause of labor. Leonora O'Reilly was taught what she had to do, and she was taught this forcefully. Yet she was not restricted in the ways she could go about achieving the end to which she was dedicated. As a result, she felt more entitled to explore widely and was more able to ponder freely and deeply than the four other women. Winifred O'Reilly's interest in ideas and the zesty intellectual fare that the O'Reillys digested together were important in molding Leonora's educative style. As a child Leonora O'Reilly had little formal schooling, but the "schooling" she received at home and at Cooper Union was more intellectually stimulating than what she would have been likely to find in an ordinary schoolroom. Thus, her ability to "engage in, move through, and combine" experiences had not been limited by the constraints inherent in a properly female education, as to a varying degree Dodge's, Nathan's, and Wald's had been; nor was it limited by the effects of a harsh reality to the extent that Schneiderman's was. And the difference between O'Reilly's educative style and that of her friends was directly related to the nature of the educational opportunities available to these women and others of their generation.

Generally speaking, despite increasing diversity, the institutionalized forms of schooling open to women in the late nineteenth century were built on the conviction that a woman's education should be designed to enhance her "natural" functions: comforting, healing, nurturing, teaching, and otherwise ministering to the needs of others. Outside of these, women could find an education in the expanding print media—books, magazines, and newspapers—or in the various media connected with the public forum—sermons, lectures, plays, and so on. Here too, however, notions of what a "true woman" could and could not do had a marked effect on both the substance and the form of the material especially directed to women, and to venture beyond such fare, women needed to be interested in questions they often had been taught to ignore. In addition, women could find an education from and in other people. They could talk to members of their families, to their neighbors, and to their friends, and to an extent, they also could purposefully seek out other people who might teach them what they wanted to know.[21]

The last of these resources—people—was by far the most significant. As an educational resource, people were extraordinarily valuable to this generation of women. Their offerings could be had with little or no cost, financial or social; they were easily available; and they often could act as conduits to further opportunity. Nonetheless, the offerings one might find in this way were as varied as the people one met, on purpose or by chance. Some women found people who helped them learn to learn according to the full spectrum of their talents. Leonora O'Reilly found such a person in her mother. Others, like Grace Dodge, Maud Nathan, Lillian Wald, and Rose Schneiderman, never found people who could help them learn to learn in ways different from the ones they could develop on their own, in interaction with the people and institutions of a society that had clear ideas about what and how women "knew" and to what ends they might use their knowledge.

The educative style of Grace Dodge, Maud Nathan, Lillian Wald, Leonora O'Reilly, and Rose Schneiderman was both a source for and an outcome of their education. Interestingly, it bears a striking resemblance to the approach to knowledge that has been associated with the entire progressive generation. It would seem, therefore, that the men who were the contemporaries of Dodge, Nathan, Wald, O'Reilly, and Schneiderman shared their interests, their concerns, and even their ways of knowing more than these women were sometimes able to realize. To analyze the similarities and differences between the thought processes of the men and women of the progressive generation would be a fascinating enterprise. And it would be even more interesting to see if one could find a relationship between these thought processes and education. Could it be, for example, that what was an educative style for Dodge, Nathan, Wald, O'Reilly, and Schneiderman was for a comparable group of men not an educative style, but a synthesis of the intellectual probings that led them to repudiate the "formal" thought of previous generations? Or could it be that the women of the progressive generation were able to "engage in, move through, and combine" experiences in ways that their male contemporaries admired partly because they learned differently, and that the educative style of progressive women was a model used by progressive men to add new ways of understanding to those they had acquired in school? One could speculate endlessly. The relationship is intriguing. Yet the point here is really nothing more than that

Dodge, Nathan, Wald, O'Reilly, and Schneiderman were progressive women and their educative style illustrates their kinship with other progressives, male and female.[22]

Finally, the educative style of these five women helps to make comprehensible the paradox of their achievement. Each of the five, in her own way, went beyond the kind of life she was expected to lead. Each ventured further into the public arena and each liberated herself from traditional conventions more than her mother had done. And in each case, education helped to make this possible. Ironically, however, in moving ahead, these women understood and justified their actions in terms that their mothers, and their fathers, would have understood and found admirable. In turning to gender-related "necessity" to explain the choices they had made, they not only acknowledged the strictures that limited them, they enshrined them. Thus, they could act as few women had done, but they could see best, comprehend most fully, and think most freely in a style that was compatible with the mental proclivities that their society thought of as uniquely and specially female. Education helped Grace Dodge, Maud Nathan, Lillian Wald, Leonora O'Reilly, and Rose Schneiderman do great things, but it did not enable them to transcend the categories of debate that had surrounded questions concerning women's roles and responsibilities throughout the nineteenth century. For women of the progressive generation, virtues that were presumed to be inherently female remained a prime rationale for the assertion of equal rights.

A Note on Method
and Sources
Notes
Index

A Note on Method
and Sources

RATHER THAN LISTING the sources upon which this study has been based, I should like to explain where and how various different kinds of literature have informed the interpretation presented in both the methodology and the argument of the book. Throughout I shall refer to specific primary and secondary works, although my purpose is to use them as examples to clarify the approach. As documentation, the notes to each chapter will serve.

Educational biography comes out of the historiographical position Lawrence A. Cremin has developed in *Public Education* (New York: Basic Books, 1976) and *Traditions of American Education* (New York: Basic Books, 1977). Its purposes are continuous with the effort to broaden the focus of educational history that began almost twenty years ago with Bernard Bailyn's essay *Education in the Forming of American Society* (Chapel Hill: University of North Carolina Press, 1960).

In an educational biography an historian investigates the experience of education: the meaning of education within the context of an individual's life. The approach is designed to bring into view the educative functions of a variety of different institutions, and to assess the effects of those institutions, as well as the effects of noninstitutionally related teaching and learning, on the individual under consideration. The importance of studying education from the perspective of the learner has been noted by many historians: see, for example, David B. Tyack, "New Perspectives on the History of American Education," in *The State of American History*, ed. Herbert J. Bass (Chicago: Quadrangle Books, 1970); the usefulness of personal documents for research in educational history has been especially well stated by Geraldine Jonçich Clifford in "History as Experience: The Use of Personal-History Documents in the History of Education," *History of Education*, 7 (1978):183-196; and the need to examine, not only the intentions of educators, but also the outcomes of education, has been repeatedly and widely stated, most insistently, perhaps by scholars such as Michael B. Katz, Colin Greer, Walter Feinberg, and Clarence J. Karier. That analyses of the process of education, as evidenced in individual lives, are a necessary complement to other modes of inquiry in the history of education is readily apparent from reviews of recent work, Douglas Sloan's "Historiography and the History of Education," in *Review of Research in Education*, ed. Fred Kerlinger, 1 (1973):239-269, being among the most comprehensive of these.

If the reasoning behind educational biography in its generic form can be found in the historiography of education, the logic for its use in studying the history of women's education can be found in recent work in women's history. In its early stages in the 1960s, women's history was primarily concerned with writing women into history in traditional terms. Pushed largely by the rebirth of a woman's movement, historians began to look for the part women had played in social movements like abolitionism and progressivism, to examine the woman's suffrage movement in greater detail, and to pay more attention to the "notable" women that were found in many other areas as well. As the field has developed, however, it has become increasingly apparent that women's history will remain obscure unless a commonsensical but important observation—that women are not in all ways the same as men—is built into both the questions historians ask and the categories of historical significance they use (see Carl N. Degler, *Is There a History of Women?* Inaugural Lecture, Oxford University, March 14, 1974, [Oxford: Clarendon Press, 1975]). The implications of this observation for women's history in general are discussed in articles such as: Barbara Sicherman, "Review Essay: American History," *Signs*, 1 (1975):461-485; Ann D. Gordon, Mari Jo Buhle, and Nancy

Schrom Dye, "The Problem of Women's History," in *Liberating Women's History: Theoretical and Critical Essays*, ed. Berenice A. Carroll (Urbana: University of Illinois Press, 1976), pp. 75-92; Gerda Lerner, "Placing Women in History: Definitions and Challenges," *Feminist Studies*, 3 (1975): 5-14; and Carroll Smith-Rosenberg, "The New Woman and the New History," *Feminist Studies*, 3 (1975):185-198.

Curiously, the relationship between the theoretical concerns of women's history and educational history has not received much attention, although articles such as Patricia Albjerg Graham's "So Much to Do: Guides for Historical Research on Women in Higher Education," *Teachers College Record*, 76 (1975):421-429, and Jill K. Conway's "Perspectives on the History of Women's Education in the United States," *History of Education Quarterly*, 14 (1974): 1-12, have suggested useful lines of research. Nevertheless, what we now know of women's history argues for taking a fresh look at what has been educationally significant for women, which can be done by deriving the educative from women's actual experience; and for including within that a careful consideration of the close, personal relationships that many different works suggest may have been especially important in the education of women: see, for example, Barbara J. Berg, *The Remembered Gate: Origins of American Feminism; The Woman and the City, 1800-1860* (New York: Oxford University Press, 1978); Nancy F. Cott, *The Bonds of Womanhood: "Woman's Sphere" in New England, 1780-1835* (New Haven: Yale University Press, 1977); Carroll Smith-Rosenberg, "The Female World of Love and Ritual: Relations between Women in Nineteenth-Century America," *Signs*, 1 (1975):1-30; and Michelle Zimbalist Rosaldo and Louise Lamphere, eds., *Woman, Culture, and Society* (Stanford: Stanford University Press, 1974). The theoretical concerns of both educational history and women's history can be addressed through educational biography, and literature from both fields has influenced this study.

In order to consider the educative significance of a wide variety of experiences and relationships an informed understanding of the process of education is important. Consequently, a third category of literature, a broad range of works all of which for my purposes may be placed under the general rubric of educational theory, also has been helpful in developing the questions I have asked.

In an educational biography, the relationship between theory and evidence should be reciprocal. For if, as Herbert Blumer has pointed out in a number of essays in *Symbolic Interactionism: Perspective and Method* (Englewood Cliffs, N.J.: Prentice-Hall, 1969), a general theoretical construct may provide a guide for one's inquiry, it is the nature of the evidence available for study that ultimately decides the specific concepts one will use. Thus, in writing the educational biographies of Grace Dodge, Maud Nathan, Lillian Wald, Leonora O'Reilly, and Rose Schneiderman, I have begun with an abstract definition of education—that education is a process of interaction by which individual potential is activated, shaped, or channeled and a change thereby produced in the self—but I have also used whichever compatible subsidiary concepts have seemed most valuable within the source material of a particular life. As a result, the five biographies differ somewhat. In each case, they reflect the same theoretical perspective, but in each case, the substantive meaning of education has been derived from the life.

All of the biographies are built around a Deweyan conception of education. The writings of John Dewey, especially *How We Think* (New York: D. C. Heath, 1910), *Democracy and Education* (New York: Macmillan, 1916), *The Sources of a Science of Education* (New York: Horace Liveright, 1929), and *Experience and Education* (New York: Macmillan, 1938), have provided the theoretical framework of this book. Obviously, therefore, all the concepts I have used, though tailored to suit the specific purposes of this study as well as the evidence, also stem from an interactionist approach to education. In analyzing each life I have drawn from an eclectic literature, for example: Gordon W. Allport, *Pattern and Growth in Personality* (New York: Holt, Rinehart and Winston, 1961); Orville G. Brim, Jr., and Stanton Wheeler, *Socialization after Childhood: Two Essays* (New York: John Wiley and Sons, 1966); Erik H. Erikson, *Childhood and Society* (New York: W. W. Norton, 1950); L. R. Goulet and Paul B. Baltes, eds., *Life-Span Developmental Psychology* (New York: Academic Press, 1970); Abraham H. Maslow, *Motivation and Personality* (New York: Harper and Row, 1954); Gardner Murphy, *Personality: A Biosocial Approach to Origins and Structure* (New York: Harper and Row, 1947); and Robert W. White, ed., *The Study of Lives: Essays on Personality in Honor of Henry A. Murray* (New York: Atherton

Press, 1963). Nevertheless, the concepts upon which I have relied most heavily are consistent with the point of view implicit in the definition of education that I have used.

For example, to find the self and its continuous transformation over time (my use of this term comes out of William James, *The Principles of Psychology* [1890; reprint ed., New York: Dover Publications, 1950], as I explain on p. 7), "style" and "metaphor" have been useful ideas. Wherever possible, therefore, I have tried to describe each woman's style, her characteristic manner of self-presentation (see note 12 on p. 186), and to discern its effects on other people. Not surprisingly, my understanding of style, what it represents and how it serves to shape experience, has been influenced primarily by scholars who write from an interactionist orientation: for instance, Erving Goffman, especially the first essay in *Encounters: Two Studies in the Sociology of Interaction* (Indianapolis: Bobbs-Merrill, 1961), and Hope Jensen Leichter, especially "The Concept of Educative Style," *Teachers College Record*, 75 (1973):239-250. Similarly, wherever possible, I have looked closely at what James Olney has called "metaphors of self" in *Metaphors of Self: The Meaning of Autobiography* (Princeton: Princeton University Press, 1972). Such constructs can be simple statements or full autobiographies, and because they are symbolic and represent an ideal sense of self more than its actuality (which is what style represents), they can provide invaluable clues to the way in which an individual wished to be seen.

In recovering the relationships and encounters that influence changes in the self, two additional concepts have proved valuable. The first is Harry Stack Sullivan's concept of "significant others." As Sullivan explains in *The Interpersonal Theory of Psychiatry*, ed. Helen Swick Perry and Mary Ladd Gawel (New York: W. W. Norton, 1953)—also relevant here are George Herbert Mead, *Mind, Self, and Society from the Standpoint of a Social Behaviorist*, ed. Charles W. Morris (1934; reprint ed., Chicago: University of Chicago Press, 1962), and Hope Jensen Leichter, "Some Perspectives on the Family as Educator," *Teachers College Record*, 76 (1974): 175-217—the appraisals of the people to whom one is most closely attached (one's significant others) serve as mirrors through which one learns to recognize one's self. If one can trace the expanding network of an individual's significant others from the primary caretakers of childhood to all those vital to that person's ongoing functioning, one can, in a sense, trace the self as it is constantly transformed over time. And such an analysis makes it possible to follow the kinds of changes that I have equated with education, and to locate the sources that have influenced such changes.

Throughout my consideration of each life, John Dewey's view of educative experience also has been central. So far as possible within the evidence, I have always tried to discern what came before any given discrete experience as well as what came after. In a sense, I have attempted to do what Dewey, in "The Child and the Curriculum" (1902), urged teachers to do: simultaneously to "psychologize" each experience—to understand its relationship to cumulative past experience—and to "socialize" it—to discern the later known outcome to which it might connect.

The degree to which I have been able to apply these concepts within each biography has varied, depending on the nature of the sources; and in most cases, I have not made the theoretical structure of the analysis explicit in the text. To do so would sacrifice the "artistic" aims of a biography more than is necessary, even in a life history that is primarily concerned with analyzing one aspect of a life. Because educational biography is like literary biography in that it attempts to present as "authentic" a portrait of individual experience as possible within its particular purpose, theory is used to provide insight, but it is usually not included as part of the story. The following monographs can be useful in understanding why this is so: Leon Edel, *Literary Biography* (Toronto: University of Toronto Press, 1957), James L. Clifford, ed., *Biography as an Art: Selected Criticism, 1560-1960* (New York: Oxford University Press, 1962), John A. Garraty, *The Nature of Biography* (New York: Alfred A. Knopf, 1957), and L. L. Langness, *The Life History in Anthropological Science* (New York: Holt, Rinehart and Winston, 1965). Generally speaking, psychobiographers are more explicit in the connections they draw between theory and evidence than an educational biographer would be. The pros and cons of this approach are discussed in Jacques Barzun, "History: The Muse and Her Doctors," *American Historical Review* 77 (1972):36-64; they are also considered at length in the symposium "The Joys and Terrors of Psychohistory," to which vol. 5 of *The Journal of Psychohistory* (1978) is almost entirely devoted; and those articles, along with the essays in Robert Jay Lifton, ed., *Explorations in Psychohistory: The Wellfleet Papers* (New York: Simon and Schuster, 1974), are among the works to which one can turn to understand the differences between the purposes of educational biography and the purposes of psychobiography.

In an educational biography, as in any biography, the ability to project imaginatively into the experience of the person about whom one is writing is as important as the more specific concepts mentioned above. Although it is always necessary to discipline and temper such transference, it is this that makes an experience "real," and therefore susceptible to understanding. Erik H. Erikson deals with the way in which transference affects one's approach to a life in "On the Nature of 'Psycho-Historical' Evidence," in *Life History and the Historical Moment* (New York: W. W. Norton, 1975), pp. 113-168; Theodor Reik, *Listening with the Third Ear: The Inner Experience of a Psychoanalyst* (New York: Grove Press, 1948), discusses the same problem in a different context; and Israel Scheffler, "In Praise of the Cognitive Emotions," *Teachers College Record*, 79 (1977):171-186, explores the question as it pertains to many different kinds of inquiry.

The ability to empathize with the experience of a historical figure depends in part on the quantity and quality of the source material; and as I have already noted, the nature of the evidence available for each life also has had a determining influence on the way in which I have applied the concepts described above. However, in writing each of the five biographies, I have used the same kinds of sources: manuscripts, autobiographies and other published articles and books by each of the five women, as well as secondary sources: biographies, institutional histories, and other more general accounts. I shall discuss this literature in that order and by category.

In writing an educational biography one tends to be more selective in one's study of manuscript collections than one would be if one were attempting to recover the details of all aspects of a life. As is always true, however, the documents in such collections provide the foundation for one's work.

Because Grace Dodge was such a private person, there are relatively few revealing documents among her papers, which can be found in the Grace H. Dodge and the Records Files Collections at the Archives of the National Board of the YWCA of the U.S.A. in New York City and in the Grace H. Dodge Papers, Special Collections, Teachers College Library, Columbia University, New

York City. The YWCA Collections contain correspondence as well as documents concerning the formation of the National Board, the reminiscences of old friends, various magazine and newspaper clippings, and drafts for magazine stories by and about Dodge and her work. Teachers College holds Dodge's "Record book, 1874-1913" (1 vol.), her "A line a day" diary, 1899-1914 (4 vols.), the 38th St. Working Girls' Society's "Meetings and Messages, November 26, 1888-August, 1915" (3 vols.), the notebook Dodge entitled "Personal work, papers and addresses, 1889-1902" (1 vol.), as well as approximately fifty letters.

Maud Nathan's Scrapbooks (12 vols.), which are the major source in the Maud Nathan Papers at the Schlesinger Library, Radcliffe College, Cambridge, Massachusetts, are invaluable for an educational biography. They contain newspaper clippings, letters, and invitations, as well as reprints of some of Nathan's magazine articles. They are not only a record of what Nathan said and did; by their very selection, they indicate what Nathan cherished and wanted remembered. The Annie Nathan Meyer Papers, American Jewish Archives, Hebrew Union College, Cincinnati, Ohio, contain many of Nathan's letters to her sister.

Lillian Wald's papers are in the Rare Book and Manuscript Library, Columbia University, the Manuscript and Archives Division of The New York Public Library, Astor, Lenox, and Tilden Foundations, and the Archives of the Visiting Nurse Service of New York. There is additional material relevant to Wald's biography in the manuscript collections of her colleagues and friends, for example, the Jane Addams Papers, Swarthmore College Peace Collection, Swarthmore College, Swarthmore, Pennsylvania. Because the Wald collections are so large, it has been most useful for my purposes to sample them selectively and rather impressionistically. The risk of such an approach is that one may miss an occasional gem; yet one need not read carefully all of the correspondence between Lavinia Dock and Lillian Wald to determine the educative significance of their relationship; nor need one read all of the many letters from Wald's "neighbors" to discover that they were a major source for her understanding of social problems. Furthermore, a quick run-through and a few indepth probes provide a sense of Wald's changing interests and style, which is what is most important in studying her education.

The Leonora O'Reilly Papers at the Schlesinger Library, Radcliffe College, Cambridge, Massachusetts, are an unusually rich collection. In addition to O'Reilly's diary (25 vols.) there are hundreds of letters to and from O'Reilly and clippings and pamphlets describing many of the organizations to which she belonged. Unlike much of Wald's correspondence, O'Reilly's tends to reflect her own life more than any organization; and, unlike the Nathan materials, the O'Reilly collection is most significant for her own reporting of events. The WTUL of New York Papers at the New York State Department of Labor Research Library, New York City, are a useful supplement to the above, as they are also to the Rose Schneiderman papers, which are at the Tamiment Library, New York University, New York City.

The Schneiderman collection is somewhat disappointing. There is relatively little correspondence and there are many pictures and White House invitations. Nevertheless, there are a few significant letters and there are a number of very helpful newspaper clippings. The Schneiderman letters in the Eleanor Roosevelt Personal Papers, Franklin D. Roosevelt Library, Hyde Park, New York, are interesting for the light they shed on her relationship with the Roosevelts as well as on her activities and point of view, especially in the 1930s and 1940s.

Leonora O'Reilly never wrote an autobiography; Grace Dodge never published one, although I have treated her "Record book" as a kind of autobiography; Maud Nathan (*Once upon a Time and Today* [New York: G. P. Putnam's Sons, 1933]), Lillian Wald (*The House on Henry Street* [New York: Henry Holt, 1915] and *Windows on Henry Street* [New York: Little Brown, 1934]), and Rose Schneiderman (with Lucy Goldthwaite, *All for One* [New York: Paul S. Eriksson, 1967] and "A Cap Maker's Story," *The Independent*, 58 [1905]:935-938) did write their own life histories. Nathan's and Schneiderman's autobiographies provide significant evidence concerning the qualities most important to their education, as do Dodge's "Record book" (its form is telling) and some of the episodes Wald described in her essentially impersonal life histories.

Generally speaking, the autobiographical writings of these women were more useful in drawing their educational biographies than their other writings, and this is probably true for any educational biography. Nevertheless, Grace Dodge's *A Bundle of Letters to Busy Girls on Practical Matters* (New York: Funk and Wagnalls,

1887) and her introduction to Annie Marion MacLean's *Wage-Earning Women* (New York: Macmillan, 1910) provide insight into what Dodge wished to do with her life. Lillian Wald's articles in *The American Journal of Nursing*, especially during her first ten years on Henry Street ("Nurses' Settlement," 1 [1901]:39; "Nurses' Social Settlements," 1 [1901]:682-684; "The Nurses' Settlement in New York," 2 [1902]:567-574; "The Treatment of Families in Which There Is Sickness," 4 [1904]:427-431; and "Best Help to the Immigrant Through the Nurse," 8 [1908]:464-467) illustrate her changing understanding of nursing and settlement work; and her "An Afterword" to Jane Addams's *Forty Years at Hull House* (New York: Macmillan, 1935) shows her respect and affection for Addams. Maud Nathan's *The Story of an Epoch-Making Movement* (Garden City, N.Y.: Doubleday, Page, 1926) testifies to her ambitious nature, as well as to the historical significance she attributed to the Consumers' League. And the articles O'Reilly wrote for *Life and Labor* exemplify her multifaceted prose style: "Are You With Us?" 2 (1912):285-286, is an example of the more angry and ironic O'Reilly; "Rahel of 'Out of the Shadow,'" 9 (1919):103-105, typifies her more gentle tone; and "Revolution-Evolution-Fraternity," 9 (1919):209-210, illustrates her ability to make a point through a vignettelike story. So far as I am aware, Schneiderman did not publish much other than her autobiography. Even if one may expect to find little that is of great moment in sources such as these, it is worthwhile to survey as many of an individual's writings as possible when writing an educational biography.

Unfortunately, there are no recent published biographies of any of these women, although Dodge, Nathan, Wald, and O'Reilly are briefly sketched in *Notable American Women* (3 vols.; Cambridge: Harvard University Press, 1971), and Schneiderman will be included in the forthcoming supplement. Abbie Graham's *Grace H. Dodge: Merchant of Dreams* (New York: The Womans Press, 1926) contains a large number of quoted reminiscences from friends, some of which tell a good deal about Dodge's personality, competence, and activities. Although the biography is uncritical, it remains the major source for Dodge's early life. Leonora O'Reilly was the subject of two undergraduate theses, Frances H. Howe, "Leonora O'Reilly, Socialist and Reformer" (Radcliffe honors thesis, 1952), and Eric L. Sandquist, "Leonora O'Reilly and the Progressive Movement'' (Harvard honors thesis, 1966); but neither is sufficient as a biography. Lillian Wald is the only one of the five who has been studied in detail. In addition to R. L. Duffus's *Lillian Wald: Neighbor and Crusader* (New York: Macmillan, 1938), which was an authorized biography, and Beryl Williams Epstein's *Lillian Wald: Angel on Henry Street* (New York: J. Messner, 1948), which is a readable but dramatized account, there are three recent very different dissertations about Wald: Jill K. Conway's ''The First Generation of American Women Graduates'' (Ph.D. dissertation, Harvard University, 1969) studies Wald in comparison with five other women; Allan Edward Reznick's ''Lillian D. Wald: The Years At Henry Street'' (Ph.D. dissertation, University of Wisconsin, 1973) examines Wald's childhood, schooling, and initial work at Henry Street; and Doris Daniels's ''Lillian D. Wald: The Progressive Woman and Feminism'' (Ph.D. dissertation, City University of New York, 1976) surveys her full life to outline the development of her feminist point of view. I differ with each of these studies at certain points, but each is detailed and careful and all have contributed significantly to my understanding of Wald's education. To an extent, an educational biography is a form of secondary analysis, that is, an attempt to tease out the educative experiences after the basic facts of a life have been established. Consequently, the kind of biographical attention Wald has received can greatly facilitate such a study.

In a number of cases, I have been able to find contemporary portraits of these women that have served not only to provide information, but also to indicate the way in which they were seen by their friends and colleagues. In this regard, Mabel Cratty's ''The Fine Profession of Being a Layman,'' in *Mabel Cratty: Leader in the Art of Leadership*, ed. Margaret E. Burton (New York: The Womans Press, 1929), pp. 121-139, and *The Association Monthly: In Memory of Grace H. Dodge*, 9 (1915), informed my view of Grace Dodge, as Jacob Riis's ''Lillian D. Wald,'' *The Survey*, 39 (1913):551-552, and Gregory Weinstein's *The Ardent Eighties: Reminiscences of an Interesting Decade* (New York: The International Press, 1928) added to my knowledge of Lillian Wald. At times, briefer descriptions, even passing mentions, were instructive. This was true, for example, of the comments about O'Reilly in Vida Scudder's *Father Huntington* (New York: E. P. Dutton, 1940) and Morris R. Cohen's *A Dreamer's Journey* (Glencoe: Free

Press, 1949), and of the comments about Schneiderman in Frances Perkins's *The Roosevelt I Knew* (New York: Viking Press, 1946).

To understand the people who were significant to each woman's education, I have again turned primarily to biographical sources. Whenever they were available, biographies of family members were useful: for example, Carlos Martyn's *William E. Dodge: The Christian Merchant* (New York: Funk and Wagnalls, 1890) and Alice Henry's "Mrs. Winifred O'Reilly: A Veteran Worker," *Life and Labor*, 1 (1911):132-136. Biographies of teachers (for example, William M. Sloane's "Sarah Porter: Her Unique Educational Work," in *When I Was at Farmington*, ed. Abby Farwell Ferry [Chicago: Ralph Fletcher Seymour, 1931], pp. 17-28), biographies of mentors (for example, Mary E. Drier's *Margaret Drier Robins: Her Life, Letters and Work* [New York: Island Press Cooperative, 1950]), and biographies of friends and colleagues (for example, Ruth Putnam, ed., *The Life and Letters of Mary Putnam Jacobi* [New York: G. P. Putnam's Sons, 1925]), often allowed me to understand the personality of an individual who was, among other things, an important role model. Finally, the biographies of people from comparable backgrounds sometimes highlighted the special qualities of the education of the person under consideration. For example, Rebekah Kohut's *My Portion: An Autobiography* (New York: Thomas Seltzer, 1925) served this purpose in studying Maud Nathan.

When possible, I have also used primary and secondary accounts to add to my understanding of the communities in which each woman grew up. Thus, histories such as Hyman B. Grinstein's *The Rise of the Jewish Community of New York, 1654-1860* (Philadelphia: Jewish Publication Society of America, 1945), Stuart E. Rosenberg's *The Jewish Community in Rochester, 1843-1925* (New York: Columbia University Press, 1954), and Moses Rischin's *The Promised City: New York's Jews, 1870-1914* (Cambridge: Harvard University Press, 1962) provided useful contextural information for the educational biographies of Maud Nathan, Lillian Wald, and Rose Schneiderman, respectively.

The educative significance of each woman's career could not have become clear without some understanding of the organizations and movements in which each participated. In some cases, it was difficult or impossible to find out as much as I should have liked. This was true for the Working Women's Society, to cite but one example. More often than not, however, I found at least some relevant information. Since most of this literature is referred to in the notes, I shall not list it again, although I would underscore the fact that institutional histories—for instance, the works pertaining to the history of Teachers College or to the history of the WTUL— were only valuable insofar as they added to my understanding of each woman's educative experience and the significance within that of her participation in a specific group. The same was true for general accounts of the labor movement—Barbara Mayer Wertheimer's *We Were There: The Story of Working Women in America* (New York: Pantheon, 1977), Alice Henry's *Women and the Labor Movement* (New York: George H. Doran, 1923), Louis Levine's *The Women's Garment Workers: A History of the International Ladies' Garment Workers' Union* (New York: B. W. Huebsch, 1924), and Joel Seidman's *The Needle Trades* (New York: Farrar and Rinehart, 1942); of the settlement movement, particularly Allen F. Davis's *Spearheads for Reform: The Social Settlements and the Progressive Movement, 1890-1914* (New York: Oxford University Press, 1967); and of the suffrage movement, for example, the *History of Woman Suffrage*, ed. Elizabeth Cady Stanton, Susan B. Anthony, and Matilda Joselyn Gage (6 vols.; reprint ed., New York: Arno Press, 1969), Ellen DuBois's "The Radicalism of the Woman Suffrage Movement: Notes toward the Reconstruction of Nineteenth-Century Feminism," *Feminist Studies*, 3 (1975):63-71, Eleanor Flexner's *Century of Struggle: The Woman's Rights Movement in the United States* (rev. ed.; Cambridge: Harvard University Press, 1975), and Aileen S. Kraditor's *The Ideas of The Woman Suffrage Movement, 1890-1920* (New York: Columbia University Press, 1965). What is more, for my purposes a document such as Louisa Lee Schuyler's "Forty-Three Years Ago: The Early Days of the State Charities Aid Association, 1872-1915" (Publication no. 135, State Charities Aid Association of New York), which reflects on Schuyler as well as on the SCAA, was often more useful than detailed secondary accounts of an organization.

Throughout each educational biography and especially in Chapter 6, I have drawn from literature in all areas of intellectual, social, and economic history. At times I have also used studies in the sociology of knowledge—Peter L. Berger's and Thomas Luckmann's *The Social Construction of Reality: A Treatise in the Soci-*

ology of Knowledge (New York: Doubleday, 1966), for example, was crucial to my understanding of a consciousness like social feminism; studies in anthropology—the view of culture presented in Clifford Geertz's *The Interpretation of Cultures* (New York: Basic Books, 1973), as well as Geertz's argument concerning "thick description" have been fundamental to this entire book; and studies in other areas of the social sciences. Where they pertain directly, specific works are mentioned in the notes.

By way of conclusion, then, I would simply reiterate that an educational biography attempts to describe the experiences from which an individual's education was derived and to assess the effects of these experiences upon his or her life. Like other new approaches to the history of education, it joins insights drawn from the social sciences with those that come from a broad survey of American culture in order to add depth to our understanding of both history and education.

Notes

Introduction

1. My use of the term "generation" rests on Karl Mannheim's point that a generation is defined by common, formative experience. See Karl Mannheim, "The Problem of Generations," *Essays in the Sociology of Knowledge* (New York: Oxford University Press, 1952), pp. 276-320. Many of the articles in *Daedalus*, 107 (1978), which is entirely devoted to the concept of "Generations," especially Annie Kriegel's "Generational Difference: The History of an Idea," pp. 23-38, deal with the difficulty of defining a generation precisely. Jane Addams discusses "subjective necessity" in *Twenty Years at Hull House* (New York: Macmillan, 1910), chap. 6.

2. Maud Nathan, *Once upon a Time and Today* (New York: G. P. Putnam's Sons, 1933), p. 309. Nathan's precise phrase was "pioneer class."

3. Rheta Childe Dorr, *What Eight Million Women Want* (Boston: Small, Maynard, 1910).

4. The census figures are from Edith Abbot, *Women in Industry: A Study in American Economic History* (New York: D. Appleton, 1915), p. 379; the comment by the foreign traveler (Harriet Martineau) is from Lois W. Banner, *Women in Modern America: A Brief History* (New York: Harcourt Brace Jovanovich, 1974), p. 6, which provides an excellent, succinct treatment of women's occupations at this time.

5. In *The New Radicalism in America, 1889-1963: The Intellectual As a Social Type* (New York: Alfred A. Knopf, 1966), Christopher Lasch argued that the men and women he studied there "articulated experiences which, whether or not they were representative experiences in the sense of being widely shared by others, were nevertheless representative in another sense: they could only have happened at a particular place at a particular time" (p. xviii). My argument that

the education of these five women can illuminate the education of the progressive generation, while not identical to Lasch's, is similar, and it has been influenced by his.

6. I am using "culture" here and also in Chapter 6 to refer to historically created "organized systems of significant symbols" that give "form, order, point, and direction to our lives." See Clifford Geertz, "The Impact of the Concept of Culture on the Concept of Man," *The Interpretation of Cultures* (New York: Basic Books, 1973), pp. 46 and 52. I am distinguishing between "culture" and "social structure" as Herbert G. Gutman does in *Work, Culture, and Society in Industrializing America* (New York: Alfred A. Knopf, 1976), pp. 15-18.

7. The literature relevant to the historiographical considerations mentioned here is discussed in the Note on Method and Sources.

8. William James, *The Principles of Psychology*, 2 vols. (1890; reprint ed., New York: Dover Publications, 1950), I, 291-401. Gordon W. Allport, in *Becoming: Basic Considerations for a Psychology of Personality* (New Haven: Yale University Press, 1955), develops the notion of "the proprium," which aptly describes what I call "the self." To define education as broadly as I do should indicate that, as I see it, education cannot be clearly separated from other processes of growth, for example, socialization and development. My definition does allow for a theoretical difference. The learning of pervasive cultural behaviors that tends to be associated with socialization and the age-related personality adjustments that tend to be associated with development *can* occur with little or no recognition of a difference in the meaning assigned to the words *I*, *me*, or *mine*, whereas, according to my definition, education always affects the meaning of these terms. But this difference, which is difficult if not impossible to discern in empirical evidence, is relatively unimportant. My primary concern is with the more rational and more intentional aspects of human growth; in other words, with that part of individual "becoming" that is education, even if, at times, it is also socialization and/or development.

1. Grace Hoadley Dodge, 1856-1914

1. Carlos Martyn, *William E. Dodge: The Christian Merchant* (New York: Funk and Wagnalls, 1890); Richard Lowitt, *William E. Dodge: A Merchant Prince of the Nineteenth Century* (New York: Columbia University Press, 1954).

2. The belief that was so central to Dodge's life was clearly stated when she wrote: "Let us study ourselves and see if we have made all we can of the talents entrusted to us . . . for the glory of our Father." Grace H. Dodge to "Friends of the Club Girls' Council," June 1, 1908, Grace H. Dodge Collection, Archives of the National Board of the Young Women's Christian Association of the U.S.A., New York, New York.

3. Grace H. Dodge, "Record book, 1874-1913," Grace H. Dodge Papers, Special Collections, Teachers College Library, Columbia University, New York, New York.

4. The quote is from Grace H. Dodge to Mabel Cratty, March 11, 1912, Records Files Collection, Archives of the National Board of the Young Women's Christian Association of the U.S.A., New York, New York.

5. The statement is from the will of William E. Dodge, Jr., which is excerpted in Edwin Wildman, "What Grace Dodge Has Done for the Working Girl," *The World Today*, December 1910, p. 5. The article, in draft form, is in the Records Files Collection, YWCA.

6. The letters are quoted in Abbie Graham, *Grace H. Dodge: Merchant of Dreams* (New York: The Womans Press, 1926), pp. 28-31. Chap. 2 of the Graham book is the best source on Dodge's childhood.

7. The quoted phrase is from ibid., p. 321.

8. Ibid., p. 34-35.

9. On Melissa Phelps Dodge see Martyn, *William E. Dodge: The Christian Merchant*, and D. Stuart Dodge, ed., *Memorials of William E. Dodge* (New York: A. D. F. Randolph, 1887). My argument about Melissa Dodge is primarily based on conversations with Esther Katz, who is writing a biography of Grace Dodge as a Ph.D. dissertation at New York University which will be entitled, "Grace H. Dodge: Women and the Emerging Metropolis." Neither Esther Katz nor I have been able to find out much about Sarah Dodge or her affliction.

10. There is a brief biography of William Earl Dodge, Jr., in *The National Cyclopedia of American Biography*, XIII, 352.

11. Graham, *Grace H. Dodge*, pp. 39-45.

12. Annette K. Baxter, "Sarah Porter," *Notable American Women*, III, 88-89; William M. Sloane, "Sarah Porter: Her Unique Educational Work," in *When I Was At Farmington*, ed. Abby Farwell Ferry (Chicago: Ralph Fletcher Seymour, 1931), pp. 17-28.

13. Sloane, "Sarah Porter," pp. 21-22 and 25. Mabel Cratty, the executive secretary of the YWCA under Dodge, wrote a sketch that draws the similarities between Dodge and Porter, although she never mentions Miss Porter. Mabel Cratty, "The Fine Profession of Being a Laywoman," in *Mabel Cratty: Leader in the Art of Leadership*, ed. Margaret E. Burton (New York: The Womans Press, 1929), pp. 121-139.

14. Between 1874 and 1913 the best sources for Dodge's activities, in addition to Graham's *Grace H. Dodge*, are her "Record book" and her "A line a day" diary, 1899-1914, Dodge Papers, Teachers College. The conversation between Grace and William Dodge is quoted in Graham, *Grace H. Dodge*, p. 57.

15. The quote is from Robert D. Cross, "The Philanthropic Contribution of Louisa Lee Schuyler," *Social Service Review*, 35 (1961):293. See also Francis Greenwood Peabody, "Louisa and Georgina Schuyler," *Reminiscences of Present-Day Saints* (Boston: Houghton Mifflin, 1927), pp. 253-273, and George M. Fredrickson, *The Inner Civil War: Northern Intellectuals and the Crisis of the Union* (New York: Harper and Row, 1965), pp. 211-212.

16. Louisa Lee Schuyler, "Forty-Three Years Ago: The Early Days of the State Charities Aid Association, 1872-1915," Publication no. 135, State Charities Aid Association of New York, p. 10.

17. Dodge's letter of resignation is quoted in the Minutes, Board of Managers, State Charities Aid Association, February 19, 1915, Records Files Collection, YWCA.

18. Dodge's conception of Teachers College is clear, for example, in the letter she wrote to Mabel Cratty on March 11, 1912: "There is no college in the country

that has much greater influence, for the friends go out to influence so many schools and colleges, and among these older women there are so many superintendents, etc." Grace H. Dodge to Mabel Cratty, March 11, 1912, Records Files Collection, YWCA. My argument should not imply that Dodge was not interested in education; the point is rather that she was especially interested in the education of women.

19. Dodge's involvement with the working girls' clubs is described in Graham, *Grace H. Dodge*, pp. 65-72, 81-100, and Lillian W. Betts, "The Beginning of the Roadway," *The Association Monthly: In Memory of Grace H. Dodge*, 9 (1915):63-65. Sheila M. Rothman, *Woman's Proper Place: A History of Changing Ideals and Practices, 1870 to the Present* (New York: Basic Books, 1978), pp. 77-79 also deals with the clubs.

20. Grace H. Dodge, *A Bundle of Letters to Busy Girls on Practical Matters* (New York: Funk and Wagnalls, 1887), pp. vii-ix.

21. Ibid., p. 105.

22. Dodge used the phrase "working *with* the girls" repeatedly. This particular quotation, as well as the one about her "wages," is from Grace H. Dodge, "Introduction" to *Wage-Earning Women*, by Annie Marion MacLean (New York: Macmillan, 1910), p. xi. Vida Scudder's comment is given in Graham, *Grace H. Dodge*, p. 114.

23. Grace H. Dodge, "A Letter to Association Girls," *Association Monthly*, n.d., Records Files Collection, YWCA.

24. Grace H. Dodge, "Paper Presented at the Labor Conference, Chicago," n.d., in "Personal work, papers and addresses, 1889-1902," Dodge Papers, Teachers College, describes the settlement movement connection; the speech to the YWCA is quoted in Graham, *Grace H. Dodge*, pp. 266-267.

25. The quote is from Grace H. Dodge, *A Brief Sketch of the Early History of Teachers College* (New York: Maynard, Merrill, 1899), p. 3. The history of Teachers College is also described in James Earl Russell, *Founding Teachers College: Reminiscences of the Dean Emeritus* (New York: Bureau of Publications, Teachers College, 1937); Richard F. W. Whittemore, *Nicholas Murray Butler and Public Education, 1862-1911* (New York: Teachers College Press, 1970); Lawrence A. Cremin et al., *A History of Teachers College, Columbia University* (New York: Columbia University Press, 1954). See also Robert J. Fridlington, "Emily Huntington," *Notable American Women*, II, 239-240, and Graham, *Grace H. Dodge*, pp. 159-204.

26. Dodge's work for the Board of Education is described in Graham, *Grace H. Dodge*, pp. 139-155, and Wildman, "What Grace Dodge Has Done for the Working Girl." The annual reports of the Board of Education for that time are not very useful in studying Dodge's education.

27. Dodge, *Brief Sketch*, pp. 21-22.

28. Dodge's comment on the honorary degree is from Graham, *Grace H. Dodge*, p. 227.

29. Nicholas Murray Butler, *Across the Busy Years*, 2 vols. (New York: Charles Scribner's Sons, 1939), I, 176-188; Nicholas Murray Butler, "Beginnings of Teachers College," *Teachers College Record*, 46 (1944):149-151; Dodge, *Brief Sketch*, pp. 3 and 27.

30. Russell, *Founding Teachers College*, pp. 42, 62-64, 73-80.

31. Dodge's assessment of what she learned in raising funds for Teachers College is described in Grace H. Dodge to Miss Geary, September 24, 1913, Records Files Collection, YWCA.

32. Marion O. Robinson, *Eight Women of the YWCA* (New York: National Board of the Young Women's Christian Association of the U.S.A., 1966), Mary S. Sims, *The Natural History of a Social Institution: The YWCA* (New York: The Womans Press, 1936), and Grace Wilson, *The Religious and Educational Philosophy of the Y.W.C.A.*, Teachers College Contributions to Education, no. 554 (New York: Bureau of Publications, Teachers College, 1933) give background on the YWCA. The quote is from Elizabeth Hamilton, "A Memory of Grace Dodge," 3 pg. ms., Dodge Collection, YWCA. See also Graham, *Grace H. Dodge*, pp. 231-286, and "A Synopsis of the Proceedings of the Conference Called at the Request of the International Board and the American Committee" and Minutes, National Board of the YWCA, 1906-1914, Records Files Collection, YWCA; Misc. Correspondence, 1907-1914, Dodge Collection, YWCA.

33. Grace H. Dodge to "Friends in the Associations Affiliated with 'The American Committee,'—with 'The International Board,' " September 15, 1905, Records Files Collection, YWCA.

34. I do not mean to imply that Dodge saw the YWCA as an alternative or competitor to Teachers College. She did not. She seems to have believed that the YWCA should supplement the education of women who could find opportunities for formal schooling while also reaching out to women who could not find such schooling.

35. Dodge, "Introduction," *Wage-Earning Women*, p. xi; Grace H. Dodge, "Practical Talks with Girls' Clubs," unpaged draft for the *Association Monthly*, September 1907, Records Files Collections, YWCA.

2. Maud Nathan, 1862-1946

1. Dodge's attitude is clear in Grace H. Dodge to Maud Nathan, n.d., Maud Nathan Scrapbooks, vol. 2, Maud Nathan Papers, Schlesinger Library, Radcliffe College, Cambridge, Massachusetts. Maud Nathan, *Once upon a Time and Today* (New York: G. P. Putnam's Sons, 1933).

2. Nathan, *Once upon a Time and Today*, pp. 19-50; Annie Nathan Meyer, *It's Been Fun* (New York: Henry Schuman, 1951), pp. 3-128.

3. Ibid.

4. The quote is from Nathan, *Once upon a Time and Today*, p. 20; Nathan's ancestors are described on pp. 19-24, 315-317.

5. Ibid., pp. 36-38.

6. Ibid., pp. 50 and 313.

7. Ibid., pp. 35 and 38.

8. Ibid., pp. 25, 22, 45.

9. Meyer, *It's Been Fun*, p. 120. When they became adults, the rivalry between Maud and Annie spilled over into the public arena (see Annie Nathan Meyer, "Letter to the Editor," *The New York Times*, February 21, 1907, and a reply by Mrs. Carrie Chapman Catt, February 22, 1907, clippings, Scrapbooks, vol. 3, Nathan Papers). Many of their publicly announced views contained only

thinly disguised efforts to undermine the other's significance. Annie made it clear that she was highly dismayed by "the tendency of the American woman to rush into the sensational and so-called reform movements" (Dora Askowith, *Three Outstanding Women: Mary Fels, Rebekah Kohut, Annie Nathan Meyer* [New York: Bloch Publishing Co., 1941], p. 35); and in *Once upon a Time and Today*, Maud hardly mentions Annie except to point out how inconsistent it was for her to be such a "progressive" woman and an antisuffragist (p. 178). But if the two sisters helped to define each other through opposition, they were also, at least later in life, able to be friends. The Annie Nathan Meyer Papers, American Jewish Archives, Hebrew Union College, Cincinnati, include many chatty and friendly letters from Maud, most of which were written after her husband's death in 1918.

10. Nathan, *Once upon a Time and Today*, pp. 30-35.

11. Ibid., pp. 103 and 25.

12. Style, as I mean it, is the characteristic manner in which one acts out one's tastes and attitudes toward one's self and the people and objects of one's world. Thus, style expresses an existing condition: one's self-perceptions relative to a particular situation or across a number of situations. And that expression not only reflects previous experience, it also shapes subsequent experience.

13. Ibid., pp. 25, 311, 49.

14. Ibid., pp. 40-41.

15. Ibid., pp. 44-47.

16. Ibid., pp. 39, 304-313.

17. Ibid., pp. 51-52.

18. Lillian D. Wald, "Speech to the Twenty-fifth Anniversary Dinner of the Consumers' League, November 18, 1915," *Proceedings*, p. 15; Robert Erskine Ely to Mr. and Mrs. Frederick Nathan, May 13, 1914, Scrapbooks, vol. 6.

19. "His Home's Happy Even Though Wife Is after the Vote," *The Cleveland News*, May 31, 1912, clipping, Scrapbooks, vol. 5; also "A Transformation," unidentified poem, Scrapbooks, vol. 6.

20. Nathan, *Once upon a Time and Today*, pp. 55-59, 53, 50.

21. Ibid., pp. 60-78.

22. Ibid., pp. 79-96; "The Fads and Ambitions of the People Who Are Enjoying Life in Saratoga," unidentified clipping, Scrapbooks, vol. 1; Jane Addams, *Twenty Years at Hull House* (New York: Macmillan, 1910), chap. 4.

23. Nathan, *Once upon a Time and Today*, pp. 100-101.

24. Ibid., pp. 101-106.

25. The Nathans had difficulty having children, and the one child they did have, Annette Florance Nathan, who was born on January 26, 1886, lived only nine years. Thus, even though Maud became active in the Consumers' League while Annette was still alive, the tragedy of her daughter's brief life would certainly seem to have influenced her increasing interest in social reform. As Nathan explained in *Once upon a Time and Today*, however, it was Lowell who made her realize that she had an important choice to make after Annette's death: "whether I was to allow my sorrow to spoil my life through selfish indulgence of grief, or enrich it through service to others" (p. 98). Even in relation to this crucial event, therefore, it was Lowell who guided Nathan's education at this time.

26. Robert H. Bremner, "Josephine Shaw Lowell," *Notable American Wo-*

men, II, 437-439; William Rhinelander Stewart, *The Philanthropic Contribution of Josephine Shaw Lowell* (New York: Macmillan, 1911).

27. Nathan, *Once upon a Time and Today*, p. 102.

28. Stewart, *Josephine Shaw Lowell*, p. 142; Maud Nathan, *The Story of an Epoch-Making Movement* (Garden City, N.Y.: Doubleday, Page, 1926), p. 19. The hyperbolic title of Nathan's history of the Consumers' League provides further evidence of her desire to do everything in an arresting fashion.

29. Nathan, *The Story of an Epoch-Making Movement*, chap. 2; Louis L. Athey, "The Consumers' Leagues and Social Reform, 1890-1923" (Ph.D. dissertation, University of Delaware, 1965), pp. 8-9.

30. Nathan, *The Story of an Epoch-Making Movement*, p. 20; Alexander M. Dushkin, *Jewish Education in New York* City (New York: Bureau of Jewish Education, 1918), p. 57.

31. Nathan, *The Story of an Epoch-Making Movement*, pp. 33-59; Athey, "Consumers' Leagues and Social Reform," pp. 8-32; Maud Nathan, "Speech to the Twenty-fifth Anniversary Dinner of the Consumers' League, November 18, 1915," *Proceedings*, p. 27; Nathan, *Once upon a Time and Today*, p. 98.

32. Athey, "Consumers' Leagues and Social Reform," p. 18; Nathan, *The Story of an Epoch-Making Movement*, p. 88.

33. *Pittsburgh Post*, October 2, 1900, clipping, Scrapbooks, vol. 2.

34. "The Heart of Judaism," Maud Nathan's speech to the New York Section of the National Council of Jewish Women, December 24, 1896, transcribed in *The American Hebrew*, clipping, Scrapbooks, vol. 1.

35. "For Preventive Charity," unidentified clipping, Scrapbooks, vol. 2; "The Ethics [?] of Money Spending," unidentified clipping, Scrapbooks, vol. 2.

36. "The key . . ." quote is also from "The Ethics [?] of Money Spending," unidentified clipping, Scrapbooks, vol. 2.

37. Nathan, *Once upon a Time and Today*, p. 176, deals with Mary Putnam Jacobi, but there are references to many other women and what they did for her throughout the book.

38. Ibid., p. 175; "Mrs. Nathan at Albany," *Evening Post*, February 25, 1915, clipping, Scrapbooks, vol. 6.

39. Nathan, *Once upon a Time and Today*, pp. 175-202; Maud Nathan, "Why I Believe in Votes for Women," *The New York Herald*, January 16, 1913, clipping, Scrapbooks, vol. 5.

40. Stephen Birmingham claims Maud's listing in *Who's Who* was longer than that of any other woman. Stephen Birmingham, *The Grandees: The Story of America's Sephardic Elite* (New York: Harper and Row, 1971), p. 260.

41. Nathan, *Once upon a Time and Today*, p. 260.

42. Nathan, *Once upon a Time and Today*, pp. 304-313.

3. Lillian D. Wald, 1867-1940

1. Lillian D. Wald, *The House on Henry Street* (New York: Henry Holt, 1915), p. 17. See also R. L. Duffus, *Lillian Wald: Neighbor and Crusader* (New York: Macmillan, 1938), pp. v-ix.

2. Duffus, *Lillian Wald*, pp. 1-15.

3. Ibid.

4. Ibid.

5. Ibid.

6. Ibid., p. 1. Allan Edward Reznick, "Lillian D. Wald: The Years at Henry Street" (Ph.D. dissertation, University of Wisconsin, 1973), describes Rochester at this time in some detail. He also discusses the changes within Judaism reflected in the Pittsburgh Platform. I have found no evidence to support his conclusion that Wald was influenced by either conditions in Rochester or developments within Judaism, except insofar as her lack of adherence to traditional Jewish custom and ritual mirrored her family's cultural location within that group of German Jews who were becoming increasingly integrated into "mainstream" American life (See Stuart E. Rosenberg, *The Jewish Community in Rochester, 1843-1925* [New York: Columbia University Press, 1954], especially Part I and Part III). Jill K. Conway, "The First Generation of American Women Graduates" (Ph.D. dissertation, Harvard University, 1969), also argues that Judaism was central to Wald's education and a significant support for her movement outside traditional female roles. And Doris Daniels, "Lillian D. Wald: The Progressive Woman and Feminism" (Ph.D. dissertation, City University of New York, 1976), makes a similar argument. Again, I have found nothing to support this argument, and I do not think that because Wald was Jewish one should assume that Judaism (as a religion) was important to her, especially in terms of educative influence.

7. Duffus, *Lillian Wald*, pp. 1-15.

8. Daniels, "Lillian D. Wald: The Progressive Woman and Feminism," p. 23.

9. Duffus, *Lillian Wald*, p. 13.

10. The prospectus is quoted in Reznick, "Lillian D. Wald: The Years at Henry Street," p. 14, and the curriculum is described on pp. 14-15.

11. Duffus, *Lillian Wald*, pp. 16-17.

12. Lillian Wald to the *New York American*, June 20, 1923, Lillian Wald Papers, Manuscript and Archives Division, The New York Public Library, Astor, Lenox, and Tilden Foundation, as quoted in Daniels, "The Progressive Woman and Feminism," p. 29.

13. Daniels, "Lillian D. Wald: The Progressive Woman and Feminism," p. 25.

14. Ibid., pp. 30-31; Reznick, "Lillian D. Wald: The Years at Henry Street," p. 43.

15. The Society of the New York Hospital, *The School of Nursing of the New York Hospital: Fiftieth Anniversary, 1877-1927* (New York, 1927), p. 9, as quoted in Daniels, "Lillian D. Wald: The Progressive Woman and Feminism," p. 42.

16. Lillian D. Wald, "Nurses' Settlement," *The American Journal of Nursing*, 1 (1901): 39. The Henry Street Settlement was called the Nurses' Settlement during its first years.

17. The quote is from *The School of Nursing of the New York Hospital*, p. 9, as given in Daniels, "Lillian D. Wald: The Progressive Woman and Feminism," p. 42. Chap. 2 of Daniels's dissertation discusses the relationship between nursing and feminism.

18. Nightingale's and Craven's books are quoted and discussed in Reznick,

"Lillian D. Wald: The Years at Henry Street," pp. 59-65.

19. Lillian D. Wald, "The Treatment of Families in Which There Is Sickness," *The American Journal of Nursing*, 4 (1904):427-431; "Best Help to the Immigrant Through the Nurse," *The American Journal of Nursing*, 8 (1908): 464-467; "District Nursing," 25 pg. ms., Lillian D. Wald Papers, Rare Book and Manuscript Library, Columbia University, New York City.

20. Wald, *The House on Henry Street*, p. 26.

21. Duffus, *Lillian Wald*, pp. 20-22.

22. Wald, *The House on Henry Street*, p. 1; Duffus, *Lillian Wald*, pp. 22-24.

23. Wald, *The House on Henry Street*, p. 1; Duffus, *Lillian Wald*, pp. 32-35. Wald's experience was remarkably like Jane Addams's experience at the bull fight she attended during her postcollege, pre-Hull House European tour (see Jane Addams, *Twenty Years at Hull House* [New York: Macmillan, 1910] chap. 4). Both were really conversion experiences, and such experiences, however brief, can be profoundly educative. For, as William James so aptly put it, "at such times there is a voice inside which speaks and says: '*This* is the real me!' " (quoted in Erik H. Erikson, *Identity: Youth and Crisis* [New York: W. W. Norton, 1968], p. 19). It is interesting to note, therefore, because it reflects on the characteristics of the progressive generation mentioned in the Introduction (and also Chapter 6), that exposure to human suffering seems to have been a common stimulus for such experiences among men and women of Addams's and Wald's generation, whereas religious revivals were a more common stimulus in an earlier generation. The secularized religious impulse in progressive social reform that so many historians have commented upon reflected an important change in American culture that included a fundamental change in education, particularly in the role and significance of the church as educator. And Wald's and Addams's conversion experiences show the effects of this in terms of individual experience.

24. Wald, *The House on Henry Street*, pp. 8-9.

25. Ibid., p. 220-228.

26. Lillian D. Wald, "The Nurses' Settlement in New York," *The American Journal of Nursing*, 2 (1902):573, is one of the many places where she used the phrase "the settlement point of view."

27. Lillian D. Wald, "Recollection," in *Charles B. Stover, 1861-1929* (New York: The International Press, 1938), p. 132; Wald, *The House on Henry Street*, p. 10.

28. Roy Lubove, "Jane Robbins," *Notable American Women*, III, 172-174; the quote is from Duffus, *Lillian Wald*, pp. 37-38. Henry Street's unique features are clear in Robert A. Woods and Alfred J. Kennedy, eds., *Handbook of Settlements* (New York: Charities Publication Committee, 1911), and Allen F. Davis, *Spearheads for Reform: The Social Settlements and the Progressive Movement* (New York: Oxford University Press, 1967); the College Settlement is described in John P. Rousmanière, "Cultural Hybrid in the Slums: The College Woman and the Settlement House, 1889-1894," *American Quarterly*, 22 (1970):45-66.

29. Reznick, "Lillian D. Wald: The Years at Henry Street," pp. 97-107.

30. Duffus, *Lillian Wald*, p. 46; Wald, *The House on Henry Street*, pp. 17-25; the quote is from Lillian Wald to Mr. Schiff and Mrs. Loeb, November 28, 1893, Wald Papers, New York Public Library.

31. Wald, *The House on Henry Street*, pp. 179-181.

32. Ibid., p. 14.

33. Wald's speech is given in William Rhinelander Stewart, *The Philanthropic Work of Josephine Shaw Lowell* (New York: Macmillan, 1911), p. 363; Jacob Riis, "Lillian D. Wald," *The Survey*, 30 (1913):551. Gregory Weinstein's autobiography, *The Ardent Eighties: Reminiscences of an Interesting Decade* (New York: The International Press, 1928), is one of the best contemporary descriptions of the Lower East Side in the 1880s and 1890s. Part II of the book is composed of portraits of the people and organizations that made up that world. Of the "Idealists and Realists" he describes, only two women are given full chapters: Lowell and Wald. And the similarities Jacob Riis draws are evident there as well. Conway, "The First Generation of American Women Graduates," p. 99, also points out Lowell's importance to Wald.

34. Jacob Schiff's character and career are described in *Jacob Schiff: His Life and Letters*, ed. Cyrus Adler, 2 vols. (Garden City, N.Y.: Doubleday, Doran, 1928). His importance to Wald at this time is clear in Wald, "The Nurses' Settlement in New York," p. 570.

35. Reznick, "Lillian D. Wald: The Years at Henry Street," pp. 84-87, 104-107; Daniels, "Lillian D. Wald: The Progressive Woman and Feminism," pp. 74-80.

36. Reznick, "Lillian D. Wald: The Years at Henry Street," chap. 4, discusses "The Ladies of Henry Street," as does Daniels, "Lillian D. Wald: The Progressive Woman and Feminism," chap. 2, "The Nursing Sisters," and chap. 5, "A Woman's World." In the early years, all residents at Henry Street were women.

37. Daniels, "Lillian D. Wald: The Progressive Woman and Feminism," pp. 44-47; Reznick, "Lillian D. Wald: The Years at Henry Street," pp. 112-116; Mary M. Roberts, "Lavinia Lloyd Dock—Nurse, Feminist, Internationalist," *The American Journal of Nursing*, 56 (1956):176-179.

38. Lavinia Dock to Lillian Wald, December 1903, December 26, 1903, Wald Papers, Columbia; Daniels, "Lillian D. Wald: The Progressive Woman and Feminism." Blanche Wiesen Cook deals at length with the friendship between Wald and Dock in "Female Support Networks and Political Activism: Lillian Wald, Crystal Eastman, Emma Goldman," *Chrysalis*, 3 (1977):43-61. One of Cook's major points is that historians have traditionally denied lesbianism and have therefore "tended to ignore the crucial role played by the networks of love and support that have been the very sources of strength that enabled political women to function." Although I agree with the argument that until recently historians have overlooked and misunderstood the importance of female support networks, I do not find it useful to apply the term lesbian to Wald or to other women of her generation who had close, affectionate, and enduring same-sex friendships, or even to define the term as broadly as Cook does (lesbians, according to Cook are "women who love women, who choose women to nurture and support and to create a living environment in which to work creatively and independently"). However that may be, the issue here is Wald's education, which, regardless of sexual relationships, was vitally influenced by Dock and other women of the Henry Street "family."

39. Reznick, "Lillian D. Wald," chap. 4; Cook, "Female Support Networks

and Political Activism: Lillian Wald, Crystal Eastman, Emma Goldman.''

40. Alice Lewisohn Crowley, *The Neighborhood Playhouse: Leaves from a Theatre Scrapbook* (New York: Theatre Arts Books, 1959), pp. 4-7.

41. Wald described the Lewisohns' contribution to the settlement in *Windows on Henry Street* (New York: Little Brown, 1934), which is dedicated to the two sisters and to Rita Wallach Morgenthau; their contribution to her education is evident throughout their correspondence, much of which can be found in the Wald Papers, Columbia.

42. Lavinia Dock wrote a detailed account of life at Henry Street in 1898, parts of which are quoted in Duffus, *Lillian Wald*, pp. 63-67; the quote is from Wald, *The House on Henry Street*, p. 8.

43. Jane Addams to Alice, February 23, 1893, Ellen Starr Brinton Collection, Swarthmore College Peace Collection, as quoted in Allen F. Davis, *American Heroine: The Life and Legend of Jane Addams* (New York: Oxford University Press, 1975), p. 94; Lillian Wald to Jane Addams, November 15, 1898, Jane Addams Papers, Swarthmore College Peace Collection, as quoted in Reznick, ''Lillian D. Wald: The Years at Henry Street,'' p. 146; Lillian Wald to Jane Addams, October 1, 1917, Wald Papers, New York Public Library.

44. Reznick, ''Lillian D. Wald: The Years at Henry Street,'' pp. 168-189; Daniels, ''Lillian D. Wald: The Progressive Woman and Feminism,'' pp. 80-81.

45. The diagram is in the ''Report of the Henry Street Settlement, 1893-1913,'' between pp. 18 and 19.

46. The quote is from Duffus, *Lillian Wald*, p. 160.

47. Lillian Wald to Ysabella Waters, August 14, 1917, Wald Papers, New York Public Library.

48. Wald, *Windows on Henry Street*, pp. 5 and 11.

49. Lillian Wald to Charles C. Cooper, January 23, 1913, Wald Papers, New York Public Library.

50. Conway, ''The First Generation of American Women Graduates,'' pp. 490-491, makes the point that Jane Addams, unlike Lillian Wald, did not age well. As old women, the two used to sit together, Wald talking excitedly about FDR, the New Deal, and the Soviet Five-Year Plans, while Addams remained silent. According to Conway, the ''efficient society'' could fit within Wald's more pragmatic approach, but could not be reconciled within Addams's ''social religion.''

4. Leonora O'Reilly, 1870-1927

1. Biographical notes written by Mary [Ryshpan] Cohen for Mary Drier, Leonora O'Reilly Papers, Schlesinger Library, Radcliffe College, Cambridge, Massachusetts.

2. Biographical notes by Mary E. Drier, O'Reilly Papers.

3. Alice Henry, ''Mrs. Winifred O'Reilly: A Veteran Worker,'' *Life and Labor*, 1 (1911):132-136.

4. Ibid.

5. Ibid.

6. Ibid.

7. It is difficult to find out much about Uncle B partly because O'Reilly pur-

posefully guarded his privacy. As she once explained, Uncle B and a number of other people who early became her teachers were "so true to the ideal of the labor movement that a few among us who know them best regard their desire to be unknown as sacred" (Leonora O'Reilly to Sarah Ollesheimer, June 1902, O'Reilly Papers). Uncle B's admonitions concerning grammar and the like are sprinkled throughout his letters; the short quotes are from Uncle B to Leonora O'Reilly, March 3, 1886; the long quote is from Uncle B to Leonora O'Reilly, December 1, 1886, O'Reilly Papers.

8. Uncle D's influence on O'Reilly's thought is especially clear in vols. 25-27 of her diary, which contain notes on her philosophy of labor and quotes from Victor Drury. The diary is in the O'Reilly Papers.

9. Gregory Weinstein, *The Ardent Eighties: Reminiscences of an Interesting Decade* (New York: International Press, 1928), pp. 165-174; Samuel Gompers, *My Life in Labor*, 2 vols. (New York: E. P. Dutton, 1925), II, 140-141; the topics and books discussed by the circle are noted throughout O'Reilly's diary, 25 vols., O'Reilly Papers.

10. Weinstein, *The Ardent Eighties*, p. 168; Leonora O'Reilly to Winifred O'Reilly, June 1913, O'Reilly Papers.

11. Morris R. Cohen, *A Dreamer's Journey* (Glencoe, Ill.: Free Press, 1949), esp. pp. 92-96, 280-281. The religious background of O'Reilly's family is not clear; her diary indicates that she did not go to church and did not subscribe to any conventional religious creed. In a way, however, O'Reilly was a deeply religious person, for whom a philosophy of labor served a function similar to the one religious doctrines can serve. And her attitudes in this regard, particularly the religious (sacred) value she placed on her secular concerns, was probably influenced by her friends on the Lower East Side.

12. The Working Women's Society is described in Nancy Schrom Dye, "The Women's Trade Union League of New York, 1903-1920" (Ph.D. dissertation, University of Wisconsin, 1974), pp. 41-44. Barbara Mayer Wertheimer, *We Were There: The Story of Working Women in America* (New York: Pantheon, 1977) discusses both the Knights of Labor, pp. 180-191, and the Working Women's Society, pp. 240 and 276. A good deal of O'Reilly's correspondence with Edward King deals with the Working Women's Society, and the group's aims are stated in Louise Perkins to Leonora O'Reilly, August 14, 1912, O'Reilly Papers.

13. Perkins probably would have agreed with Lowell that the members of the Working Women's Society had "had a practical education in life . . . but of course . . . need a great deal of advice." See William Rhinelander Stewart, *The Philanthropic Work of Josephine Shaw Lowell* (New York: Macmillan, 1911), p. 136. The short quotes are from Louise Perkins to Leonora O'Reilly, January 2, 1896, O'Reilly Papers.

14. The Perkins-O'Reilly correspondence collected in the O'Reilly Papers is voluminous. It spans the years from approximately 1886 to 1927. The description above is gleaned from this correspondence. Perkins does not appear in any of the standard biographical references.

15. The quote about "the rich" is from Leonora O'Reilly, "The Story of the Little Brown House," unidentified ms., O'Reilly Papers.

16. O'Reilly diary, August 3, 1897.

17. Louise Perkins to Leonora O'Reilly, July 29, 1894, and April 2, 1896; O'Reilly diary, August 3, 1897, O'Reilly Papers.

18. Louise Perkins to Leonora O'Reilly, September 24, 1894, O'Reilly Papers; J. K. Paulding, "His Life and Personality," in *Charles B. Stover, 1861-1929* (New York: International Press, 1938), p. 26, describes the Social Reform Club.

19. The quotes are from O'Reilly dairy, n.d. [1896?], O'Reilly Papers. Father James O. S. Huntington, the Christian socialist reformer, met O'Reilly during this period and sent her to Hadley, Massachusetts, several times for vacations with his family. Characteristically, she enjoyed herself, but wrote to her mother that the Huntingtons' two "helpers" must see her as " 'A dirty O'Neal' " (Leonora O'Reilly to Winifred O'Reilly, July 19, 1897, O'Reilly Papers); O'Reilly's relationship with Father Huntington is described in Vida D. Sudder, *Father Huntington* (New York: E. P. Dutton, 1940), pp. 120-121.

20. The quote is from Perkins to Lillian Wald, August 16, 1897; the salary is discussed in Louise Perkins to Leonora O'Reilly, May 22 [1897?], December 21, 1898, January 18, 1899, August 2, 1899, and December 7, 1920, O'Reilly Papers.

21. The best description of the workshop was written by one of O'Reilly's students: Rose Cohen, *Out of the Shadow* (New York: George H. Doran, 1918); it is also described in R. L. Duffus, *Lillian Wald: Neighbor and Crusader* (New York: Macmillan, 1938), pp. 67-68.

22. O'Reilly wrote frequently of the Henry Street "family" in vols. 3-7 of her diary, O'Reilly Papers.

23. On Pratt see esp. O'Reilly diary, June 1, 1900, June 21, 1900, September 19, 1900; the long quote is from O'Reilly diary, April 20, 1900; a copy of the thesis is also in the O'Reilly Papers.

24. There is a copy of the first prospectus in the O'Reilly Papers. See also Leonora O'Reilly, "Notes for letter to Mrs. O. [llesheimer]," n.d.; Virginia Potter to Leonora O'Reilly, October 9, 1902; Sarah Ollesheimer to Leonora O'Reilly, June 1, 1902; all in the O'Reilly Papers. The school is described in various clippings from *The Outlook, Charities and Commons*, and similar periodicals, also in the O'Reilly Papers.

25. Leonora O'Reilly to Virginia Potter, n.d. [1902?]; O'Reilly's views on how the school should be run are clear in O'Reilly diary, February 1, 1905, and "Notes for letter to Mrs. O.," n.d., O'Reilly Papers. See also Robert J. Fridlington, "Mary Raphael Schenck Woolman," *Notable American Women*, III, 663-665.

26. Duffus, *Lillian Wald*, p. 67; O'Reilly's increasing disenchantment is clear in correspondence with Mary Woolman: Leonora O'Reilly to Mary Woolman, May 1905, and Mary Woolman to Leonora O'Reilly, May 26, 1905, O'Reilly Papers. The Manhattan Trade School for Girls was incorporated into the New York City public school system in 1910. Since O'Reilly's wish to resign was evident well before her actual resignation in 1909, knowledge of the pending merger was probably unimportant in her decision.

27. The quote is from Dye, "The Women's Trade Union League of New York," p. 65. The WTUL has a significant organizational history that has received a good deal of recent attention. In addition to the Dye study see Allen F. Davis, "The Women's Trade Union League: Origins and Organization," *Labor*

History, 5 (1964):3-17; Jack Meyer Stuart, "William English Walling: A Study of Politics and Ideas (Ph.D. dissertation, Columbia University, 1968); Eleanor Flexner and Janet Wilson James, "Mary Keeney O'Sullivan," *Notable American Women*, II, 655-656; Robin Miller-Jacoby, "The Women's Trade Union League and American Feminism," *Feminist Studies*, 3 (1975):126-140, and Wertheimer, *We Were There*, chap. 15.

28. The quotes are from Dye, "The Women's Trade Union League of New York," pp. 90, 110, 111; chaps. 2 and 3 of the Dye study are relevant in their entirety. Between 1909 and 1913, when there were large general strikes in the garment industry, which the WTUL supported, an increasing number of workers did join unions. How much of the credit for this should be given to the WTUL, however, rather than to the militance created by the strikes themselves, is difficult to know.

29. On the importance of industrial education, see O'Reilly diary, December 7, 1904, O'Reilly Papers; the problems the league encountered and its strategy are clear in Minutes, Executive Board, Women's Trade Union League of New York, 1905-1909, Women's Trade Union League of New York Papers, State Department of Labor Research Library, New York City.

30. Leonora O'Reilly to Gertrude Barnum, December 29, 1905, O'Reilly Papers; Minutes, Executive Board, Women's Trade Union League of New York, July 25, 1906, Women's Trade Union League of New York Papers. William L. O'Neill, *Women at Work* (Chicago: Quadrangle Books, 1972), pp. 3-303, is a reprint of *The Long Day*.

31. Leonora O'Reilly to Gertrude Barnum, December 29, 1905, and Gertrude Barnum to Leonora O'Reilly, February 13, 1906, O'Reilly Papers.

32. Louise Perkins to Leonora O'Reilly, June 14, 1906, O'Reilly Papers.

33. The Driers' background and work is described in Mary E. Drier, *Margaret Drier Robins: Her Life, Letters and Work* (New York: Island Press Cooperative, 1950).

34. Leonora O'Reilly to Winifred O'Reilly, n.d. [c. 1900], O'Reilly Papers.

35. Mary Drier to Winifred O'Reilly, January 16, 1908, O'Reilly Papers.

36. Louise Perkins to Leonora O'Reilly, September 13, 1895, March 18, 1896, June 14, 1906; Mary Drier to Winifred O'Reilly, January 16, 1908; Leonora O'Reilly to Winifred O'Reilly, n.d. [c. 1900]; all in O'Reilly Papers.

37. Leonora O'Reilly to Mary Drier, August 31, 1915, and Mary Drier to Leonora O'Reilly, September 6, 1915, O'Reilly Papers. Throughout its history, the WTUL had an uneasy alliance with the AFL and its affiliates. See Dye, "The Women's Trade Union League of New York," chap. 5, and Wertheimer, *We Were There*, pp. 284-289.

38. The quote is from Gretchen [Margaret Drier Robins?] to Leonora O'Reilly, July 13, 1919, but all of this can be seen throughout the correspondence between O'Reilly and other league members that has been collected in the O'Reilly Papers. Over the years the WTUL reordered its priorities in much the same way O'Reilly did. As Dye explains in the introduction to her study, the WTUL changed from "a self-defined labor organization that downplayed women's special concerns in the work force into a women's organization that emphasized specifically feminist issues and demands, namely, woman suffrage and protective

labor legislation" ("The Women's Trade Union League of New York," p. 2).

39. O'Reilly noted the problems she had with male trade unionists throughout her diary; see also Leonora O'Reilly, notes for a speech on "Loyalty among Women Workers," n.d., O'Reilly Papers. O'Reilly had experienced the indifference of male trade unionists before the league was founded, especially in relation to her efforts to organize a women's shirtwaist local within the United Garment Workers (United Garment Workers' Local 16), see O'Reilly diary, vol. 2, O'Reilly Papers.

40. O'Reilly diary, n.d. (follows May 11, 1909, entry), April 26, 1911, September 5, 1911, O'Reilly Papers.

41. The quotes are from O'Reilly diary, February 8, 1911, May 30, 1911, June, 19, 1911, and from Leonora O'Reilly, "Report on Peace Conference—International Congress of Women," typed draft, p. 15, O'Reilly Papers.

42. Aileen S. Kraditor, *The Ideas of the Woman Suffrage Movement, 1890-1920* (New York: Columbia University Press, 1965), chap. 6, explains the attitude of working women to suffragists and vice versa. The New York City Wage Earners' Suffrage League is described in Misc. Correspondence, Leonora O'Reilly to Mary Beard, 1912, O'Reilly Papers; *Life and Labor*, 2 (1912):318; Wertheimer, *We Were There*, p. 282.

43. The quotes are from Leonora O'Reilly, "Labor Movement and Ballot," typed ms., n.d., and Leonora O'Reilly, "Notes from trip to the Hague, May 11, 1915." See also O'Reilly diary, September 15, 1911, O'Reilly Papers.

44. O'Reilly diary, May 26, 1909, O'Reilly Papers.

5. Rose Schneiderman, 1882-1972

1. Alex Rose to Rose Schneiderman, March 3, 1937, Rose Schneiderman Papers, Tamiment Library, New York University, New York City.

2. Rose Schneiderman with Lucy Goldthwaite, *All for One* (New York: Paul S. Eriksson, 1967), pp. 11-30. In *Current Biography*, 1946, Rose Schneiderman's parents' names are given as Adolph Samuel and Dora (Rothman) Schneiderman.

3. Rose Schneiderman, "A Cap Maker's Story," *The Independent*, 58 (1905):935-938. The quote is on p. 936.

4. The quotes are from Schneiderman, *All for One*, pp. 11-12, 15, 46, and 53.

5. Ibid., p. 16.

6. Ibid., pp. 83, 28-29.

7. Ibid., pp. 31-32.

8. Ibid.

9. Ibid., pp. 32, 30-31, 13, 17, 26. I do not mean to imply that Schneiderman literally "forgot" these aspects of her childhood, but rather that she "forgot" them in the sense of choosing not to mention them or to think of them, in the sense of purposefully putting them out of her mind. And the shame she initially seems to have felt about her family's poverty (see pp. 124-125) and later slowly outgrew probably also influenced her changing memories.

10. Ibid., pp. 35-43; the quote is from p. 34.

11. Ibid., pp. 38-40.

12. Ibid., pp. 45 and 43.

13. Ibid., pp. 43-44.

14. Charlie Schneiderman to Rose Schneiderman, July 24, 1912, Schneiderman Papers. See also Schneiderman, "A Cap Maker's Story," p. 936, and *All for One*, pp. 38, 54, 226.

15. Ibid., pp. 46-47, 41, 29, 50.

16. Schneiderman, "A Cap Maker's Story," p. 936.

17. Schneiderman, *All for One*, pp. 48-50.

18. Ibid., pp. 41-42, 53.

19. Ibid., p. 42.

20. Ibid., pp. 67-68.

21. Ibid., pp. 54-55, 76. Except for the remark about her mother's fears concerning conversion, Schneiderman made few references to Judaism in *All for One*. Her family did celebrate religious holidays and their values and aspirations did reflect their cultural tradition, but Rose does not seem to have been a very religious person.

22. Ibid., pp. 77-78.

23. Ibid., p. 78. Margaret Drier did not become Margaret Drier Robins until 1905, although I have used her married name throughout.

24. The tensions that plagued the WTUL are described in Nancy Schrom Dye, "The Women's Trade Union League of New York, 1903-1920" (Ph.D. dissertation, University of Wisconsin, 1974), chaps. 6 and 7. Schneiderman discussed the league's closing in *All for One*, pp. 247-251, and described the "sad news" in a letter to Eleanor Roosevelt, May 22, 1950, file no. 3862, Eleanor Roosevelt Personal Papers, Franklin D. Roosevelt Library, Hyde Park, New York.

25. Schneiderman described the three women in *All for One*, pp. 77-79, 184, and also in Bessie Beatty, "Rose Schneiderman Plays Major Role in Decent Standard Endeavor," *Consumers Apparel Label Guide*, 1 (1937):1, clipping, Schneiderman Papers.

26. Schneiderman's most famous speech, one she gave at a meeting in the Metropolitan Opera House following the 1911 Triangle Fire, is reprinted in *All for One*, pp. 100-101; and her general effect as a speaker is clear in M. A. Sherwood to Mrs. Upton, July 15, 1912, Jeannette Eaton to Rose Schneiderman, October 28, 1935, Clara Somerville to Rose Schneiderman, March 6, 1937, and Charles W. Ervin to Rose Schneiderman, April 7, 1949, Schneiderman Papers. The "forgiving soul" quote is from Helen Marot to Rose Schneiderman, January 2, 1911, Schneiderman Papers; the vacation is described in Schneiderman, *All for One*, pp. 81-82.

27. Margaret Drier Robins to Rose Schneiderman, n.d., Leonora O'Reilly to Rose Schneiderman, November 30, 1917, Margaret Drier Robins to Rose Schneiderman, January 1, 1915, Schneiderman Papers. These letters are from a later period than the one I am describing, although it seems safe to assume that they reflect what was communicated, primarily in conversation, during Schneiderman's early years in the league.

28. Margaret Drier Robins to Rose Schneiderman, January 1, 1915, Rose Schneiderman to Mrs. Dorothy Canfield Fisher, May 7, 1943, Schneiderman Papers. The relationship between Schneiderman's wish to be a teacher and her later work is mentioned in Oliver Pilat, "Teacher to the Community," *New York*

Post Magazine, April 28, 1949, clipping, Schneiderman Papers.

29. Schneiderman, *All for One*, p. 96.

30. For the problems in the league at this time see Dye, "The Women's Trade Union League of New York," chap. 4; for the 1909-1910 strike, Louis Levine, *The Women's Garment Workers: A History of the International Ladies' Garment Workers' Union* (New York: B. W. Huebsch, 1924), pp. 144-167, and Barbara Mayer Wertheimer, *We Were There: The Story of Working Women in America* (New York: Pantheon, 1977), pp. 293-309.

31. Rose's interests and activities at this time are clear from misc. news clippings and the following letters: Max Fruchter to Rose Schneiderman, March 5, 1911; Joseph E. Cohen to Rose Schneiderman, November 8, 1911, and May 29, 1912; Alice [Bean?] to Rose Schneiderman, June 13, 1912; M. A. Sherwood to Mrs. Upton, July 15, 1912; Anna H. Shaw to Rose Schneiderman, July 24, 1912; Rose Schneiderman to Benjamin Schlesinger, February 6, 1916; all in Schneiderman Papers.

32. Dye, "The Women's Trade Union League of New York," p. 369; the quote is from *News-Democrat*, July 25, 1912, clipping, Schneiderman Papers. Schneiderman once said that she had been greatly influenced by " 'Alice Kimball,' a novel which gave an idea of the terrible status of women in the early 19th century, and 'What Is to Be Done,' by Tchernitzky [sic], which she says opened her eyes as to what women had to do to improve their condition" (Pilat, "Teacher to the Community," Schneiderman Papers). Reading of this sort may account for the fact that Schneiderman was more interested in suffrage than many working-class women. On her problems with the ILGWU see: Rose Schneiderman to Benjamin Schlesinger, February 6, 1916 and Rose Schneiderman to Abraham Baroff, December 1, 1916, Schneiderman Papers.

33. Schneiderman mentions the significance of O'Reilly's philosophy in Beatty, "Rose Schneiderman Plays Major Role in Decent Standard Endeavor," p. 1; her views in the 1930s and 1940s are clear in "The Union Was My School, Says Rose Schneiderman," *New Leader*, March 13, 1937, and "Woman Unionist to Quit Post Here," *The New York Times*, April 7, 1949, clippings in Schneiderman Papers.

34. Frances Perkins, *The Roosevelt I Knew* (New York: Viking Press, 1946), pp. 30 and 32. See also Joseph P. Lash, *Eleanor and Franklin* (New York: W. W. Norton, 1971), pp. 280-281, 288. Rose Schneiderman to Eleanor Roosevelt, May 27, 1937, and "Memorandum for Mr. McIntyre" from E. R., June 2, 1937, file no. 1440, Eleanor Roosevelt Personal Papers, illustrate the way in which Schneiderman's information was gotten to FDR.

35. Schneiderman was self-conscious in her effort to learn even at this time. She said of her "thrilling" and interesting job at the NRA, for example: "It's like an extension university course giving me a tremendous opportunity to learn about industry in all its phases" (Arthur T. Weil, "Women Who Do Things in Washington," *American Hebrew and Jewish Tribune*, January 4, 1935, clipping, Schneiderman Papers).

36. The first quote is from Charlotte Baum, Paul Hyman, and Sonya Michel, *The Jewish Woman in America* (New York: Dial Press, 1976), p. 160, and the second, from Schneiderman, *All for One*, p. 257. *The Jewish Woman in America*,

chap. 5, discusses Schneiderman's life in comparison to other women of similar background.

37. According to Lucy Goldthwaite, the writer who helped Schneiderman with her autobiography, Schneiderman dictated the whole book and Goldthwaite changed nothing of any significance. Indeed, Goldthwaite was irritated because Schneiderman would not let her do more. Interview with Goldthwaite June 22, 1976.

38. Schneiderman, *All for One*, pp. 50 and 227; the "if you think" quote is given in Dye, "The Women's Trade Union League of New York," p. 270.

39. Schneiderman, *All for One*, p. 264.

6. The Education of a Generation

1. The influences that probably shaped William Dodge's pedagogy and less directly that of Annie Florance Nathan and Minnie Wald are described in Anne L. Kuhn, *The Mother's Role in Childhood Education: New England Concepts, 1830-1860* (New Haven: Yale University Press, 1947), and Bernard Wishy, *The Child and the Republic: The Dawn of Modern American Child Nurture* (Philadelphia: University of Pennsylvania Press, 1968). On Catharine and Lyman Beecher see Kathryn Kish Sklar, *Catharine Beecher: A Study in American Domesticity* (New Haven: Yale University Press, 1973), especially pp. 3-55.

2. One could cite a good deal of primary and secondary material here: in the first category, Catharine Beecher, *The American Woman's Home* (1869; reprint ed., New York: Arno Press, 1971), is illustrative; in the second, Barbara Welter, "Coming of Age in America: The American Girl in the Nineteenth Century," *Dimity Convictions: The American Woman in the Nineteenth Century* (Athens: Ohio University Press, 1976), pp. 3-20.

3. Daniel Walker Howe, "American Victorianism as a Culture," *American Quarterly*, 27 (1975):507-532.

4. To place Mrs. O'Reilly in context see Herbert G. Gutman, "Class, Status, and the Gilded Age Radical: A Reconsideration," *Work, Culture, and Society in Industrializing America* (New York: Alfred A. Knopf, 1976), pp. 260-292, and Robert H. Wiebe, *The Search for Order, 1877-1920* (New York: Hill and Wang, 1967), pp. 66-75; for Samuel Schneiderman see Irving Howe, *World of Our Fathers* (New York: Harcourt Brace Jovanovich, 1976), and Moses Rischin, *The Promised City: New York's Jews, 1870-1914* (Cambridge: Harvard University Press, 1962).

5. The distinction I am drawing rests in part on the difference between "sponsored" and "contest" mobility discussed in Ralph H. Turner, "Sponsored and Contest Mobility and the School System," *American Sociological Review*, 25 (1960):855-867. On women's occupations see Lois W. Banner, *Women in Modern America: A Brief History* (New York: Harcourt Brace Jovanovich, 1974); Barbara Mayer Wertheimer, *We Were There: The Story of Working Women in America* (New York: Pantheon, 1977); Robert W. Smuts, *Women and Work in America* (New York: Columbia University Press, 1959); and Peter Gabriel Filene, *Him/Her/Self: Sex Roles in Modern America* (New York: Harcourt Brace Jovanovich, 1974).

6. The history of benevolent organizations can be found in works such as

Robert H. Bremner, *From the Depths: The Discovery of Poverty in the United States* (New York: New York University Press, 1956), and Roy Lubove, *The Professional Altruist: The Emergence of Social Work as a Career* (Cambridge: Harvard University Press, 1965). Of course, O'Reilly and Schneiderman had to work. But the avowed aims of reform groups supported their sense of having been "called" to their work for reasons beyond immediate economic need.

7. Female friendship in the nineteenth century is discussed especially well in Nancy F. Cott, *The Bonds of Womanhood: "Woman's Sphere" in New England, 1780-1835* (New Haven: Yale University Press, 1977), pp. 160-196; Christopher Lasch and William R. Taylor, "Two 'Kindred Spirits': Sorority and Family in New England, 1839-1846," *New England Quarterly*, 36 (1963):23-41; and Carroll Smith-Rosenberg, "The Female World of Love and Ritual: Relations between Women in Nineteenth-Century America," *Signs*, 1 (1975):1-30.

8. George McGregor to Leonora O'Reilly, n.d. [c. 1902?], O'Reilly Papers.

9. Mary Ryshpan Cohen's life is clear from Leonora Cohen Rosenfield, *Portrait of a Philosopher: Morris R. Cohen in Life and Letters* (New York: Harcourt Brace, 1948); Mary Wolfe to Leonora O'Reilly, January 22, 1918; Mary Drier to Winifred O'Reilly, January 16, 1908, O'Reilly Papers.

10. Mary Drier to Leonora O'Reilly, September 16, 1916, O'Reilly Papers.

11. Grace H. Dodge to Leonora O'Reilly, January 31, 1908, and March 28, 1912; Mrs. O'Reilly's opinions are described in O'Reilly diary, January 4, 1911, O'Reilly Papers.

12. Peter L. Berger and Thomas Luckmann, *The Social Construction of Reality: A Treatise in the Sociology of Knowledge* (Garden City, N.Y.: Doubleday, 1966), and James Hitchcock, "The Dynamics of Popular Intellectual Change," *American Scholar*, 45 (1976):522-535, have helped me make sense of the function and dynamics behind a consciousness of this kind.

13. So far as I am aware, the term "social feminism" was originated by William L. O'Neill in *Everyone Was Brave: A History of Feminism in America* (Chicago: Quadrangle Books, 1969), and then picked up and further developed by J. Stanley Lemons in *The Woman Citizen: Social Feminism in the 1920s* (Urbana: University of Illinois Press, 1973).

14. The "mother instinct" quote is from Rose Schneiderman, unidentified clipping, Schneiderman Papers; the long quote is from Leonora O'Reilly, "Report on Peace Conference—International Congress of Women," typed draft, p. 15, O'Reilly Papers.

15. Jill K. Conway makes a similar argument in "The First Generation of American Women Graduates" (Ph.D. dissertation, Harvard University, 1969), and I have been strongly influenced by her work. I think, however, that Conway overdraws the distinction between what she calls the "scientist" type and the "sage" type. In my opinion, many women of this generation, including some of the ones Conway considers, fit into both categories. See also Jill Conway, "Women Reformers and American Culture, 1870-1930," *Journal of Social History*, 5 (1971-72):164-177.

16. Poem by Mary E. Drier, *Life and Labor*, 5 (1927), clipping in the O'Reilly Papers.

17. For Kelley's life see Dorothy Rose Blumberg, *Florence Kelley: The Making*

of a Social Pioneer (New York: Augustus M. Kelley, 1966), and Josephine Gold-
mark, *Impatient Crusader: Florence Kelley's Life Story* (Urbana: University of
Illinois Press, 1953). The clearest statement of Kelley's point of view is Florence
Kelley, *Some Ethical Gains through Legislation* (New York: Macmillan, 1905).
Conway, ''The First Generation of American Women Graduates,'' discusses Kel-
ley's influence at Henry Street and Hull House.

18. Lillian D. Wald to Jane Addams, November 15, 1898, Jane Addams Pa-
pers, Swarthmore College Peace Collection, as quoted in Conway, ''The First
Generation of American Women Graduates,'' p. 220; Jane Addams, *Twenty
Years at Hull House* (New York: Macmillan, 1910), illustrates Addams's style;
Allen F. Davis, *American Heroine: The Life and Legend of Jane Addams* (New
York: Oxford University Press, 1973), discusses Addams's influence.

19. Hope Jensen Leichter, ''The Concept of Educative Style,'' *Teachers College Record*, 85 (1973):239-250.

20. See Richard Hofstadter, *Anti-intellectualism in American Life* (New York:
Alfred A. Knopf, 1962), p. 25, for the difference between intellect and intelligence.

21. On women's schooling see Thomas Woody, *A History of Women's Education in the United States* (New York: Science Press, 1929), I, 329-459, 519-551,
II, 137-320; on collegiate education see Patricia Albjerg Graham, ''Expansion
and Exclusion: A History of Women in American Higher Education,'' *Signs*, 3
(1978):759-773; on the print media, the public forum, and the attitudes that
pervaded women's education generally, see Barbara Welter, ''The Cult of True
Womanhood: 1800-1860,'' and ''Anti-intellectualism and the American Woman,'' *Dimity Convictions: The American Woman in the Nineteenth Century*,
pp. 21-41 and 71-78, respectively; also Ann Douglas, *The Feminization of American Culture* (New York: Alfred A. Knopf, 1977).

22. There is a large literature on the progressive mind, but my view of it has
been most influenced by Richard Hofstadter, *Anti-intellectualism in American
Life*; Morton G. White, *Social Thought in America: The Revolt against Formal-
ism* (New York: Viking Press, 1949); Lawrence A. Cremin, *The Transformation
of the School: Progressivism in American Education* (New York: Alfred A.
Knopf, 1961); and David W. Noble, *The Paradox of Progressive Thought* (Min-
neapolis: University of Minnesota Press, 1958).

Index

Addams, Jane, 2, 44, 59, 81-82, 111, 159; writings by or about, 174, 176
Adler, Felix, 98, 147
Adult education, 151-159. *See also* Social feminism; Sororal education
All for One, *see* Schneiderman, Rose, writings and papers
Alliance Employment Bureau, 102
Allport, Gordon W., 170, 182n8
American Federation of Labor, 95, 108, 110, 136
American Journal of Nursing, The, 176
American Union Against Militarism, 84
Apprenticeship, 147-151; in Dodge's education, 18-21; in Nathan's education, 45-49; in Wald's education, 76-77, 190n33; in O'Reilly's education, 96-99; in Schneiderman's education, 128-131, 132
Arthur, Helen, 80
Asacog Settlement, 101-102
Association Monthly, The, 177

Bailyn, Bernard, 167
Baltes, Paul B., 170
Barry, Charles P., 65

Barry, Mrs. Charles P., *see* Wald, Julia
Barzun, Jacques, 172
Beecher, Catharine, 143
Beecher, Lyman, 143
Bellevue Training School for Nurses, 19
Berg, Barbara J., 169
Berger, Peter L., 179-180
Biography, *see* Educational biography; Literary biography; Psychobiography
Blumer, Herbert, 170
Braut, Bessie, 123
Brewster, Mary, 71, 72, 73, 78
Brim, Orville G., Jr., 170
British Women's Trade Union League, 103
Bryn Mawr Summer School for Working Women, 134
Buhle, Mari Jo, 168-169
Butler, Nicholas Murray, 25, 26, 27

Central Labor Union of New York, 124
Charities, 75
Childhood education, *see* Early education; Familial education; Schooling
Children's Bureau, 84
Choate, Mrs. William G., 45

Clifford, Geraldine Jonçich, 168
Clifford, James L., 172
Cohen, Morris Raphael, 94, 95, 153, 177-178
Cohen, Mrs. Morris Raphael, *see* Ryshpan, Mary
College Settlement (NYC), 73-74, 75
Collegial education, *see* Sororal education
Commons, 75
Comte Synthetic Circle, 93-95, 99, 142
Consciousness, 154-159. *See also* Social feminism
Consumers' League, 1, 20, 33, 95, 176; in Nathan's education, 47-52, 55; national, 80, 152
Conway, Jill K., 169, 177
Cooper Union, 91, 95, 162
Cott, Nancy F., 169
Cratty, Mabel, 177
Craven, Darcré, 68-69, 72
Cremin, Lawrence A., 167
Cyprus, Anne, 124, 125

Daniels, Doris, 177
Davis, Allen F., 82, 179
Degler, Carl N., 168
Development, 182n8
Dewey, John, 170, 172
Dock, Lavinia, 79, 80, 81, 99, 100, 174
Dodge, Grace Hoadley, 1-5, 33, 99; familial education, 9-16, 138-147; religion, 10, 11, 12, 15, 18, 21, 29-31; work, 10, 18-31; schooling, 11, 16-18; tutorial education, 11-12; apprenticeship, 18-21, 147-151; sororal education, 21-24, 151-159; reading and study, 30; consciousness, 154-159; educative style, 160-164; writings and papers, 10-11, 18, 22-23, 28, 33, 173-174, 175-176; writings on or relevant to, 176, 177, 178, 179
Dodge, Melissa Phelps, 14
Dodge, Sarah Hoadley, 9, 11, 14, 17, 183n9

Dodge, William Earl, Jr., 9, 11, 15, 18-19; pedagogy characterized, 138-147 passim
Domesticity, 144-145
Drier, Margaret, *see* Robbins, Margaret Drier
Drier, Mary E., 106-107, 157-158, 178; on sisterhood, 108-109, 153; as mentor, 128-131, 133, 136, 147, 149
Drury, Victor, 92-94, 95, 97, 104, 107
DuBois, Ellen, 179
Duffus, R. L., 61, 62, 64, 103, 177
Dye, Nancy Schrom, 168-169

Early education, 138-147. *See also* Familial education; Schooling
Edel, Leon, 172
Education, definition of, 5-7, 170, 182n8
Educational biography: definition of, 4-7, 167; historiographical considerations, 4, 167-169, 180; theoretical considerations, 5-7, 13-14, 70, 170-173; use of primary and secondary sources in, 173-180; as a form of secondary analysis, 177
Educative style, 160-164
Epstein, Beryl Williams, 177
Erikson, Erik H., 170, 173
Ethical Culture Society, 98, 102, 152

Familial education, 138-147; in Dodge's education, 9-16; in Nathan's education, 34-41, 185-186n9; in Wald's education, 59-67; in O'Reilly's education, 90-92; in Schneiderman's education, 115-118, 119, 121-122
Farmer-Labor party, 134
Farmington, *see* Miss Porter's School
Feinberg, Walter, 168
Female friendship, 150-154, 169. *See also* Sororal education
Feminism: in Dodge's education, 16, 20-21, 22-24, 28; in Nathan's education, 34, 40, 52-53; in Wald's

education, 68, 79; in O'Reilly's education, 108-112; in Schneiderman's education, 123, 133. *See also* Social feminism; Sororal education; Suffrage
Flexner, Eleanor, 179

Garraty, John A., 172
Geertz, Clifford, 180
Generation: definition of, 1-2, 181n1, 181-182n5. *See also* Progressive generation
George, Henry, 100
Goffman, Erving, 171
Gompers, Samuel, 93, 103
Goodrich, Annie W., 80
Gordon, Ann D., 168-169
Goulet, L. R., 170
Graham, Abbie, 13, 176
Graham, Patricia Albjerg, 169
Greer, Colin, 168
Grinstein, Hyman B., 178

Hebrew Free School Association, 48
Hebrew Sheltering Guardian Society, *see* Schneiderman, Rose, orphanage experience
Henry, Alice, 90, 178, 179
Henry Street Settlement, 1, 59, 152, 159; and nursing, 67-68, 69; in Wald's education, 72-86; in O'Reilly's education, 99-101, 154
History of Woman Suffrage, 179
House on Henry Street, The, see Wald, Lillian, writings and papers
Howe, Frances H., 176
Hubert, John Baptist, 92-94, 95, 104, 107, 141, 191-192n7
Hull House, 81, 158

Industrial Education Association, 25, 27. *See also* Teachers College, Columbia University
International Conference of Working Women, 112
International Congress of Women (1915), 111, 155

International Ladies' Garment Workers' Union, 132, 133

Jacobi, Mary Putnam, 51-52, 178
James, William, 7, 171
Journal of Psychohistory, The, 172

Karier, Clarence J., 168
Katz, Michael B., 168
Kelley, Florence, 80, 103, 126, 157-159
King, Edward, 73, 93, 94, 97, 100, 107
Kitchen Garden Association, 19, 20, 21, 27. *See also* Teachers College, Columbia University
Kittredge, Mabel Hyde, 80
Knights of Labor, 92-93, 95, 142, 145, 146
Kraditor, Aileen S., 179

Labor Advisory Board (NRA), 1, 135
Labor movement: in O'Reilly's education, 90-93, 103-105, 106, 108-112, 145-146; in Schneiderman's education, 115, 123-125, 126, 128, 134, 135; writings on, 179. *See also* American Federation of Labor; Knights of Labor; Women's Trade Union League
Lamphere, Louise, 169
Langness, L. L., 172
Leichter, Hope Jensen, 171
Lerner, Gerda, 169
Lesbianism, 190n38
Levine, Louis, 179
Lewisohn, Alice, 80
Lewisohn, Irene, 80
Lewisohn, Leonard, 80
Life and Labor, 109, 176
Life history, *see* Educational biography
Lifton, Robert Jay, 172
Literary biography, 5, 172
Loeb, Mrs. Solomon, 74
Long Day, The, 105
Low, Seth, 152
Lowell, Josephine Shaw, 95, 96, 99,

108, 192n13; as mentor, 45-49, 76-77, 147-148, 150
Lower East Side, 48, 71-86, 94-95, 126, 131-132, 147
Luckmann, Thomas, 179

McDowell, Helene, 80, 100
McGregor, George, 152-153
MacLean, Annie Marion, 176
Manhattan Liberal Club, 126
Manhattan Trade School for Girls, 152, 193n26; in O'Reilly's education, 102-108
Marriage: attitudes toward, 65, 122, 136-137, 152-153
Martyn, Carlos, 178
Maslow, Abraham H., 170
Mazzini, Giuseppe, 100
Mead, George Herbert, 171
Mentors, 147-151. *See also* Drier, Mary E.; Lowell, Josephine Shaw; O'Reilly, Leonora; Perkins, Louise S. W.; Robbins, Margaret Drier; Schuyler, Louisa Lee
Mercantile Inspection Act (1896), 152
Metaphors of self, 171
Meyer, Annie Nathan, 37-38, 174, 185-186n9
Mikol, Maurice, 124
Miss Cruttenden's School, 60, 64-66, 70, 141
Miss Porter's School, 16-18, 21, 140
Moody, Dwight L., 15, 18, 141
Morgenthau, Rita Wallach, 80
Mt. Sinai Hospital School of Nursing, 44
Murphy, Gardner, 170

Nathan, Annette Florance, 48, 186n25
Nathan, Annie, *see* Meyer, Annie Nathan
Nathan, Annie Florance, 34, 35, 36, 37, 38, 39; pedagogy characterized, 138-147 passim
Nathan, Frederick, 41-43, 54
Nathan, Maud, 1-5, 76, 98; religion, 34-35, 38-39, 49-50; familial educa-tion, 34-41, 138-147, 185-186n9; schooling, 38-30; reading and study, 40; marriage, 41-44, 49-50, 54-55; work, 42-55; travel, 43, 49, 54, 55; apprenticeship, 45-49, 147-151; sororal education, 47-48, 51-52, 151-159; consciousness, 154-157; educative style, 160-164; writings and papers, 33-34, 35, 42, 55-56, 174, 176; writings on or relevant to, 176, 178, 179
Nathan, Robert Weeks, 34, 36-37
National American Woman Suffrage Association, 55, 132
National Association for the Advance-ment of Colored People, 152
National Board, *see* Young Women's Christian Association
National Consumers' League, *see* Con-sumers' League
National Industrial Recovery Adminis-tration, *see* Labor Advisory Board (NRA)
National Women's Trade Union League, *see* Women's Trade Union League
New Deal, 134, 135, 136, 157
New School for Social Research, 112
New York Association of Working Girls' Societies, *see* Working Girls' Clubs
New York City Board of Education, 10, 25, 72
New York City Wage Earners' Suffrage League, 108, 111
New York College for the Training of Teachers, 26. *See also* Teachers Col-lege, Columbia University
New York Consumers' League, *see* Consumers' League
New York Exchange for Women's Work, 44-45
New York Hospital School of Nursing, 60, 66, 67-70, 71
New York State Department of Labor, 1, 135
Nightingale, Florence, 67, 68-69, 72

Notable American Women, 176
Nursing, 66-72

Olney, James, 171
Once upon a Time and Today, see
   Nathan, Maud, writings and papers
O'Reilly, Alice, 110-111
O'Reilly, Leonora, 1-5, 89, 126;
   schooling, 89, 93, 101; work, 89,
   95-112, 141; familial education, 90-
   92, 138-147; reading and study, 93-
   95, 110, 112, 157; apprenticeship,
   96-99, 147-151; sororal education,
   99-100, 109-110, 151-159; as mentor, 128-131, 133, 134, 136, 147,
   148; consciousness, 154-159; educative style, 160-164; religion,
   192n11; writings and papers, 174-
   175, 176; writings on or relevant to,
   176-177, 178, 179
O'Reilly, Winifred, 89-92, 97, 100,
   101, 107-108; compared with
   Deborah Rothman Schneiderman,
   121; pedagogy characterized, 138-
   147 passim
O'Sullivan, Mary Kenney, 103

Parental padagogy, *see* Familial educa-
   tion
Pentecost, Hugh, 126
People's Institute, 152
Perkins, Frances, 135, 178
Perkins, Louis, S. W.: as mentor, 96-
   99, 100, 107, 147, 148, 192n13
Porter, Sarah, 16-18, 20, 30
Pratt Institute, 101
Progressive generation: characteristics
   of, 2-4, 189n23; education of, 138-
   164. *See also* Generation
Protestant evangelical tradition, 9-10,
   143, 144
Psychobiography, 5, 172-173

Reading and study: in Dodge's education, 30; in Nathan's education, 40;
   in Wald's education, 68-69, 75; in
   O'Reilly's education, 93-95, 110,

112, 157; in Schneiderman's educa-
   tion, 120, 123-124, 197n32
Reik, Theodor, 173
Religion, 189n23; in Dodge's educa-
   tion, 10, 11, 12, 15, 18, 21, 29-31;
   in Nathan's education, 34-35, 38-
   39, 49-50; in Wald's education, 62,
   188n6; in Schneiderman's educa-
   tion, 119, 126, 196n21; in
   O'Reilly's education, 192n11
Reznick, Allan Edward, 177
Richardson, Dorothy, 105
Riis, Jacob, 75, 77, 177
Rischin, Moses, 178
Robbins, Jane, 73, 74, 103
Robbins, Margaret Drier, 112; as men-
   tor, 128-131, 133, 136, 147, 149
Roosevelt, Eleanor, 135, 136, 175
Roosevelt, Franklin, 135, 136, 178
Rosaldo, Michelle Zimbalist, 169
Rosenberg, Stuart E., 178
Russell, James Earl, 26, 27-28
Ryshpan, Mary, 94, 153

Sandquist, Eric L., 176-177
Sanitary Commission, 18, 45
Scheffler, Israel, 173
Schiff, Jacob, 74, 77-78, 82
Schneiderman, Charlie, 116, 122
Schneiderman, Deborah Rothman,
   115-118, 123, 124, 126; compared
   with Winifred O'Reilly, 121
Schneiderman, Harry, 116
Schneiderman, Jane, 116
Schneiderman, Rose, 1-5; familial
   education, 115-118, 119, 121-122,
   138-147; schooling, 116, 117, 118,
   119, 120, 124-125; orphanage experience, 116, 118-120, 141; religion, 119, 126, 196n21; work, 120,
   121, 126-137, 197n35; reading and
   study, 120, 123-124, 197n32; apprenticeship, 128-131, 132, 147-
   151; sororal education, 128-137,
   151-159; consciousness, 154-159;
   educative style, 160-164; writings
   and papers, 116, 120, 136-137, 175,

198n37; writings on or relevant to, 178, 179

Schneiderman, Samuel, 115-118, 119, 124; pedagogy characterized, 138-147 passim

Schooling, 6, 162; in Dodge's education, 11, 16-18; in Nathan's education, 38-40; in Wald's education, 64-71; in O'Reilly's education, 89, 93, 101; in Schneiderman's education, 116, 117, 118, 119, 120, 124-125

Schuyler, Louisa Lee, 45, 141, 179; as mentor, 18-21, 26, 30, 147, 148, 150

Schwartz, Maud, 135

Schwarz, Goodman, 60, 61, 63, 139

Schwarz, Samuel, 60, 61, 63, 139

Scott, Melinda, 132

Scudder, Vida, 23, 177

Seidman, Joel, 179

Settlement movement, 23-24, 73-74, 75, 81-82. *See also* Asacog Settlement; College Settlement (NYC); Henry Street Settlement; Hull House; University Settlement

Shirtwaist strike (1909), 131-132

Sicherman, Barbara, 168

''Significant others,'' 171-172

Sisterhood, *see* Feminism

Sloan, Douglas, 168

Sloane, William M., 178

Smith-Rosenberg, Carroll, 169

Social feminism, 154-159, 199n15

Social Reform Club, 95, 98, 99, 101, 102, 152

Socialism, 132-133, 134, 158

Socialization, 182n8

Sororal education, 151-159; in Dodge's education, 21-24; in Nathan's education, 47-48, 51-52; in Wald's education, 68, 78-82; in O'Reilly's education, 99-100, 109-111; in Schneiderman's education, 128-137

State Charities Aid Association, 18-21, 24, 25, 45, 179

Stover, Charles, 73, 93, 98

Style: as aspect of education, 39, 171, 186n12. *See also* Educative style

Suffrage, 2; Frederick Nathan on, 42; in (Maud) Nathan's education, 51-52; in Wald's education, 79; in O'Reilly's education, 111-112; in Schneiderman's education, 132-133; as aspect of social feminism, 154; writings on, 179

Sullivan, Harry Stack, 171

Survey, The, 75

Sutliffe, Irene, 67, 69-70

Synthetic Circle, *see* Comte Synthetic Circle

Teachers College, Columbia University, 1, 102, 179; Dodge's view of, 20, 30, 183-184n18; in Dodge's education, 24-28

Thirty-Eighth Street Working Girls' Society, *see* Working Girls' Clubs

Trade union movement, *see* Labor movement

Transference: in writing educational biography, 173

Triangle fire (1911), 111

Tyack, David B., 168

Uncle B, *see* Hubert, John Baptist

Uncle D, *See* Drury, Victor

United Cloth Hat and Cap Makers' Union, 123-124, 125, 126, 132, 134

University Settlement, 73, 74, 103

Vassar College, 60, 64, 66, 71

Visiting Nurse Service, 1, 59, 174

Vocational education, 147-151; O'Reilly on, 101-104. *See also* Apprenticeship; Work

Wald, Alfred, 61, 63-64

Wald, Gus, 61

Wald, Julia, 61, 66

Wald, Lillian, 1-5, 41, 93, 98, 99, 100, 103, 107; familial education, 56-67, 138-147; religion, 62, 188n6;

schooling, 64-71; sororal education, 68, 78-82, 151-159; reading and study, 68-69, 75; work, 71-86; apprenticeship, 76-77, 147-151, 190n33; consciousness, 154-159; educative style, 160-164; writings and papers, 60, 85-86, 177, 178, 179; writings on or relevant to, 61, 177, 178, 179

Wald, Max D., 59, 60, 61, 62

Wald, Minnie Schwarz, 59, 60, 61, 63, 64, 72; pedagogy characterized, 138-147 passim

Walling, William English, 103, 152

Waters, Ysabella, 80, 84

Weinstein, Gregory, 177

Wertheimer, Barbara Mayer, 179

Wheeler, Stanton, 170

White, Robert W., 170

Wilson, Woodrow, 79

Windows on Henry Street, see Wald, Lillian, writings and papers

Women's Medical College, 71

Women's Trade Union League, 1, 100, 106, 152, 153, 194nn28, 38; national, 1, 128, 133-134; in O'Reilly's education, 103-105, 107-110; in Schneiderman's education, 128, 129, 130-133; papers, 175

Woolman, Mary Schenck Raphael, 102

Work: occupational choice, 2-3, 149-151; in Dodge's education, 18-31; in Nathan's education, 42-55; in Wald's education, 71-86; in O'Reilly's education, 95-112; in Schneiderman's education, 126-137

Working Girls' Clubs, 1, 10, 19, 21, 152; in Dodge's education, 21-24

Working Women's Society, 108, 152, 178, 192n13; in Nathan's education, 47-48; in O'Reilly's education, 95-96, 109, 142. *See also* Consumers' League

Young Women's Christian Association, 1, 20, 99, 152, 185n34; in Dodge's education, 26, 28-31